LAST THINGS
FIRST

Also by Sydney J. Harris
Majority of One
Strictly Personal

Sydney J. Harris

LAST THINGS

FIRST

In practical philosophy, the final end is the first principle.
ARISTOTLE

HOUGHTON MIFFLIN COMPANY BOSTON

*For Barbara
with love*

CONTENTS

LAST THINGS
FIRST

I

OF THE

MIND AND PASSIONS

Keep Control of Your Personality

I WALKED with my friend, a Quaker, to the newsstand the other night, and he bought a paper, thanking the newsie politely. The newsie didn't even acknowledge it.

"A sullen fellow, isn't he?" I commented. "Oh, he's that way every night," shrugged my friend. "Then why do you continue being so polite to him?" I asked. "Why not?" inquired my friend. "Why should I let *him* decide how I'm going to act?"

As I thought about this little incident later, it occurred to me that the operating word was "act." My friend *acts* toward people; most of us *react* toward them.

He has a sense of inner balance lacking in most of us frail and uncertain creatures: he knows who he is, what he stands for, and how he should behave.

No boor is going to disturb the equilibrium of his nature; he simply refuses to return incivility with incivility, because then he would no longer be in command of his own conduct, but a mere responder to others.

When we are enjoined in the Bible to return good for evil, we look upon this as a moral injunction, which it is; but it is also a psychological prescription for our emotional health.

Nobody is unhappier than the perpetual *reactor*. His center of emotional gravity is not rooted within himself, where it belongs, but in the world outside him. His spiritual temperature is always being raised or lowered by the social climate around him, and he is a mere creature at the mercy of these elements.

Praise gives him a feeling of euphoria, which is false, because it does not last and it does not come from self-approval. Criticism depresses him more than it should, because it confirms his own secretly shaky opinion of himself. Snubs hurt him, and the merest suspicion of unpopularity in any quarter rouses him to bitterness or aggressiveness or querulousness.

Only a saint, of course, *never* reacts. But a serenity of spirit cannot be achieved until we become the masters of our own actions and attitudes, and not merely the passive reactors to other persons' feelings. To let another determine whether we shall be rude or gracious, elated or depressed, is to relinquish control over our own personalities which is ultimately all we possess. The only true possession is self-possession.

My friend is a model of balanced conduct, and few of us can hope to attain his kind of surefootedness. But we can at least adjust our weight to lean less heavily upon the world's giddy gyrations.

A Person's Worth Doesn't Change

No OTHER article I have written in a year has evoked so much comment as my recent piece on "acting and reacting." Hundreds of readers wrote in to tell me how much they like it; it has been widely reprinted, and used as a text for many sermons in the last few weeks.

I mention this not by way of boasting, but to point out that the individual today is deeply concerned with his personal and social character: he knows the kind of person he wants to be, but he doesn't know how to reach this goal.

As a corollary to my previous piece, may I suggest that one of the impediments to becoming an "actor" instead of a mere "reactor" is what I call the "pulley system" of evaluating people, including oneself.

On the pulley system, we go up when someone else goes down, and we go down when someone else goes up. We have no inner stability, because our emotional position keeps shifting in relation to the outside world.

If I meet a man who writes better than I do, this does not diminish my talents. I still have exactly what I had before, no more and no less. His own gifts do not devalue mine, nor do mine devalue somebody else's.

Yet most of us judge ourselves on this false relativistic basis. If we meet someone richer, we feel poor; someone handsomer, we feel ugly; someone more fluent, we feel tongue-tied. If they are up, we are down.

Conversely, many of us cannot feel comfortable unless we are pulling others down. We rise only by their lowliness: if he is uglier, I am handsomer; if he is poorer, I am richer; if he is ineffectual with women, I am a Casanova.

Those who have a tremendous need to depreciate others are doing it not because they feel genuinely superior, but because this is the only way they can achieve any emotional parity with the world. Unless others are made to feel inferior, these people cannot feel even normal.

But human society is not a pulley system. Each person has his own value, his own place, his own distinctive gifts and limitations. A pretty women is no less pretty because a beautiful one enters the room; I am no poorer because I am lunching with a millionaire. My own writing does not become despicable when I am reading Shakespeare.

Things remain what they were; only our opinions of them change. To act, and not merely to react, implies the acceptance of God's world, and knowing that only He is the ultimate judge of our real worth.

An Open Mind Is the Healthiest One

PEOPLE who are merely suspicious often imagine they are shrewd. But the price paid by the suspicious mind is a high one; for, as C. S. Lewis somewhere says, "suspicion often creates what it suspects."

If you imagine that people are cheating you, they will begin to cheat you. Have you noticed that it is the most worldly men who are often the most taken in? Innocence protects most of us from fraud, but the cunning operator is most likely to be victimized by a yet more cunning one.

A child who is suspicious, wary, and overprotective of his possessions usually finds them wrested away by other children, while the child who shares is allowed to play peacefully with his things. It is no accident that playmates gang up on the boy who thinks everyone is always ganging up on him.

A highly suspicious wife, I have no doubt, can drive a faithful husband into adultery, on the theory that if he has the name he might as well have the game. And when citizens expect a politician to be crooked, his incentive for remaining straight is scarcely compelling.

In our conformist society, anyone who demonstrates genuine individuality is deemed a prig or a crank; and this reaction has, in reality, turned many individualists into prigs and cranks. If we are suspicious and inhospitable toward differences, then we cannot blame those who are different from emphasizing their differences in a dramatic, shocking or sullen way.

Indeed, even the problem of what we call "insanity" is affected by the suspicion of the community. Inmates, we are beginning to learn, who are locked up and treated as potential menaces behave much more "crazily" than those kept in open wards and allowed a more normal routine. We become as mad as others think we are.

This is one reason why witch hunts of any kind produce more witches than existed before. "Suspicion creates what it suspects," and if we live in a repressive society which is seeking out Communists, for instance, the very repression will drive some weak personalities into communism.

The open mind, like the open society, is the healthiest; it is better to be gullible than to suspect, better to be fooled than to withhold trust; for the loss of a possession is trifling compared with the loss of human contact.

It's the Way You Say It That Counts

WE HEAR a great deal about "communication" these days — about our need to listen more carefully, to read more skillfully, to grasp the essence of what another person is trying to say. But it seems to me that communication, even more than charity, begins at home. The most important person to listen to is oneself, and our most important task is to develop an ear that can really hear what we are saying.

Anyone who has ever listened to a playback of a hidden tape recorder will know what I mean. It seems impossible that these are our voices — these babbling, incoherent sounds, more like monkeys than human beings. Is that raucous tone our own? How did self-pity sneak into that sentence? And listen to that phrase, unctuous with hypocrisy, or vibrating with false heartiness.

Without refraction, the voice cannot hear itself, any more than the eye can see itself. The whining wife does not know she whines, the bellowing husband is unaware of his bellow, the self-satisfied prig cannot detect the smugness dripping from his lips.

Just as we do not know what we sound like in timbre and cadence of voice, so we do not hear the unconscious attitudes that are revealed to others by our speech — the hostility thinly masquerading as humor, the fear hiding behind cool precision, the pomposity or envy or greed or any other unlovely trait we desperately try to conceal from others and from ourselves.

To communicate well and meaningfully it is not enough to make one's meaning plain to a listener. It is, first of all, to make one's meaning plain to oneself, to understand the real motives for our attitudes, to hear the half-tones and flats and sharps of our own prejudices, and to separate (however imperfectly) the voice of reason from the voice of childishness.

This is the hardest job of all, and this is where all genuine communication must begin. For people do not so much listen to what we say as to how we say it; the expression of a statement carries a stronger charge than its content; two men can make the same observation, and one will be accepted, the other met with suspicion or disbelief.

The world listens to the secret language of our emotions, and not to the bald denotations of the words themselves. And mastering that secret language calls for a true ear as much as for a true heart.

A Severe Conscience Can Be Crippling

IT WAS NOT until I began looking upon myself as a baseball player, about a dozen years ago, that I was able to achieve any repose about my work.

What I mean is that I ceased to regard the quality of my columns on a day-by-day basis, and went on a "seasonal batting average" kind of system. If a player hits .400 he is doing remarkably well; this is two hits out of five times at bat. I go to bat five times a week, and if I strike out, pop up, or foul the ball three times, I can live with it — so long as I get two clean hits out of five tries.

Until I adopted this long-range view, I was agonized at the appearance of a column that I felt was a wash-out. I judged my own output more harshly than any reader did, and bitterly castigated myself when the day's product fell below my own private standard of craftsmanship.

But nobody can continue to live with so rigid a conception of value. We fluctuate with the tides, the weather, our personal metabolism, the blood count, the bank balance, the shape of the week, or the shapelessness of the weekend. And I realized, collaterally, that every job involves a great deal of nonsense, of empty flourishing, of routine motions; that the moments of genuine meaning and creativity are recurrent, but not constant; and, in my own case, that nobody can hope to express an idea daily without much of the time simply spouting wind.

I mention this autobiographical material by way of illustration, and not to point to the special hazards of my craft. For all around me I see men who feel themselves judged on a day-by-day basis when they are not. Each failure is to them the end of the world, each mistake a repudiation of their entire past, each act of silliness a mockery of their good judgment.

The fault of the wastrel is that he does not judge himself harshly enough; the fault of the hard-working person is that he judges himself too harshly. A severe conscience can be as crippling as no conscience at all; when a man serves as his own judge and jury, the verdict is almost always "guilty."

But the world around us, fortunately, does not assay us daily, or even monthly; we are regarded across a perspective of years, and the strike-outs and pop-ups are forgotten and forgiven when the seasonal average is consistently high. It is comforting, on bleak days, to know that the umpire outside of us is more just than the one within us.

Best Listener Is a Good Talker

"WELL, I may not know a lot," said the man smugly, "but at least I'm a good listener."

It often seems to me that the man who prides himself on being a good listener isn't good at much else. I like men who are tuning forks rather than sounding boards.

A dog is a good listener. He fixes those big brown sympathetic eyes upon you and lets you pour out your woes to him, sometimes even licking your hand during the recital. But I don't know anyone who has solved his problems by having a one-way seminar with a dog. You might as well talk into a tape-recorder, which is the most faithful listener, and will play back to you exactly what you said, with all the gratifying intonations of pity and anger and self-justification.

An expert bartender is a superlative listener — or seems to be, even when he doesn't comprehend a word you are saying. He knows just when to put in the knowing "Ah!" and the approving "How true!" and the consoling "That's life for you!" But a man has to be pretty drunk to believe that he is achieving any real communion across the bar.

What we need are more *discriminating* listeners: and these are hard to find. We need people who know how and when to break in with "That's not so," or "You're deluding yourself," or "What do you *really* mean by that remark?" These are the people who keep us on pitch, who force us to try to harmonize our conflicting emotions, and are not mere echo chambers for our unresolved fears and our infantile wishes.

And, contrary to popular belief, it is usually the good talker who makes the best listener. A good talker (by which I do not mean the egomaniacal bore who always talks about himself) is sensitive to expression, to tone and color and inflection in human speech. Because he himself is articulate, he can help others to articulate their half-formulated feelings. His mind fills in the gaps, and he becomes, in Socrates' words, a kind of midwife for ideas that are struggling to be born.

This is why a competent psychiatrist is worth his weight in gold — and generally gets it. His listening is keyed for the half-tones and the dissonances that escape the untrained ear. For it is the mark of the truly good listener that he knows what you are saying often better than you do; and his playback is a revelation, not a recording.

A Jerk Can't See Himself as Others Do

I DON'T KNOW whether history repeats itself, but biography certainly does. The other day, Michael came in and asked me what a "jerk" was — the same question Carolyn put to me a dozen years ago.

At that time, I fluffed her off with some inane answer, such as "A jerk isn't a very nice person," but both of us knew it was an unsatisfactory reply. When she went to bed, I began trying to work up a suitable definition.

It's a marvelously apt word, of course. Until it was coined, not more than twenty-five years ago, there was really no single word in English to describe the kind of person who is a jerk — "boob" and "simp" were too old hat, and besides they really didn't fit, for they could be lovable, and a jerk never is.

Thinking it over, I decided that a jerk is basically a person without insight. He is not necessarily a fool or a dope, because some extremely clever persons can be jerks. In fact, it has little to do with intelligence as we commonly think of it; it is, rather, a kind of subtle but pervasive aroma emanating from the inner part of the personality.

I know a college president who can be described only as a jerk. He is not an unintelligent man, nor unlearned, nor even unschooled in the social amenities. Yet he is a jerk *cum laude*, because of a fatal flaw in his nature — he is totally incapable of looking into the mirror of his soul and shuddering at what he sees there.

A jerk, then, is a man (or woman) who is utterly unable to see himself as he appears to others. He has no grace, he is tactless without meaning to be, he is a bore even to his best friends, he is an egotist without charm. All of us are egotists to some extent, but most of us — unlike the jerk — are perfectly and horribly aware of it when we make asses of ourselves. The jerk never knows.

Nor does he feel the common pangs of remorse or humility.

He is locked snugly in his tight little shell and looks out at the world with smug, uncomprehending eyes. He has no real sense of humor, because he thinks the only things that are funny are the things he laughs at, and he has no real sense of values, because he thinks the only things that are true are the things he believes in.

The most serious indictment against the jerk is that he is always trying too hard to get people to like or respect him, without trying to like or respect them at all. It can't be done, but it's impossible to explain this to a jerk. That is what makes him one.

Don't Bottle Up All Your Emotions

ANOTHER "model mother" has done it. It happens quite a few times a year. This time a "model mother" in Connecticut killed her three children, to the utter consternation of all her friends and neighbors.

A model mother, as you may know, is one who is always calm and quiet, never shouts at her children, patiently endures their whims and waywardness.

She is usually held up as an example of all a mother should be — this tender and smiling creature. Yet, in an astonishing number of cases, her children grow up more disturbed and rebellious than the offspring of a screaming mother.

For what a child fears and resents most of all are hidden feelings, which he can sense in a parent who never gives them free expression. A child can cope with shouting or anger or even nagging, for these are emotions out in the open; what make him uneasy and troubled are exasperations and hostilities which the mother never permits herself to express.

It is only in rare cases, of course, that this repression builds up such a head of emotional steam that the parent is driven to the final insanity of child murder. But it happens.

In an interesting book published a few years ago, called *Paradoxes of Everyday Living*, a child psychiatrist included a chapter dealing with the neurotic child in the "happy" home.

He pointed out that the quiet, polite, well-organized home is not necessarily the happy one; and, contrariwise, that children who grow up in homes where a great deal of emotion is volubly expressed do not seem to be hurt by this.

I know many parents who think their children are "well behaved" when they are merely repressed; who confuse surface politeness with warmth of heart; who imagine that good social manners imply sound character. Such parents are usually in for a grim awakening when their children go through the turbulence of adolescence.

Please do not write to tell me that I am condoning bad manners, or shouting, or screaming, or rage, in a household. These are all unattractive traits. I am simply pointing out that their opposites are not necessarily good; that "model mothers" might benefit themselves and their children more if they let themselves go occasionally, if they disclosed some of the ugly feelings we all have at times.

Self-control is an admirable virtue, but if carried to an immoderate degree, it must in the end lead to a dangerous loss of all control.

Why There's Danger in Extremism

A MAN I KNOW, whom I have always considered a calm and stable personality, told me recently that he is regarded in some quarters as a wild-eyed radical, and in other circles as a stony conservative — when actually he is neither. "It's an irresistible urge I have when I get together with extremists," he said. "I promptly swing over to the other extreme, just because I am so irritated with their one-sided view."

I was delighted to learn that somebody else reacts that way, too. For years I have deplored my own tendency to do this. In most cases, it gives a false impression of my views — but when I am confronting an extremist, I become a passionate defender of the opposite view.

With ice-cold reactionaries, I sound like a rabid bolshevik; with professional liberals, I take on the tone of a fascist; with the ardent culture-vultures, I pretend to read nothing but comic books and lovelorn columns; with pugnacious lowbrows, I refer haughtily to the French symbolist poets and the ontological existentialism of Kierkegaard. This, of course, is a senseless way to behave; it is overreacting to a situation. But, in all fairness, there is something about extremism that breeds its own opposite.

The complacency of the bourgeoisie makes me yearn for the bohemian life; the sloppiness of the bohemians brings out my primness; loud-mouthed patriots prompt me to take a stand for the French way of life; and moist-eyed lovers of all things European give me the urge to hop on a chair and begin waving Old Glory.

The danger of extremism is that it forces its opponents to adopt an equally extreme view — thus hurting its own cause more than it realizes. The Reign of Terror during the French Revolution was a natural historical result of the repressive monarchy; the satanism of Stalin sprang out of the soil of Czarist cruelty.

No single way of living is exclusively right. Combination

is all. Life is the art of mixing ingredients in tolerable proportions, so that all the varied needs of man are somehow satisfied, and no important hunger is neglected. This is what all extremists forget, with their too-simple slogans for the good life.

Hate Is Rarely a Personal Matter

A FRIEND of mine was complaining at lunch that somebody hates him, and he couldn't understand why. "He probably doesn't hate you," I tried to console him. "You may just remind him of something he hates."

And I remembered an observation that a wise doctor made to me some time ago: "One is rarely lucky enough to be hated for oneself." This puzzling remark makes more sense the more you think of it. Usually, if we hate, it is the shadow of the person that we hate, rather than the substance.

We may hate a person because he reminds us of someone we feared and disliked when younger; or because we see in him some gross caricature of what we find repugnant in ourself; or because he *symbolizes* an attitude that seems to threaten us.

To be hated for oneself alone is almost a tribute; at least you feel that the person knows you and estimates you (however harshly) as an individual. But most of what passes for hate is merely an illusion. We are hated as a type, as a symbol, as a fantasy of the past, not as a person.

The French may be straining the truth in their famous saying that "to understand all is to forgive all," but it is certainly true that the more we know of any given person, the harder it becomes to hate him. We may begin seeing him as a type, but further intimacy reveals him in the nakedness of his individual personality — and there is always more there to pity than to scorn. Hateful people are pathetic, and no harm they do to others is so great as the harm they do to themselves.

I have known, as you have, a number of unpleasant and unattractive persons — but not more than one or two who seemed hateful in their very essence, whose souls seemed corroded at the core. Most of us wistfully want to be better than we are; and there is a kind of redemption in this wish.

The only way to cope with hate that is directed against oneself is to realize that it is rarely (strange as this may sound) a personal matter; that the object is only a pretext for hating; that any other convenient symbol might serve the hater just as readily; and that refusing to return hate for hate is not only a great moral precept but the wisest piece of psychological advice ever handed down to man.

Here's True Test of Good Breeding

LIKE MOST people, I used to think that the real test of good breeding was the way we behave toward those less fortunate than ourselves — toward the poorer, the weaker, the men and women lacking the advantages we have known.

This is important, surely, but I now think there is a truer test of good breeding. After all, it is relatively easy to behave in a normal and kindly fashion toward someone we feel superior to. Where most of us fall down is in our reactions to those *more* fortunate than ourselves — toward the richer, the stronger, the celebrated men and women who are known to us as *personages* rather than as persons.

Genuine breeding (which is as rare as it is delightful) consists in regarding a celebrity (distasteful word!) with the same naturalness and ease we would approach any ordinary person. Persons in the limelight have a heavy cross to bear.

They are subjected to the most searching scrutiny by strangers; and by the time we meet them, we have already formed some opinion of them, which may be nothing like their real characters at all. When we approach them, at a dinner or a party or a public event, most of us do so defensively or fawningly or with a tremendous concern for the impression we will make upon them. Thus, from the first, a person-to-person relationship is impossible — not because the celebrity is aloof, but because we ordinary mortals refuse to treat him in an ordinary way.

Good breeding (which I can admire more than I can imitate) accepts each person for what he is, and does not hastily type him as belonging to this "class" or representing that "kind." Nobody, at bottom, is a class or a kind; our surfaces have been formed by the society we have lived in, but our distinctive personalities are as individual as our fingerprints.

And the celebrity — no less than the humblest worker — wants to be regarded, and accepted, as an individual, not as an inflated dollar sign, or a mighty brain, or a magnificent piece of flesh. The most miserable women I have ever seen in my life were Hollywood beauties who bitterly resented being tagged and typed by all who met them — and never achieving a normal, easy relationship with people.

In the end, the most crushing price one can pay for a famous name or a famous face is to be known *to* millions, but known *by* nobody.

Temperament Bigger Than Talent

TWO ACQUAINTANCES of mine work for different companies in the same line of business. Both men have the same title —

an impressive title. But one is influential and the other is little more than a highly paid flunky. This discrepancy is not so much a difference in the companies as in the character of the men themselves. Even in this anonymous, mass-produced age of ours, the force of personality still counts for a good deal.

I know many men who are bucking for a promotion, for a new title that will presumably give them authority and prestige. But authority and prestige are not automatic — they may come with the promotion, but they do not necessarily stay with it.

Here, temperament is often more important than talent. Disgruntled subexecutives sometimes feel they have been passed over in favor of men with less talent, which may be true. But, for an executive, knowing how to get the best out of other men is as important as knowing how to get the best out of oneself.

An honest self-evaluation of one's own personality early in one's career might save a lot of resentment and heartache. This is why I have continually stressed that the knowledge of one's limitations is fully as important as the awareness of one's capacities.

I myself would not want the responsibility of ordering other men around, nor do I like to be ordered around. I work best in splendid solitude, left to my own peculiar devices. No money on earth could persuade me to become a Mover and Shaker. This self-knowledge has saved me a lot of grief, and in addition has permitted me to do what I do best with a minimum of friction. The peace of mind that this affords is worth, to me, far more than all the titles and perquisites and badges of authority. For genuine authority is not something given to us with a name on the door, but a gift, like musical talent or mathematical prowess. If it comes naturally to us, then we can gracefully assume responsibility; if it does not, we merely look pathetic and ineffectual in the role, and may wind up acting the tyrant — which is always a sign of impotence rather than of strength.

Sadly enough, our society is so arranged that it offers its largest rewards to the manipulators rather than to the creators — which is why so many creative men try vainly to fit their round heads into square jobs.

Good Workmen Are Never Crude

THE MOST obvious truths in the world are often the hardest to grasp. The simplest facts of human relations are often the most difficult to make some people see.

Such as the equation: the more respect you give, the more respect you get back. Since everybody wants respect from others — indeed, the struggle for money and prestige is simply a means of trying to attain respect — why don't more persons try this easy, proven method?

I have had lots of men working around the house since I bought it early this summer. Two or three of them have been Old World characters, who did their jobs not only with competence but also with dignity and courtesy. The others have been the brash and sloppy workmen we have become so used to these days. They roll into the house as if doing the homeowner a favor, are dirty in their habits, crude in their deportment, and even seem contemptuous of their own skills.

When they are treated in the manner they seem to invite — for everyone is treated in the manner he seems to invite — they build up a further supply of resentment, and the vicious circle begins anew.

The other workmen — and I am sorry to admit that they are not of native birth, but bring with them a sense of craftsmanship from Europe — are treated with the respect they earn and deserve. They carry an aura of dignity that gives them stature as human beings. They are courteous and deferential, not because they are weak, but because they are strong and can afford the emotional luxury of politeness. When a man has genuine respect for his own person and his powers, he then has enough respect to spare for others.

Crassness is always a sign of weakness; the blusterer is full of fear; the sullen workman who is afraid of being imposed upon is secretly convinced of his own inferiority — when he has to say, or think, "I'm as good as any man," he doesn't quite believe it himself.

The good workmen never doubt their status, either as human beings or as craftsmen. They think well of themselves, and therefore are thought well of by the people they work for.

It is a curious psychological fact that the man who seems to be "egotistic" is not suffering from too much ego, but from too little. When the ego is strong and well developed, there is no nagging need to impress others — by money, by rudeness, or by any other show of false strength.

How to Get Your Way on Big Issues

PERHAPS the most valuable lesson I have learned about handling young children is this — if you give them their way in matters of little importance, they will let you have your way in matters of great importance.

I have seen too many parents who said "No" to small requests, simply because they wanted to assert their authority, or because they didn't care to be bothered, or because some slight personal discomfort to themselves was involved. What they are doing, actually, is setting up a pattern of refusal in the child as well, who nurses these little grievances and petty injustices until they explode in some vast (and otherwise un-explainable) rebellion.

All human relations are a subtle system of barter and exchange. Children have an inborn sense of fairness. If a parent is fair, reasonable and pliant in matters important to the child, the child will reflect that attitude in matters important to the parent.

Much the same may be said of marriage. The happiest and most smooth-running marriages I have ever known were those in which the wife tried to please her husband in dozens of small ways. In return, the husband is quite willing to go along with his wife on major decisions. Most men retain a core of childishness: they are pleased by trivial attentions, and it is only when these are refused that they become difficult about important matters.

A skillful wife can win her way in almost every area of living, so long as she makes her husband feel that she is catering to his everyday needs. In this respect, the European woman (even long before she had the vote or any property rights) achieved a great deal more satisfaction out of life than her often disgruntled and neglected American sister.

A husband confronted with stale bread in a sandwich is likely to exact a ridiculously high price for his minor annoyance. Of course, his vexation is all out of proportion to the cause — but that rational animal called man has always been more animal than rational.

It is surprising how few couples understand that in a marriage the little things loom much larger than the big ones. A small concession by the wife, a slight word of praise from the husband — these are worth more than their weight in gold. And there is no return in casting stale bread upon the waters of matrimony.

When Rebellion Becomes Bondage

I KNOW a man who grew up in a stuffy midwestern atmosphere of Victorian piety, and who rebelled at an early age. He is now fifty, and still rebelling.

His old family home was cluttered; so his own home is starkly simple. His parents were fanatically devout; so he is fanatically irreligious. His relatives were dogmatically conservative; so he is dogmatically radical. This man thinks himself a "free soul." He thinks he has burst the bonds of his enslavement to the past. But he is wrong — for he is *overreacting* to the past, and is still chained to it by his hostility.

A hundred years before Freud, G. C. Lichtenberg, the German essayist, made the shrewd observation that "to do exactly the opposite is also a form of imitation." To do exactly the opposite is also a form of bondage. This is something that young people generally do not understand. To free oneself from parental domination does not mean to defy them or despise them, but to accept them for what they are, and to make life decisions that are based on one's own ideas, and not on blind rebellion.

In physics, we speak of negative and positive attractions. The same is true in psychology. The woman who hates the man she once loved is not free, but as much a slave to her negative passion as she formerly was to her positive passion.

The young man who rebels from Babbitry to bohemianism because it is exactly the opposite of what his father tried to cram down his throat is allowing his decision to be made by somebody else. This is why such bohemians eventually become bitter and aimless creatures.

Every person, as he grows up, must liberate himself from the past, but must at the same time learn to conserve what was good in the past — which is only another way of saying that a balanced person is both a liberal and a conservative.

To be free, in the fullest sense, does not mean to reject what our fathers believed; it means to discriminate, to select, to take on the difficult task of separating our principles from our passions. Many a man makes the lifelong mistake of elevating his neurosis into a creed.

Each generation, in some measure, rebels against the last. It is normal and natural and healthy. But it is necessary to know that the aim of rebellion is civil peace within the soul, and not perpetual revolt.

Masks Can't Hide the Real Self

"I WONDER what they're like when they're home alone," said the woman across the breakfast table from me. "How do you suppose they act when the masks are off?" She was referring to a couple we had seen at a party the night before, and had seen perhaps a half dozen times previously. Each time, they have been effusive, enthusiastic, and exhaustingly gay.

I replied that they were probably the same way in private by now. If a social mask is worn long enough, it hardens into a permanent cast of reality.

We become what we do. It is an error to suppose that

somehow we retain an "essence" of ourselves that is different from our daily existence. Our character consists of the way we act and react with other people, because man is primarily a social animal.

Some persons think they keep a core of integrity and self-honesty within themselves while they deal with the world falsely or hypocritically. They try to separate the "real self" from the social self, but this is as impossible as managing to keep dry while drilling a hole in the bottom of your rowboat.

People like the couple we were discussing, who are perpetually on the make socially, soon cease to be real persons, even to themselves. They become totally absorbed in what they are doing, and social success (which ought to be merely a pleasant by-product of the personality) turns into an all-consuming end.

In this way, many persons are dehumanized by taking one function and converting it into the total personality. They are pathetically lopsided, about making the most money, or being seen at the "best" places, or whatever other partial and paralyzing goal they have decided upon.

And, before long, the public mask they have adopted for this purpose becomes indistinguishable from their own features. They are driven by their drives, instead of controlling them — just as the heavy "social drinker" may wake one morning and discover that he is no longer in charge of his desires, that he is an alcoholic.

Virtue, said Aristotle, is a habit. We cannot be good in private; we cannot keep an inner part of ourselves separate from our daily conduct. To show a mask to the world is the surest way of losing that precious identity by which each individual soul carries the special mark of God.

Self-Doubt Is One Mark of Sanity

It is PART of the common wisdom of the human race to recognize that "everybody is a little crazy." It is this knowledge,
about ourselves as well as others, that keeps us in touch with
sanity. And it is one of the paradoxes of mental health that
the person who never questions his own sanity is the one most
likely to lose contact with reality.

I was speaking with a lawyer the other evening, and he remarked that he has had to deal with scores of clients who, in
his opinion, were over the line. "And they all had one thing
in common," he reflected. "They never doubted that they
were right."

This is why I am so negative about all those believe-in-
yourself books and courses and inspirational lectures. The
paranoid is a person who believes in himself — and in nobody
else. He has complete faith in his utter sanity, and that is the
mark of his madness.

It is not only useless, it is harmful, to believe in oneself until
one truly *knows* oneself. And to know oneself means to accept our moments of insanity, of eccentricity, of childishness
and blindness. In a family, for instance, when one of the
mates voluntarily goes to seek psychiatric help, it often turns
out that the other mate needs it more desperately. The rigidity of the paranoid personality never questions its own sanity,
but may easily drive a mate into questioning his own.

It is true that many disturbed people lack "confidence" in
themselves. But confidence cannot be achieved by a magic
incantation, by resolving grimly to "believe" in oneself. Self-
confidence can be won only by treading the path of self-
discovery — by learning all the twists and turns and dark
corners of our emotional nature.

A tightrope walker gains confidence by practice, by becoming aware of his skills *and his limitations*, by a realistic acceptance of the dangers involved — not by repeating to himself, "I can, I can," and then foolishly attempting a stunt for which he is not prepared.

The man who thinks he can do anything if he *wills* it hard enough is crazy. The man who thinks he is always right is crazy. The man who believes that if only those around him would change, then everything would turn out fine — he is closer to the edge of insanity than the self-doubting creature who timidly visits a doctor to learn if he is losing his mind.

Tough: Adjusting to Readjustment

A FELLOW NEWSPAPERMAN, who works in an office with three other chaps, was complaining that he couldn't get much work done "because of the noise." Yet, years ago, when he worked in the city room with one hundred other men, he had no difficulty in concentrating. "It was so noisy there that nothing bothered me," he explained.

It is important to understand that strange phenomenon. If any pressure is constant enough, we soon cease to find it a pressure; it is only when the pressure comes and goes that we find it intolerable. Working with three other men, my friend gets used to periods of quiet — and then rapidly has to adjust to other phone conversations and interruptions, which throw him off his stride.

But when the level of noise is continually high, we do not hear it any more. It becomes part of the accustomed background, and a reporter can easily take a complex message over the phone while a score of typewriters are clacking all around him.

People can adjust to almost any conditions; what they *cannot* adjust to is frequent readjustment. A rat can be conditioned to jump at a circle, even though he gets a mild shock from it; but he collapses when he is forced to shift from circles to squares to triangles.

What we popularly call a "nervous breakdown," I am convinced, does not come so much from steady pressure as from frequent shifts in stresses and strains, so that we do not know what to expect at any given time.

Children who become schizophrenic, it has been shown, are not so much the victims of cruel parents as of inconsistent parents. A child can adapt itself to cruelty, as a tangible and constant atmosphere of life. It cannot, however, cope with wildly fluctuating moods and attitudes on the part of parents. To be "loved" on Monday and rejected on Tuesday is frightening and bewildering to the human organism, which (if subjected to a great deal of this stress) will simply retreat from the world of reality. Likewise, the most precarious marriages are those in which the couples sharply swing from affection to hostility.

Steadiness is the prime condition of emotional health; even the strident steadiness of a pneumatic drill can be endured by the driller.

Our Songs a Sign of Sick Society

THE MAN who said he didn't care who wrote the nation's laws so long as he could write its songs lived a long time before the era of the juke box.

If our nation's popular songs are any indication of our state of mind, then we have become the most immature civilization the world has ever known.

Almost every song I hear on the car radio as I drive to work is the plaintive call of a baby asking for love. "I want" and "give me" and "need you" are the invariable refrains of all these melodies.

This is not love; it is what we call "egocentricity" in a baby, and what we call "neurotic dependence" when it persists in an adult. True love is not a taking as much as it is a giving.

Modern popular songs, almost without exception, are pathetic cries for attention, for protection, for comfort, for assurance — in short, for all the needs an infant must get from its parents.

Love songs of the past — from the odes of Horace to the sugared sonnets of Shakespeare — were exactly the reverse of this. They promised attention and protection and comfort to the beloved; they poured out love like a fountain, and did not soak it up like a sponge.

Those who object to rock-and-roll music are holding the stick by the wrong end. The music, no doubt, is barbarous and idiotic — but the lyrics are a more serious symptom of emotional sickness than the tunes. Young people today grow up saturated in this atmosphere of false romanticism. They think that love is something that "happens to you," instead of something you have to make yourself, in a creative and generous fashion.

If the songs a nation sings are more important than its laws — and there is a measure of truth in this — then our songs reveal a shocking infantilism in our approach to love and marriage. For it is an absolute psychological fact that the more love we are desirous of getting, the less love we are capable of giving. When the question is "What can you do for me?" instead of "What can I do for you?" then we have only a neurotic perversion of love, a greediness of the heart, a self-seeking passion that can never be satisfied.

Love, to mean anything, must be directed outward toward an object; and most popular songs are directed inward toward the subject. "I want, I want, I want" is a proper refrain for a baby screaming for its bottle; when it becomes an adult's theme song, our emotions are still in the cradle.

Why We Accept Opinions As Facts

IN HER RECENT BOOK *The Humanity of Words*, Dr. Bess Sondel who lectures on Communication at the University of Chicago tells about a test she gave to thirty top-ranking executives of a large industrial company. The purpose of the test was to determine whether or not these men could make the distinction between "facts" and "opinions." Their average grade was 35 — only seven correct out of twenty questions.

Dr. Sondel then gave the test to a ten-year-old girl, who made a grade of 95. The girl apologized for her failure to make 100 by saying she didn't know the meaning of the word "prestige," and therefore couldn't answer correctly.

Here are two statements that were part of the test given to the executives: (1) "Last year the records show a loss of $20,000 on the Alaska project." (2) "That was a lot of money to lose."

Everyone called the first statement a fact, which it is. But only four of the thirty executives called the second statement an opinion, which it clearly is. And these men are responsible for the policies and practices of an international industrial organization.

We talk disparagingly of the "ten-year-old-mentality" which popular entertainment is supposed to be aimed at. But the mentality of a ten-year-old, while poor in experience, is

rich in clarity. It has not yet been clouded or blunted or perverted by adult prejudice.

As we grow older, we acquire more information — but we
also run the grave risk of losing the candid gaze of childhood.
In our daily business, we pretend to worship facts; but often
we cannot distinguish a fact from an opinion, because we are
defending a position instead of defining a situation.

It becomes emotionally necessary for us to believe that what
we are doing is right. In order to believe it, we must hypnotize
ourselves into accepting our opinions (or the opinions of our
superiors) as facts.

Children do not do this, on the whole, for they do not have
an emotional investment in society; they have no status to be
defended, no position to be protected. And this is why adolescents, especially, seem so clear-eyed and cynical about the
pretensions and hypocrisies of their parents.

And this is why the Bible tells us we must become like
little children, who play their games more honestly than we
play ours.

Formula Is Out in Love or Politics

MENTIONING Ortega's new book, *On Love*, as I did recently,
reminded me of a remark that Albert Einstein made a few
years before he died. He was asked how it was that we have
made such strides in physics, and in science generally, but we
have not come very far in politics, and still squabble as childishly as the Greeks and Trojans did.

Einstein replied, quite directly: "This is because politics is
harder than physics."

Ortega makes the same observation in his book, saying

that the two subjects which everyone presumes to know —
love and politics — "are the ones which have progressed
least."

We look upon math and physics and astronomy as "difficult" subjects, but in a sense they are not really difficult; they
are merely complex. It takes time and patience to understand
them. But both politics and love — which seem so simple and
clear-cut to most people, who consider themselves experts on
both subjects — are infinitely more difficult to understand
and to cope with in a mature way.

It is almost the tragic irony of mankind that everybody
has a decided opinion about love and about politics, and these
two subjects have created 90 per cent of the world's turmoil
since the beginning of time.

The reason for this is not hard to see. There is no emotion
involved in a mathematical formula; one mathematician can,
without much trouble, convince another mathematician that
he is wrong. But love and politics are inextricably involved
with our emotions. One of the hardest tasks in the world is
to separate what is fact from what is desire — whether we
desire a certain person or a certain way of life.

We have traveled an enormous distance from the Greeks
and Trojans in terms of our knowledge of the external world,
but scarcely an inch in terms of the knowledge of our own
inner motives.

The greatest discoveries of the future, I am sure, will have
nothing to do with outer space or the basic composition of the
atom — for these will not help us solve the perennial human
problems of lust and possessiveness. It is only when we apply
ourselves — soul and mind together — to the study of the
human personality that we can begin to crawl along the road
toward our social salvation.

Quite Often It's Healthier to Be Sick

A MILWAUKEE DOCTOR, in a recent report to the American Association for Surgery of Trauma, has suggested that prospective employees should be given "thorough lower back X-rays" before being hired. Industry and insurance companies, he said, would save themselves considerable money, time and trouble if they rejected applicants who showed "probable future back disability."

One Milwaukee company began pre-employment back X-rays four years ago, and 31 per cent of the applicants were turned down on the findings, thus saving some $22,000 in treatment fees.

This strikes me as a shallow and shortsighted approach to the problem of industrial illness and absenteeism. I scarcely know a man past his middle thirties who has not had some lower back trouble; and most of them are suffering from little more than tension and anxiety. It is not so much organic physical illness that is responsible for high medical bills and low production rates as it is emotional disorders and the stresses of living in a frantic age. The major cause of "illness" in this country lies in the head, not in the rest of the body.

Any internist will readily tell you that more than half the patients coming to him with vague and persistent complaints — often a "nagging backache" — show absolutely no evidence of illness in laboratory tests and X-rays.

Indeed, those who *do* show some organic flaw are much more easily treated and cured. The 31 per cent who were rejected are precisely those who have the best chance of recovery, for a doctor can often cure an ailment he can put his finger on.

It is the others — those who showed no signs of bodily weakness — who comprise the great majority of patients these days. They troop from doctor to doctor, hoping to find a specific diagnosis — eyes, or pinched nerve-ends, or anemia, or thyroid, or whatever happens to be the currently fashionable explanation for a hole in the head.

Men and women with concrete physical illnesses are often the best workers, for they are dogged and diligent and seriously take care of their condition. The unreliable (and thus expensive) employes are those who suffer from the common malaise known as Unwillingness to Take a Hard and Honest Look at Oneself.

The Idea of a Thing Isn't the Thing

BETWEEN a thing, and the *idea* of a thing, there often lies a world of difference; and it is this difference that drives some persons to divorce, despair, drink and nervous breakdowns.

Many young people believe they would like to be married; but what really appeals to them is the *idea* of marriage, which is a quite different thing. And, likewise, many young wives think they want a child; but what they actually want is the *idea* of having a child — and a living, crying, demanding infant in no way resembles their abstract ideal.

Mark Twain once observed that "a classic is a book that everybody wants to have read, and nobody wants to read." His shrewd comment applies to a great deal more than literature.

We want something in the past tense, not in the present. The mother wants *to have had* a child, not to have one. Confronted with the immediate reality, she is liable to collapse — for she has been living with an idea, and is not emotionally prepared to accept a real object.

Many marriages fall apart because the couples have conceived of marriage as something *accomplished*, a fact behind them, once they are legally sealed. But a living relationship is never accomplished, it is always in process, always changing, always subject to stress, always becoming something different from what it was.

The idea of marriage is a permanent and stable one, but even the best marriage itself is up-and-down, in-and-out, to-and-fro. Ideas are static, but all life is motion, and motion can be terribly frightening to some personalities.

Heraclitus, the ancient philosopher, made the famous statement that we never step into the same river twice — for the river is always changing. He might have added that we are never the same, either, and the person who steps into the river in autumn is different — however subtly — from the one who stepped in in the summer.

A dependence upon abstract ideals can be fatal in the world of human relationships. The bright-eyed pink-cheeked baby on the magazine cover is an abstraction, and the mother who expects only this will plunge into despair when faced with a red-eyed, pale-cheeked baby screaming with colic at four o'clock of a cold morning.

Learn to Team up Your Horse Sense

As SOME anonymous French wit once said, most of us use ideas the way a drunk uses a lampost — for support, and not for illumination.

Consider the two contrary notions of "common sense" and "expert knowledge." Which do we believe in? Whichever one happens to suit us best at the time. When we disagree with expert knowledge, we call upon common sense. When common sense seems to be against us, we take refuge in expert opinion.

I know a woman who used to drive her children nearly crazy this way. When they were ill, and the doctor recommended something she disapproved of, she would say, "Well, the doctors don't know everything — you sometimes have to rely on your common sense." However, at other times, when the children rebelled at some medicine the doctor had prescribed, she would say, "You have to follow medical advice — after all, the doctor's paid to know what's best for you."

Such inconsistency is ludicrous and infuriating; but most of us do much the same sort of thing in our daily lives. What we fail to realize is that neither common sense nor expert opinion is sufficient unto itself. The two continually need to be joined together in a sensitive blend. Common sense can take you only so far, and then it comes up against the blank wall of ignorance. Without some study and specialized knowledge, the most perceptive mind in the world is working without adequate tools.

Likewise, the *expertise* of the professionals cannot exist in a vacuum. The world is full of educated fools who think that their titles or degrees give them a command of their subjects, and who lose sight of the human application of their theories.

A balanced personality is one which knows how to reach a delicate equilibrium between the two — neither scorning the intellectual approach of the expert, nor despising the intuitive attitude of the ordinary man.

Whenever I hear a person praise "common sense," I suspect he is an ignoramus; and whenever I run across a smug expert citing "authorities," I suspect he would be lost without his reference books. The only man who can help us — the only man who can help himself — is the one who can drive these two horses together, with an easy hand on the reins.

Grads: *Money Isn't All in Hunt for Job*

THE THOUSANDS of graduates who are now looking for jobs — or, more likely, evaluating different job offers — ought to be told the emotional facts of life, which go far beyond the economic facts of life.

Perhaps one per cent of the graduates will ever get rich. They get rich by accident, by inheritance, or by some rare and special combination of skills. For most of us, a decent comfort is all we can expect. This being the case, the most appealing factor about a job opportunity ought to be the kind and depth of pleasure it affords. Yet we hardly ever hear anyone counseling college graduates about this.

To obtain a genuine gratification from one's work is worth many thousands a year. This is what every middle-aged man has learned the hard way. For we find that, as our income goes up in arithmetical progression (1, 2, 3, 4, etc), our expenses go up in geometrical progression (1, 2, 4, 8, etc.).

Our income gets higher; but our expenses get both higher and wider. In our economy, at least, the more we make, the more we spend; the race is endless, and there is no turning back, once a luxury has become a "necessity."

To go into a field because it offers more money can be the most fatal of illusions. Money is necessary, but it is never sufficient. If it were, the richest people would be the happiest, and quite obviously they are not.

I have listened to medical students trying to decide on their specialty in terms of the ease of hours and the rate of fees; and while they think they are being "realistic," it seems to me that they are shockingly unrealistic — because they ignore their own deepest psychological needs.

A man whose work is emotionally satisfying can cope with a great deal of tension in other areas of his life. If he feels he is making a contribution, if he feels that the intangible returns from his work compensate for the long hours and the lesser pay, he has a secret source of strength to sustain him, while his more prosperous but disgruntled fellows fall victim to ulcers or alcoholism or some other symptom of personal dissatisfaction.

This is not the trite plea to ignore the economic appetite, which is strong and important. But it is a suggestion that, beyond a decent minimum level, money fails to bring us what we think it will. Only pleasure in the performance of our craft can do that.

Cause or Effect—Which Is Which?

WE OFTEN SPEAK glibly about "the law of cause and effect," but sometimes it is difficult to tell the one from the other. Especially in regard to medical "evidence."

I read a recent survey showing that heavy smokers tend to have more nervous breakdowns than light smokers and non-smokers. What, exactly does this prove? It might indicate, of course, that heavy smoking brings on a nervous condition; but it might just as plausibly be argued that people with nervous dispositions tend to smoke heavily.

Does the smoking cause the nervousness, or the nervousness the smoking? Nobody yet knows.

Likewise, I attended a lecture given by a Swedish scientist who has found that patients with schizophrenia show blood reactions that are strikingly different from "normal" people.

He is convinced that something chemical in the action of the blood "causes" schizophrenia. I wonder whether the opposite might not be true — that people who suffer from mental derangement also undergo some chemical changes.

We know that when a person is angry or fearful, his glands discharge a great deal more adrenalin than when he is placid. Here, the physical condition is induced by the mental state. May it not be just as possible that schizophrenics produce similar changes in their blood composition?

The biologist who insists that all mental illness comes from physical causes is as absurd, dogmatic and one-sided as the psychiatrist who insists that all mental illness is "psychic" in origin.

We simply do not know enough yet about the subtle interplay between body and mind. We do not know enough yet about the constitutional factors at birth which may push us in a certain direction and make us vulnerable to special diseases of the mind or body. "Cause" is a simple word, but an elusive concept.

The human tendency to oversimplify is the great enemy of progress on all fronts. The roots of any trouble are usually deep and intertwined. It may make us feel good, or smart, to point to a single "cause," but it adds nothing to the world's stock of permanent, useful knowledge.

And, in response to most basic questions about human behavior, isn't it time the scientists gave us the only scientifically honest answer, which is: "We simply do not know enough yet"? But scientists, being also men, are fond of pretending otherwise.

Intelligence: A Word of Many Facets

A COUPLE dropped in while I was playing chess the other evening, and the woman made the customary remark that she wasn't "intelligent" enough to take up the game.

Yet, although I have been playing since I was ten, with duffers and experts alike, I have not seen the slightest relation between chess ability and general intelligence. Indeed, I have seen some Masters who barely knew enough to tie their shoelaces properly away from the chessboard. They can beat me blindfolded every game, but their non-chess intelligence is scarcely visible to the naked eye.

I suggest that the word "intelligence" is not a single unitary thing, but is rather a composite made up of many strands. There are different *kinds* of intelligence, and one is not necessarily better than the other.

There is social intelligence, for instance, which few intellectuals possess — the ability to understand how other people feel and to live and work with them in reasonable peace.

There is mechanical intelligence, which I don't possess an iota of — the ability to manipulate and conquer physical objects, to make, to repair, to take apart and put together.

There is mathematical intelligence, of which chess is a part — the ability to visualize abstractions in space. This is a rare gift which has sometimes been given to men who are otherwise idiots.

There is verbal intelligence — the ability to use words with force and clarity; but some of the writers who are best at this (Hemingway comes to mind) are appallingly poor thinkers and have evolved a philosophy of life that would scarcely do credit to a high school sophomore.

And there is a deep intelligence of the blood and the bone, which is not articulate, which cannot express itself verbally, but which knows what to do in practical situations where a genius might find himself helpless or hysterical.

We must not be bluffed or intimidated by a word. "Intelligence" can cover a wide spectrum of human aptitudes; and, besides, this spectrum is so colored with our emotional lives that many people seem dumb (to themselves as well as to others) because they are merely fearful and confused.

No real gauge of intelligence has yet been devised; the I.Q. test is a makeshift device, heavily weighted in favor of those who can express themselves deftly and swiftly. But millions of others have simply not learned to use more than a fraction of the intelligence they have.

Smut Is the Sign of a Sick Society

I AM FORCED to disagree with those well-intentioned defenders of public morality who insist that "pornographic literature" exercises a dangerous effect upon young minds. There has never been the slightest evidence that what a person reads influences his basic motives — but there is plenty of reason to believe that a person's basic motives determine his choice of reading matter.

It is typical of the thoughtless observer to blame something obvious and extreme — such as trashy comic books — for perverting and degrading the minds of young people. This is one way of relieving ourselves of the responsibility for the spiritual atmosphere we have created in our whole society.

America today is enormously, and frighteningly, sex-oriented. Scarcely a movie, or a magazine story, or an advertisement, reaches the public eye without stressing the female figure as an object of allure and glamour and the ultimate in desirability.

It is these "respectable" elements in our social order that reflect our immature preoccupation with sex. And it is this preoccupation that opens the door to obscene comic books and cloacal postcards. Pornography is always a symptom, not a cause. The breakdown in values begins at the top, among the arbiters of taste, and filters downward to the young and impressionable. The purveyors of pornographic literature are merely filling a demand that we have stimulated; they are not creating it.

This is not to say that the public does not have the right, and the duty, to protect youngsters from such filth. But doing this alone would be an ineffectual and hypocritical gesture so long as adults themselves continue to adulate the mammary glands, to sell products keyed to sexual symbolism, and to confuse physical attraction with love.

Young people are astonishingly clearsighted. They can readily see through our humbug, and despise us straightforwardly for it. They know that much of our social and economic dynamo is driven by an excessive emphasis on sexuality, no matter how piously we proclaim otherwise. And they want to go along for the ride.

It was good, and healthful, that the Freudian revolution should have released sex from its dark and festering corner. It is bad, and sick, that we have manipulated and exploited this new freedom for quick gains and cheap pleasures. The publishers of pornography are merely taking a soiled leaf from our own book.

Sign of Immaturity: Blaming Others

READING THE MANUAL of Epictetus for a Great Books assignment last week, I came across a lovely sentence that anticipates — two thousand years ago — much of what we know about modern psychology:

"To accuse others for your own misfortunes is a sign of lack of education; to accuse yourself shows that your education has begun; to accuse neither yourself nor others shows that your education is complete."

What does this admirably compact sentence mean? First of all, obviously, it expresses a thought we all recognize and accept today — that the really bad things in our lives are mainly caused by our own motives and actions, not by external circumstances or by other people. But, more than that, it wisely points out that self-accusation is only the beginning of knowledge. While it is good and healthful to know that we ourselves are responsible for what happens to us, this admission must never become an excuse for persisting in flaws and failures.

People who blame others are immature; but people who constantly blame themselves are indulging in a kind of neurotic pleasure — they do something wrong, feel pangs of remorse, castigate themselves, and then feel purged to go out and repeat the same wrong actions over again.

Genuine education — of the emotions, and not merely of the mind — goes beyond blame. It tries to *understand* why we do the things we do, and only by understanding them, in their deepest meanings, can we acquire the resolve to alter our pattern of behavior.

This is why, for instance, so many alcoholics fail to break

their tragic habit. After a bout with the bottle, they engage in a paroxysm of self-blame; but the paroxysm itself is simply a way of getting rid of guilt feelings; then, when these feelings are discharged, the alcoholic resumes his doleful fugue.

Blaming others is an obvious means of escaping responsibility. But blaming oneself is a more subtle device for refusing to change. "I can't help myself," or "I'm just built that way," or "It's in my blood," are just verbal barriers to avoid coming to grips with some central problem in the personality.

The human mind is a devilishly complex organism, full of tricks and disguises, which we can begin to see even in a small child, who learns quite early how to win approval and yet satisfy his own pleasures. And we are not grown up until we accept reality by relinquishing the pleasure of blaming ourselves as a substitute for facing ourselves.

Matter of Giving Is a Rare Art

WE ARE TOLD, in the Book, that it is more blessed to give than to receive, which is a spiritual truth. But it is a psychological truth that sometimes it is harder to give tactfully than to receive gratefully.

The art of charity, for instance, has been mastered only by those rare souls with an innate sense of tact. When most of us give, we do so clumsily or smugly or, worst of all, with a brazen announcement of our own generosity. This is why the poor or the needy seem so often to resent our Lord and Lady Bountiful roles. They recognize — and resent — that beneath our charity lies a hard core of superiority, which poisons the gift at the source.

The French are a frugal people, but they have raised tact

to a high level, and when they do give they know how to do it so that the recipient almost feels that he is conferring a favor upon the donor.

One of the loveliest examples is the note that Corot, the painter, sent to his friend Daumier, who was nearly blind and facing eviction on his sixty-fifth birthday:

"Old Friend — I have a little house at Valmondois which I could not, for the life of me, think what to do with. Suddenly I thought to give it to you. Liking the idea, I have had your ownership legally confirmed. I had no idea of doing you a good turn. The whole scheme was carried out to annoy the landlord. Ever yours — Corot."

And Daumier wrote gratefully in reply: "You're the only man from whom I can take such a present and not feel humiliated."

Much of our present-day organized philanthropy lacks this essential person-to-person tact, and therefore makes its recipients both greedy and sullen at the same time. The poor know that it is much easier to give money than to give kindness and a little thought.

It is difficult, said Ruskin, to be wisely charitable, "to do good without multiplying the sources of evil." And when doing good becomes vast and institutional and even fashionable, then the human element has given way to the "sociological" — and we are helping Unfortunates instead of men and women and children much like ourselves.

People in underdeveloped countries resent American largess as much as they need it. How to give without humiliating may well be the chief perplexity of our foreign aid policy.

Cause of Divorces? Who Knows?

SOME FRIENDS were discussing the possible reasons that a couple we know are getting divorced, and I recalled what a wise woman of Dr. Allan Gregg's acquaintance once told him: "You never know the true inwardness of sombeody else's marriage; you only know your own — in fact, you only know half of that."

We can call this woman wise because, like Socrates, she knew how ignorant she was, and how ignorant everybody else is, of the "true inwardness" of other people's relationships.

There is much gossip and chatter and conjecture about such things, and all of us are equally guilty. We toss around psychological terms with light abandon; we make generalizations that not only sweep but also soar; we project our own needs and fears and desires into other people's lives. And it is a sober fact that, in most cases, we scarcely know the true inwardness of our own marriage. How many "contented" husbands are amazed when a faithful wife of twenty years suddenly moves out and declares she wants a divorce? How many wives with "happy" marriages are shocked to learn their husbands are involved in an illicit affair of long standing?

It is an unfortunate truism that deep communication between couples exists during the courting period, if at all, and then disappears in a welter of practical problems — the home, the children, the bills, the doctors and dentists and clubs and summer plans. The sheer *mechanics* of domesticity often take the place of the *dynamics* of emotions that brought the couple together in the first place.

Nietzsche, that unhappy genius, understood the basic need for communication in a lifelong relationship when he advised men: "At the beginning of a marriage ask yourself whether this woman will be interesting to talk to from now until old age. Everything else in marriage is transitory; most of the time is spent in conversation — or in sullen silence."

How are we to fix the "responsibility" for a broken marriage? Even in gross cases of cruelty or drunkenness or promiscuity, the facts that appear in court or over the cocktail tables merely scratch the surface of the relationship. Certainly no stranger, probably no friend, and sometimes not even the partners themselves can elucidate the deeper reasons for the break. It is more than an impertinence, it is sheer intellectual arrogance, to make such judgments. But we will all continue to make them.

2

OF CUSTOMS
AND TABOOS

Woman's Mind Is Like Abstract Art

ONE OF THE MINOR difficulties in the relation between the sexes is that women speak a language without nouns. Their minds work so freely and intuitively that they feel pronouns are enough to tell you what they are talking about.

In one of C. S. Lewis' early novels, he observes: "If two men are doing a bit of work, one will say to the other, 'Put this bowl inside the bigger bowl which you'll find on the top shelf of the green cupboard.' The female for this is 'Put that in the other one there.' And then if you ask them, 'In where?' they say, 'In *there*, of course.' "

While undressing at home after a party, a wife will often reflect aloud to her husband, "She really didn't look very well, tonight." "Who didn't?" the husband asks. "Why, Priscilla, of course," the wife replies shortly, "Who else would I mean?"

A woman's mind jumps gaps, like an electric spark, while a man's mind has to travel through a conductor. He needs some vehicle for transmitting the current of thought; she easily dispenses with logical connections, like an abstract expressionist painter.

It ordinarily takes many years for the slow, ponderous mind of a man to grasp the content of this idea-painting. He is normally used to literal, photographic impressions of people and the world. "Did you notice anything about Daphne tonight?" his wife will say. "That was a pretty pink dress," her husband answers dutifully. "It wasn't pink," she says, "and besides, I meant her *attitude*, not her dress."

Ten minutes after entering a room at a dinner party, a woman can tell if any of the couples had a quarrel that day; a man would have to see a husband hitting his wife over the head with a plate before he realized something was amiss. This almost-animal perception is what makes women talk without nouns — they just assume you have followed their unconscious train of thought.

A couple may be sitting in the living room reading the paper after dinner when she remarks, "It doesn't feel right." "What doesn't?" her husband asks. "The arrangement around the fireplace, naturally," she retorts impatiently. "Why didn't you say so?" he asks. "I did," she answers. And so she did — whose fault was it that he couldn't follow?

We males are clumsy materialists in a world of exquisite female sensibility — a sensibility that goes far beyond facts and logic and even proper nouns; and no marriage can be called a success which ignores this profound emotional disparity.

Inaction Is Deficiency of Democracy

I WAS TRAVELING back from St. Louis in a daycoach, when the man across the aisle asked the porter if he could lower the temperature in the car. Several passengers had muttered darkly about the heat, but only among themselves.

The porter ignored his request. About ten minutes later he asked another porter, and received the same summary treatment. By this time he was mad, and he charged in full pursuit of the conductor to make a complaint.

The feelings of the rest of the passengers were mixed. We, too, had been suffering from the heat in the car, but no one else spoke up. The complaining passenger both pleased us and embarrassed us. He was in the right, and yet no one supported him openly.

I think it is this attitude, on a large scale, that makes our democratic society so deficient. We are ashamed or afraid to complain; we are unwilling to make nuisances of ourselves, unless the provocation is extremely great. And so we sit by passively until minor annoyances snowball into huge injustices.

We let the cranks or the crackpots or the aggressively offensive people do our protesting for us. None of us others wants "to make a fuss." And yet resentment grows inside us until it explodes in some vast irrational action, more in the nature of a mob revolt than an orderly petition for justice.

In some ways England, with all its aristocratic heritage, is more democratic than the United States. England has a long tradition of individual protest: the average citizen will sit down and write a letter to the president of a railway about a minor grievance. We will not complain; we will just stop using that railway after a while.

The English are intensely jealous of their individual rights, while we submit to the most outrageous treatment without a murmur. Americans are treated like cattle in many situations, but they rarely apply their high ideals of "freedom" to specific situations in their daily lives.

The man in the coach was doing what all of us should have done; but because we were too timid or too lazy he grew excessively wrathful and defeated his own cause. What we have yet to learn is that when we refuse to make a fuss about minor matters we soon lose our power to rectify major injustices without a diabolic revolution.

Collecting Completely Baffles Syd

A RECENT ADVERTISEMENT for dictating machines showed Raymond Moley in his office, the walls of which were covered with framed (and presumably signed) photographs of famous persons.

I have never understood this need or desire on the part of so many people to surround themselves with the visible signs of importance. It is a harmless vanity, I grant you, but one that is simply inexplicable to me. I have met a fair number of significant men and women in my time, but it never occurred to me to document our relationship with an autographed picture.

Collecting the signatures of the great leaves me equally baffled. What in the world would I do with the signature of a famous person on a sheet of paper? It means nothing, even if I get him to scribble "To my dear friend . . ." above his signature.

Likewise, first editions or books autographed by their authors leave me utterly cold. I am interested in the contents of a book, and it doesn't matter to me if it is printed on cardboard and is the umpteenth edition.

Some temperaments, I am sure, receive much warmth and contentment from this vicarious association with greatness: like the people who patiently stand in line for hours to shake hands with some luminary, so that they can tell their friends and children of their feat. I would be embarrassed to shake hands with a man who did not know me from Adam's off ox and who was just performing some impersonal ritual.

It pleases me, frankly, when readers come up to shake my hand after a lecture, and to tell me they enjoyed it. But this is just a friendly and spontaneous gesture, and not what I am talking about. I am referring to the dedicated celebrity hunter, the picture collector, the signature clutcher, the autographed-edition hound.

My office walls, by now, could be filled with the portraits of famous authors and actors and musicians — but to what purpose, except to look around on wan days and assure myself that I know them? I know that I know them; if we are genuinely friends, I don't need their faces on the wall; if we aren't, then the pictures are a fraud to impress others.

Which reminds me of the author who boasted to an acquaintance, "My first editions are very rare." Yes," he was answered, "and your second editions are even rarer."

Is Push to Masculinity Too Rapid?

I WAS PLEASED to see an off-beat item in the paper last week: in London, the heavyweight wrestling champion of Scotland Yard revealed that his "secret hobby" is designing wedding dresses.

What pleased me was this acknowledgment by a robust masculine figure that he unashamedly practices a craft considered "feminine" by most. In our country, a man who designed a dress or knitted a sweater would be looked upon with scorn or amused contempt.

There is too sharp a division in our minds between "masculine" and "feminine" activities. Nobody is pure male or pure female; all of us have slight tendencies of the other sex, which require healthy expression. Yet boys in our culture are not permitted to express this. The girls, during the twentieth century, have abdicated many of their traditional roles: it is now not considered unfeminine for a girl to engage in sports, or drive a car, or smoke a cigarette, or even wear pants.

The boys, however, have no outlet for their passive tendencies. It is considered "sissy" for a boy to be anything but a rough, roistering figure with a good left hook and a few missing teeth. At the tenderest ages, parents make these definite distinctions between the sexes.

The competition among boys to grow up fast and grow up tough has been accelerated in our society to the danger point. Sometimes it seems as if we are afraid of our masculinity, for we feel such a need to assert it and to implant it early in our male children, instead of accepting it quite naturally.

I think that this exaggeration has two opposite results: with some sensitive little boys, it makes them withdraw from male competition and drives them further away from normal masculinity; with others, it gives them the false idea that toughness and aggressiveness are the true marks of manhood. Much of what we call "juvenile delinquency" is motivated by this inflated idea of how a "real man" should behave.

We are, of course, the most sex-conscious country in the world; all one has to do is to flip through the ads of any general magazine to see the proof of that. Yet with all our com-

mercial emphasis on feminine desirability and masculine drive,
we have succeeded in producing more cold women and more
immature men than we had ever believed was possible.

The reasons for this, no doubt, are deep and complex; but
one factor we cannot ignore is our relentless pushing of small
children to become "little women" and "little men" before
they are ready to adopt either role. When we do this, we can
scarcely blame our adolescents for playing these roles to the
dangerous hilt.

An Unlisted Phone Locks the Door

THE NEW YORK TELEPHONE COMPANY has just begun to charge
its subscribers fifty cents a month for performing a non-service
— keeping their numbers out of the telephone book.

It may surprise you, as it pleased me, to learn that 400,000
phone subscribers in the New York metropolitan area have
unlisted numbers. This propensity for privacy on the part of
telephone owners has created extra work for the company,
including a separate set of records. Thus the "non-service"
charge.

I think it is well worth it. My own number has been out of
the book for a dozen years, and what a blessed relief it has
been. There are several other Sydney Harrises in the local
book, however, and reports have reached me that they are
frequently afflicted with calls meant for me.

None of these calls, I am sure, was of the slightest importance. Before I delisted myself, I was plagued with salesmen,
solicitors, drunks who wanted me to settle barroom bets, and
miscellaneous pests with nothing better to do than invade the
privacy of a stranger's home.

It is encouraging that nearly a half million New Yorkers

feel the same way and have deleted their presence from the directory. It was Robert Lynd, the sociologist, who described the telephone as "the greatest nuisance among conveniences, and the greatest convenience among nuisances." An unlisted number, to my mind, preserves the convenience while removing the nuisance.

A magazine I much enjoy, the quarterly *The American Scholar*, published by Phi Beta Kappa, has lately been running a series of articles on "the concept of privacy" in modern American life. The consensus of its distinguished contributors has been that Americans are the most victimized people in the world. Everywhere we turn, we are assailed by the relentless competition for our attention, from people selling products, ideas, emotions, prejudices; by tests, surveys, polls, contests; and the home, which used to be a man's castle, has become an open-air forum.

The families who have pulled their names out of the phone directory are not suffering from snobbism, nor are they dodging creditors. For the most part, they are seeking a little peace and quiet in the one refuge that is left to them. I applaud the good sense of Telephonics Anonymous.

Think Twice—Then Don't Say It!

ANY STATEMENT that begins: "When I was a boy . . ." will not be listened to by young people today, who rightly suspect sentimental nostalgia and distortion of the past.

Any statement that begins: "There are two sides to every question . . ." is generally an attempt to make the weaker side sound as plausible as the stronger side.

Any statement that begins: "If I were in charge of things . . ." is scarcely worth hearing out — for when we take charge of things we soon sound like those who are in charge of things.

Any statement that begins: "You only live once, so . . ." is bound to be a defense of the sensual life as against the rational life, and a concealed apology for doing as we like, and not what we know to be right.

Any statement that begins: "I'll make you a handsome offer . . ." is bound to be more handsome in appearance than in substance, and more generous verbally than actually.

Any statement that begins: "I'll never forget the day . . ." usually introduces an anecdote about a day that would be better off forgotten.

Any statement that begins: "We've been keeping an eye on you, my boy . . ." signifies that an employee is going to get a raise in prestige, but not necessarily in pay.

Any statement that begins: "I want to tell you something as a friend . . ." will contain a piece of unsolicited, unnecessary and offensive advice that displays about as much unconscious enmity as open friendship.

Any statement that begins: "I don't like to brag about my own children, but . . ." is a downright lie. (Personally, I enjoy nothing more than bragging about my children, when I can trap an audience in a weakened condition.)

Any statement that begins: "That's funny, I have a brother-in-law with the same complaint, and the doctor told him . . ." indicates that you have just fallen into the deepest of conversational pits — the one cunningly dug by a "Health Bore," who has staked out rare, complicated and macabre diseases as his own special field of misinformation.

Any statement that begins: "If you ask me, the Russians are going to . . ." is invariably made by someone you would not dream of asking even what language the Russians speak.

"Model" Home? Don't You Believe It

THE ONLY THING wrong with those new "model homes" is that they don't come fully equipped with model children. After a few weeks, those lovely plans for "comfortable living space" might as well have been drawn in vanishing ink.

My own ménage has spacious quarters. The little ones have their own rooms, with a connecting bathroom. There is plenty of play space. Also, Mama and Papa have a separate wing: bedroom, study, hall and two bathrooms "for grownups only."

And where do you suppose Michael and Barbara park themselves all day long? Naturally — in Mama's bedroom, in Daddy's study, and in the bathrooms that don't belong to them.

I have yet to shave in the morning without two little ones twining themselves around my legs, tossing a sailboat in my washbasin, tangling themselves in the electric shaver cord.

In our "private" hall, I continually stumble over drums, tractors and doll beds. In my study, when I look for a copy of Fowler's *Modern English Usage*, I have to wade through *Chicken-Licken*, *The Rattle-Rattle Dump-Truck*, and an assorted mound of coloring books.

You would think that the children's own rooms were perpetually quarantined. Nothing is duller to them than an area that is not inhabited by adults. "Go to your room and play" sounds to them like a death knell; they would much rather punch holes in my hi-fi speaker, or climb up the draperies in the living room.

And these are, on the whole, tractable and obedient children. But, good as they are, they are children — and to a child, unless he is severly repressed, there's no business like the old folks' business.

If the phone in my study rings, Barbara is there to perform her incoherent answering service. If the doorbell rings, Michael the Butler is out in the hall (usually trouserless) to greet the startled visitor.

If we had put them into airless dungeons, with prison bars and snarling tigers ready to leap out at them, the children couldn't be more disinclined to stay in their rooms. On the rare occasions when they do, we immediately phone the doctor; illness has set in.

This is just a friendly note to young inexperienced parents about to make delicious plans for a "model home." Don't believe it. Until the kids have reached the adolescent stage of being utterly bored by all adults, there won't be an inch of space in the house you can call your own. I'm writing this while sitting in the children's bathroom.

Why Mr. H. Calls Strangers "Mister"

A FRIEND OF MINE insists I am stuffy because I resent the use of first names between persons who know each other only slightly. "It's just a friendly and informal American habit," he protests.

Strangely enough, I don't think it is informal at all; I think it is quite formal — because it is a mere formality, without any true meaning. When I meet a man and begin calling him "Dick" instead of "Mr. Johnson" within a half hour, I am conforming to a false standard of intimacy. The man is a stranger to me, and I have no right to presume on a friendship that does not exist.

Like the words "darling" and "sweetheart" in theatrical

circles (which mean absolutely nothing, since they are applied to everyone indiscriminately), first-naming of strangers is a cheapening and debasement of true friendship. When an actor calls everybody "sweetheart," what is left to call his sweetheart? When I address a stranger by his first name, what is left to call my dearest friends? How then can I signify the gradations of feeling from politeness to deep devotion?

My objection to first names on early acquaintance does not indicate that I am unfriendly; far from it. It indicates that I value friendship so highly that I am unwilling to bestow its symbol upon a stranger. I think friendship must be earned and won, and not conferred loosely.

Language is a tool — our greatest tool — and can be blunted and broken like any other tool. A man would be a fool to use a fencing sword to cut butter with, or a butter knife to hack down a tree — yet we abuse the tools of language even more violently and senselessly.

If we call every minor writer a "genius," then we have lost a word to apply when a genuine genius comes along; if every performer in show business is "great," how do we define true greatness? And if every transitory amour is called "love," we must seek for some other word to describe that rare, elevated and abiding passion.

It used to be, when a man called you by your first name, you knew it signified a change in the relationship — that he accepted you at your worth, considered you a friend, and could be relied upon to help.

This is precisely what it should mean; but among today's Dicks and Toms and Sams, it is only a formal salutation of false conviviality. "I'm sorry, Dick, we have to let you go," says Tom, the boss, smiling heartily and pulling out the rug from under his good old pal.

When a Smile Is Worth a Scowl

WHILE I WAS ADDRESSING a medical convention last month, a newspaper photographer stopped in to take pictures of the great men. He posed several of the doctors around a chart they had been studying, and commanded them, "Now, let's all have a big smile on our faces!"

I saw the photo a few hours later; the medical men were grinning in delight at the chart, which had the bold legend written above it: "Infant Mortality Rate in Illinois for 1958."

There is a wonderfully sardonic moral in this picture of the doctors beaming ruddily about the newborn babies who had died in Illinois hospitals last year — and the moral is: "Don't Keep Smiling."

Each profession has its own clichés, and the newspaper business is no exception. People in pictures are supposed to be smiling, unless they are "bowed by grief." What they are smiling about doesn't matter, as long as the "stiffness" is taken out of the picture.

But what is the point of replacing the stiffness of a solemn face with the stiffness of an artificial smile? Why should men be grinning while they point at a chart, any more than two contesting candidates should be grinning while they shake hands and privately wish each other were dead?

The next day I saw another picture in the paper. A department store had opened a new bank of elevators, and several of the officers were "operating" one of the elevators, with enormous smiles and ecstatic hand-wavings. It looked like the phoniest picture of all time, because none of the men was behaving as he normally would. Elevators are run by operators or by pushbuttons, not by presidents and vice-presidents;

just as tractors are run by farmers and not by senatorial candidates.

But one of the most entrenched clichés of journalism is that people in pictures have to be "doing something," even if it is only smiling at a chart about dead babies. It is true that, in a photo, action is better than inaction; but inaction is better than false action.

What a photographer wants is a "natural" shot, and I don't see how you get this by creating an artificial pose. A strained smile is worse than an honest scowl; it is not without reason that the finest personality photograph in recent years was one of Callas, the opera singer, bearing her fangs at a summons server. An ordinary photographer would have waited until she had given him a dazzlingly operatic smile.

What Makes a Good Teacher Good?

THE GALLUP POLL not long ago said that if the general public set the policy, America's schoolteachers would be given pay increases based on their teaching ability rather than on the length of their service.

This idea sounds clear, fair and plausible — until you begin to examine it. What exactly is "teaching ability," and how do we begin to measure it?

Is a "good teacher" one who stuffs her students full of facts, who loads them with homework, who forces them to memorize huge chunks of her subject? Or is it one who inspires in pupils an appetite for learning, who makes them intellectually curious, who gives them a lifelong zest for improving their minds?

Very few teachers can do both of these at the same time.

My own teachers who crammed me with facts were dull and spiritless creatures, while the ones who maintained my interest in a subject were less concerned about memorization and repetition.

The reason that "teaching ability" cannot be evaluated fairly is that it is as much a matter of personality as of knowledge. One teacher may *know* twice as much about a subject as another, but if she cannot communicate, if she has no rapport with her pupils, then she cannot impart her knowledge in a manner that will stick.

I have long recommended that prospective teachers be given rigorous personality tests — which are more important, to my mind, than academic tests. If a teacher lacks humor, perspective, flexibility of viewpoint, she will not make her subject appealing, no matter how hard she forces the pupils to work. They may get higher grades than pupils in another class, but high grades mean only that a pupil has committed a course to memory, not that he necessarily understands it or cares about it.

Students must be taught to *care* about what they are learning, to grasp its relevance to the world at large, to comprehend what it means to be an educated person. The teachers I most remember are those who made their subjects come alive for me — subjects I am still interested in.

But how could the school system evaluate these teachers except on grades and examinations, which mean little? Ultimately, only the pupils know who the really good teachers are; they cannot be fooled.

Conversation No Road to Success

I WISH I COULD HAVE believed the advertisement I saw in a magazine last week. It was offering a correspondence course in conversation, holding out the promise of "new heights in the business and social world" to those who mastered the course. "In your conversation," the ad vibrated, "may lie the opportunity for social and business advancement . . . new contacts . . . promotion . . . in short, SUCCESS."

Would that it were so. But I can't think of anything less important or decisive than conversation in the modern world — and especially in modern America. The few charming conversationalists I have known were failures in the eyes of the world; and the most successful men have been nearly inarticulate. Most of them could not even verbalize their own businesses.

Conversation is a dying, if not a dead, art. We are too busy getting and spending, listening and watching professional entertainers, to develop our own powers of communication. And when a delightful talker does come along, we sullenly suspect him of being frivolous and insincere.

Our social conversation, in the main, is as deadly as our business talk. The most "fashionable" parties I have attended were accompanied by conversation scarcely above the Cro-Magnon level; but if the liquor is flowing freely, nobody seems to care.

Somebody once said that good conversation should be like a tennis match, with each player gracefully sending the ball back across the net; instead, most conversation is like a golf game, with each player stroking only his own ball, and waiting impatiently for the other to finish.

Success, in the worldly sense, depends upon one thing only (beyond a minimum of cunning), and that is: single-mindedness. You have to care about nothing else, think about nothing else, talk about nothing else. This monomania is guaranteed to take you straight to the top, without the need of any correspondence course — but it will do little to expand your talent for self-expression.

It is the manipulation of *things*, not the mastery of words or ideas, that characterizes our society. We mistake solemn dullness for profundity; and dismiss the verbal graces as mere trifling. Today, the good talker is out selling things for the grunter who makes them.

At Last—A Do-It-Yourself Speech

As a FREE PUBLIC SERVICE to all newly elected club officials, and others who may from time to time be called upon to make a brief talk, I am herewith presenting a Master Speech, guaranteed to fit all organizations and all occasions equally well. Just fill in the blanks yourself:

"I want to thank you for giving me the opportunity to say a few words before this worthy group of ——. I'm not much of a speechmaker, but what I have to say comes from the heart.

"It seems to me the important thing is to pull together. Nothing can be accomplished without teamwork, as our past efforts on behalf of the —— have shown us.

"We must face the future with hope and confidence. Nothing gets done without faith, and as long as we continue to have faith in this —— work of ours, I have no doubt we will forge ahead and make real progress in the coming years.

"And let's try to remember the other fellow's point of view. Nobody is perfect, and nobody is always right, and so it behooves us to work together cooperatively toward our —— goal.

"After all, life is a matter of give and take, and if you can do your best and keep smiling . . . why, then you've done your best, and who can do better than that?

"I didn't mean to get philosophical in these remarks, but just think what a better world this would be if only the people in it could be a little better. That's the thing we have to keep in mind all the time.

"Let's try to be less selfish and more considerate of others. It was Patrick Henry — or was it Daniel Webster? — who said 'we must hang together or we will hang separately.' There's a thought in that for everybody.

"Well, that's about all I have to say . . . except I want to thank —— for his splendid work the past year, and also ——. There are many others too numerous to mention, and I thank them all for being real folks.

"As I said, I'm just an ordinary person, and not much of a speechmaker, but I sure appreciate the honor you've bestowed on me tonight, and I'll do everything in my power to see that —— continues to live up to its ideals of ——. Thank you very much."

Answers to Ponderous Questions

TODAY'S ESSAY is devoted to answering ponderous questions from perplexed readers:

"Dear Mr. Harris: Do you believe a tall girl should marry a very short man?"

No — if God wanted the short people and the tall people to marry each other, He would have made them all the same height.

"Dear Mr. Harris: What is your opinion of the recent novel, *Exodus*."

Sorry, but I am still working my way through Genesis.

"Dear Mr. Harris: How can I get my sixteen-year-old son to mind me?"

I answered this same question several years ago, but I am happy to repeat it for the benefit of newcomers: Shrink him down to six months and start over, differently.

"Dear Mr. Harris: How can we prevent Puerto Ricans from moving into our neighborhood?"

Strike back by moving to Puerto Rico.

"Dear Mr. Harris: In view of the fact that I hope to enter the medical profession, can you recommend a journal for me to read?"

The doctors I have met personally seem to prefer the *Wall Street Journal* three to one.

"Dear Mr. Harris: Who, in your opinion, is the most representative American of our time?"

Lawrence Welk, the hope of the free world.

"Dear Mr. Harris: Do statistics show that capital punishment acts as a deterrent to crime?"

Every statistic that has been gathered conclusively proves that not a single person who has suffered capital punishment has been indicted a second time.

"Dear Mr. Harris: Our five-year-old son likes to put on dresses and walk around the house in them; should we be concerned about him?"

Not necessarily — he's probably seen his mother wearing pants most of the day, and is just making a natural inference.

"Dear Mr. Harris: Don't you think a little depression might be healthy for the nation?"

A little depression is like a little pregnancy.

The Biggest Snob: No-Snob Snob

IF ONE WERE WRITING a book of snobs, as Thackeray once did, it would be necessary to include that modern type — the No-Snob Snob. Today he has become the most prevalent member of the species *homo snobbimus*.

The No-Snob Snob, as his name indicates, feels superior about his inferiority. He is proud of his humility. He revels in the knowledge that he knows little. He feels exceptional to be so ordinary.

If he reads a book that is somewhat beyond him, he does not blame his own limitations for failing to understand it; rather, he says beamingly, "I don't go for those authors who won't write English for the common men." If he hears a piece of music too intricate for his ears, or sees a painting too subtle for his perception, he does not resolve to cultivate his taste in these arts; rather, he puffs himself up and declaims proudly, "Those fellows just don't know how to communicate to the public."

In the political realm, the No-Snob Snob distrusts and derides any candidate with a good command of language, urbane manners, and a background that does not encompass the bowling alley and the beer hall. And if he does elect a Rockefeller to office, it is only after Rockefeller demonstrates that he can eat as many hot dogs, kiss as many babies and pump as many moist palms as the grizzled ward-heelers of the River wards.

The No-Snob Snob has lost sight of the Jeffersonian goal of democracy, which was to raise every citizen to the level of excellence; to him, democracy means lowering every citizen to the common denominator of amiable mediocrity.

He condemns the intellectual for his "arrogance," and the aristocrat for his "pride," but actually he is the most arrogant and proud of any. The intellectual is arrogant about knowledge, which is a good thing; the aristocrat is proud of tradition, which is a good thing; but the No-Snob Snob is arrogant about ignorance and proud of self-centeredness, which are bad things.

As a poor man, the No-Snob Snob is merely pathetic; as a rich man, he is intolerable, for he assumes that his ability to make money has conferred upon him the wisdom of Solomon and the authority of St. Paul. He feels competent to make majestic pronouncements in all fields of human endeavor, on the false assumption that his pecuniary shrewdness is a mark of God's special favor. Snobbery can go no further than this.

Why Modest Ol' Syd's a Good Emcee

A FRIEND RECENTLY asked me to what I attribute my vast popularity as a toastmaster and chairman of banquets, meetings and assorted social functions. "Is it charm, brilliance, humor, wit," he inquired, "or simply your overpowering presence and unrivaled handsomeness?"

Tempted though I was to reply in the affirmative, a remnant of honesty in my nature struggled for supremacy and won. "None of these," I admitted. "Although I might with modesty lay claim to all these virtues, actually it is a vice of mine that has brought me unsurpassed success on the rostrum and before the microphone."

"And what is this vice?" he prompted.

"Lack of patience," I said. "Except where small children are concerned, I am the most impatient of men. Speeches bore me — including my own. I cannot tolerate long-winded introductions. I will not, as toastmaster, put up with a scheduled two-minute response that drones on for ten minutes. I am highly allergic to sound without sense."

"How has this brought fame, fortune, and the most beautiful women in the Western world to your feet?" my friend pressed on.

"Easily," I waved. "Americans are being strangled by verbosity and suffocated by ponderosity. They go to a dinner at seven, are through eating at eight, and then suffer through two and a half hours of stale smoke, staler quips, idiotic oratory, and the prolonged introduction of everybody in the room except the bus boys.

"When, some years ago, word leaked out that there was available — even at a staggering fee — a toastmaster of massive impatience, who enjoyed nothing better than to slice an hour of ceremonies down to fifteen minutes, the bidding for my services became indecently riotous. Program chairmen flung themselves on my chest, sobbing deliriously, with greenbacks clutched in both moist paws.

"There's a bitter lesson for moralizers in this," I continued, "for all my splendid virtues have merely nudged me closer to the precipice of bankruptcy, while my salient vice — this raw edge of impatience — has been the only thing keeping me solvent.

"Were I suddenly to lose this, were I overnight to become bland and tolerant of gaseous public speaking, my mortgage would be foreclosed in a month, my wee ones left homeless."

"It's an astonishing story," said my friend. "Let me tell you about my . . ." but I had already vanished. He was talking too much.

A Nook a Need in Modern Homes

ALTHOUGH I HAVE a high opinion of most modern architecture — indeed, I think that America's only contribution to the arts in the twentieth century has been in the field of architecture — I deplore the increasing lack of privacy that seems to mark most modern homes.

Wide expanses of glass, walls that open and combine two rooms into one, family areas with floating partitions — these all may make for spaciousness and graciousness, but they rigidly ignore the psychological needs of people. I firmly believe that doors were invented for closing, that each member of a family is entitled to be alone when he wants to, that "togetherness" should be a matter of emotional rapport and not mere physical proximity.

In this respect, the old-fashioned house is far superior to its modern counterpart. It may have been ornate and cluttered and dark, but at least it provided the inhabitants with places of refuge when the spirit of solitude descended upon them.

Children, especially, require all the privacy they want, in these times of overorganized activities and the desperate race to "adjust" to others. Emerson's words of advice are still cogent: "Be not too much a parent; trespass not on the child's solitude."

The French wisely recognize these needs, and most French homes are designed to give each member of the family the maximum of privacy. In fact, the "boudoir" was invented to supply the lady of the house with a place to remove herself to at times of pique; *bouder* means "to pout" in French, and the *boudoir* was literally a sulking room for madame.

It appalls me to see so many new homes going up with more

space devoted to the car than to the children, with a large area for a barbecue pit and no study for the father, with an all-electric kitchen for the mother to work in, and no cranny for her to escape to. The great charm of old houses does not consist in the elegance of the living room or the graceful curve of the staircase, but the cool refuge of the basement, the redolent mustiness of the attic, the alcoves and turnings and just plain hiding places from the world.

People who live in glass houses can't help throwing stones at one another if they have no secret nook in which to brood or exult or daydream or simply withdraw from the mounting pressure of planned chaos.

Compliment Often Food for Thought

AN ATTRACTIVE young woman was sitting next to me at a party when a friend of hers came up and burbled, "Your hair looks just lovely tonight — and I've never even noticed it before!"

When the woman next to me had mumbled her thanks, and the friend had sidled away, she turned to me and exclaimed: "I always feel odd when I get a compliment like that — it's supposed to make me feel good, but it doesn't."

"Why not?" I asked, as a curious male who doesn't receive two compliments a decade.

"Well," she said, "I always wonder what I looked like before. My hair must have been a mess for years, and nobody ever told me. I get upset at the thought that until I changed my hairdo, I was probably an object of pity and derision."

"Surely that's your imagination," I tried to comfort.

"No," she said. "Most people compliment you in a way

that's more upsetting than gratifying. For instance, when I took off ten pounds, all my friends commented on how lovely and svelte I looked. It immediately occurred to me that I must have looked like a fat slob before I trimmed down — I never realized it."

"You just don't have enough self-confidence," I put in.

"Maybe you're right," she reflected, "but then I don't think most women have a lot of self-confidence about their personal appearance. And I also think that when a woman compliments another, she is also in some subtle way turning the knife in her back."

"How do you mean?" I asked.

"Just what I said — the implication of a compliment about a new hairdo or a nice suntan or a new dress is often a way of suggesting that in the past your hair was a fright, your complexion was sickly sallow, and your clothes bagged where they shouldn't have."

"But aren't you pleased that you've corrected these possible flaws?"

"Yes and no," she answered. "It makes me wonder, too, what else there is wrong with me that I don't know about. Maybe two years from now, someone will come up and compliment me on my new flattering make-up and I'll be stricken with the thought that all these years I've worn colors that looked ghastly on me, and not a woman friend would tell me."

I hastily caught the bartender's eye and bade him bring liquid sustenance for this lovely creature. Then I excused myself. "I have to go to the powder room," I said, "to muss up my hair and rumple my collar. I couldn't bear it if someone complimented me tonight."

Whoever Heard of "Mr. Accident"?

A READER IN Michigan has asked me to use my massive influence with the U.S. government and prevent the Weather Bureau from employing feminine names to designate tropical storms and hurricanes.

She thinks it is fine that we name ships for women, and call them "she," because ships, in her mind, are associated with "beauty, generous living, peace and commerce." But her indignation boils over at the thought of using feminine names to indicate natural forces resulting in death, property damage and untold misery.

What this good woman fails to realize is that the human race has always applied the feminine gender to capricious and willfull objects in nature. In recorded history, it is as old as Homer, and doubtless goes back even farther than that.

Ships — and later trains, cars and planes — have been called "she," in nearly every language, in recognition of both the loving qualities and unpredictability of these vehicles. A man looks upon his car with a mixture of affection and exasperation.

Countries have often been called "she" — like La Belle France and Britannia. It is true that both Britain and the U.S. have been personified by John Bull and Uncle Sam, but these have been for cartoon purposes, and speakers generally refer to a nation in the feminine gender.

Hurricanes have been given girls' names not in any way to disparage the feminine sex, but simply to suggest that variability of their nature which reminds meteorologists of a woman's swift transition from smiles to tears, from ardor to anger. It is a metaphor, not an insult.

"He" is almost never used to designate an object or a natural activity. It is either "she" or "it." Things and events are called "it" when they have no personality and arouse no feelings in the beholder. But lovely, powerful, or potentially dangerous objects are usually "she" — proving again that language is not logical, but reflects the emotions of the men who make it.

We even speak of "Lady Luck," or "Dame Fortune," but nobody refers to "Mr. Accident" of "Sir Misfortune." Astronomers have long spoken of the moon and planets as "she"; likewise, workmen fondly refer to their familiar tools in the feminine. And now it's time to stop pounding my typewriter for the day — she's getting tired.

Why Professionals Seem Cynical

I HAD TAKEN a friend to lunch at the Press Club, and as we were finishing our coffee he couldn't help overhearing a party of newspapermen and criminal lawyers at the next table discussing a particularly messy murder case.

"They're so cool and detached about it," he said to me as we left. "Don't they have any feelings about the defendant or the victim?"

What my friend failed to understand is that all professionals quickly learn to discuss cases without reference to the personalities involved. Some tasks are so upsetting emotionally that unless we can approach them in an impersonal manner we cannot do our jobs well. A doctor called in to handle an auto accident emergency has to concentrate on the injury; if he thinks about the tragedy, in a poignant personal way, he is no longer able to operate at peak performance.

When lawyers discuss a gory murder trial, they consider the persons in the case only in regard to their credibility as witnesses. They're concerned with legal and technical points, and don't speculate as to whether the defendant is innocent or guilty.

Likewise when a surgeon refers to a "beautiful ulcer," he is talking as a professional, and his relationship to the patient is not a personal one, but a clinical one. The doctor is no more "hardened" to disease than the lawyer is "hardened" to crime or the reporter to disaster. He just knows it is necessary to place a certain distance between himself and his work in order to keep his sense of balance and perspective.

Even an actor soon learns that his profession — which seems to call for deep emotional involvement — requires a cool objectivity. An actor who "throws himself" into a role almost always gives a bad and hammy performance. It is when he is most detached that he gives the impression of passionate intensity.

Reporters so often seem to be cynical on the surface because they are protecting their emotions from being flicked on the raw. To do a competent and conscientious job while observing ninety dead children being carried out of a burning schoolhouse calls for a thick layer of protective gauze over the heart and nerves.

Some professionals, it is true, remove themselves at too great a distance from the objects of their practice, and forget that they are fundamentally dealing with persons and not with wounds or warrants.

But this is the danger inherent in any calling where a man in his daily life is surrounded by grim reminders of our tragic mistakes and our fragile mortality.

You Very Often Are What You Do

A WOMAN I KNOW — know very well — marched in a parade last month to protest the atomic-bomb testing. The march was sponsored by the American Friends Service Committee, known as Quakers to the laity.

"When we assembled at headquarters before the march," she told me, "we looked like a quite respectable and responsible group. But as soon as we got out on the street, with our badges and placards, we looked like a band of ragged crackpots."

It is a curious, but undeniable, fact that people change in appearance with their different functions. A well-dressed doctor looks impressive carrying his medical bag down the street; he looks ludicrous carrying a sign, "Ban the Tests!" no matter how worthy his ideals. Likewise, every family looks shabby and seedy while moving in or out of an apartment. Some people moved in down the street from us last week, and although the apartment is expensive and their furniture was good, the whole affair resembled a bankruptcy sale: every crack and sag and spot in their belongings immediately leaped to the eye.

I have noticed the same transition in a posh hospital I occasionally visit for X-rays and other probings into my hypochondria. The people sitting and waiting in the out-patient clinic invariably resemble candidates for public relief funds, although most of them are just as well-heeled as the patients in private rooms. But there is something so essentially demeaning about the atmosphere of a hospital clinic that all the patients take on the aura of charity cases — and, alas, are often treated that way by the brusque attendants.

It is only a half-truth to say that clothes make the man, or the woman. We are judged more by function than by physical appearance — for instance, no matter how winningly dressed a woman may be, if she is ferociously chewing gum in public, she will fail to gain the approval or admiration of those from whom she most desires it.

The marchers protesting the bomb tests were no longer individuals, and neither their faces nor their apparel were evident to the onlookers — only the badges and placards proclaiming them as "cranks" of some sort or another.

This is obviously unfair and unjust, but while we demand the right to be judged as individuals, we all want to reserve the privilege to judge others as indistinguishable members of a group.

Why Must It Be Either Up or Out?

AT DINNER RECENTLY, I was talking with a doctor who does some "medical review" work for several large corporations — that is, he examines their executives (junior and senior) every six months or so.

"Most of these men's symptoms," he confided, "come from stress. And the stress often comes from going ahead faster than they are able to, or even willing to."

"How do you mean?" I asked.

"I mean," he said, "that many companies have a policy of 'Up or Out' for their executives. After a certain period, the men are promoted — they're sent to a higher office, and the door is, in effect, locked after them. There is nowhere to go but up. They can't go back — this would be a terrible admission of failure — and they can't even stand still. Some of them would be happy on their present plateau, but if the escalator is rising, they have to rise with it."

"It seems to me," I put in, "that a lot of executives are looking for promotion, and feel even worse if they don't get it. What about that kind of stress?"

"Exactly," he said. "They feel bad if they don't get it — and they often feel bad when they do get it. What creates stress is the knowledge that you're not determining your own pace, but it's being determined for you — by the structure of the business, or the demands for 'success,' or a gnawing sense that others are forging ahead faster.

"This is true in many organizations," he continued. "I did some similar work for a university some years ago, and there too it was 'Up or Out.' The assistant professors had to make full professorship within a specified number of years, or find another job — even though some of them were much better off operating at a lower level."

"Do you think this has anything to do with the rising rate of coronaries and high blood pressure among men in their forties?" I asked.

"Well, it's partly better diagnosis, and earlier diagnosis," he said, "but I'm sure a lot of it can be attributed to the feeling of isolation when the door is locked behind you and the only vista in front of you is Up.

"Have you ever noticed," he concluded as we rose from the table, "that the most cheerful-looking men in a big office are the window-washers? The thought of their falling isn't somehow as terrifying as the constant specter in the minds of the men at the desks."

"I'll Bet You Don't Remember Me"

ON BEHALF of all the unfortunate people like myself who have atrocious memories for names and faces, let me tell you my private test for determining whether any stranger I meet is really well-bred or not.

The persons who possess tact and breeding may be introduced to me at a party or come up at a social gathering, and say, "I'm So-and-So. We met at such-and-such."

Whereupon I am able to rearrange my face into an impression of cordiality, and reply, "Of course, I remember — and how are you?"

The others (by far, alas, the vast majority) barge up and snap, "I'll bet you don't remember me!" Or, even worse, "Do you know who I am?" Since I never remember, I am caught flat-footed and flat-mouthed.

The essence of social manners is to put others at their ease. This is especially true with someone who may meet hundreds of people a month and is not running for public office so that he has no ulterior reason for remembering all of them.

Just as there are different kinds of intelligences, so there are different kinds of memories. No better or worse, just different. For instance, I can remember lines of poetry I haven't read for twenty years, but I can't remember a person I met only a week ago. Or the telephone number we had when I was in grade school, but not the faces of the girls I danced with at the Senior Prom.

It is an awkward and embarrassing deficiency, but those few who are blessed with total recall for names and faces should recognize this as a deficiency and not ascribe it to boorishness or snobbishness.

We non-rememberers of people are crippled in some part of the mind, and we deserve, if not compassion, at least a touch of consideration — just as we make allowances for a stutterer or any other socially handicapped person.

Groucho Marx at a party once saw a dreadnaught of a woman bearing down upon him with that familiar gleam in her eye. And, sure enough, she clawed his arm and shouted victoriously, "I'll bet you don't remember me!" Groucho gave her an evil leer, blew out a black cloud of cigar smoke, bowed and replied, "Madam, I never forget a face — but in your case I'll make an exception."

Syd Scores a Hit on a Foul

THERE IS A DOORMAN on our block who is wild about baseball. He also knows that I am vaguely associated with some newspaper, perhaps in an exalted sporting capacity.

Each morning he greets me with a little baseball observation, and I haven't had the heart to inform him that I know less about baseball than I do about the second law of thermodynamics — about which I know nothing except the name.

I have found, however (and I suspect that millions of other American men also have) that it isn't necessary to know a single thing about the game in order to conduct a fairly intelligible conversation about it. Our regular morning dialogues run something like this:

Doorman: "Well, I see where Frizzle got two out of four at bat yesterday. Guess he's out of that slump now."

Harris: "You just have to ride them out, I guess. You can't force a thing like that."

Doorman: "That's very true. Lookit how Schmangerpamf

picked up when he was sold to the Carnals. Best switch hitter in the league now."

Harris: "Of course, a good coach makes a lot of difference, too."

Doorman: "And how. Remember how in '54 Osskewitz was tightening up at the plate until Chicken Licken Jones got him relaxed? He'll murder 'em with that short Los Angeles fence now."

Harris: "Boy, you can't argue with the facts."

Doorman: "You said a mouthful. Those Frisco Pygmies are really zooming up there — whaddayuh think of that Chris Cringle making an unassisted double-play yesterday?"

Harris: "Helluva player that Cringle. He can play on my team any day."

Doorman: "Mine, too. And didyuh notice that new sinker ball Les Fauves is using this year? He oughta win twenty easy this season, if they plug up that hole in center field."

Harris: "They sure gotta plug up that hole, all right; you could drive a fleet of trucks through there right now."

Doorman: "You're not kiddin'. They never shoulda sent Buddy Myopia to the minors — that manager is a moron."

Harris: "Well, that's the way the ball bounces. We ought to pick up steam pretty soon."

Doorman: "I hope so. And if you run across a coupla passes you're not using — don't forget me, Mr. Harris."

The Degradation in Graduation

A FRIEND OF MINE has a daughter who was "graduated" from kindergarten last month — white gown, mortarboard, diploma and all.

Now I suppose that the theory behind this cute and cunning ceremony is that it makes the children feel important as they step into the primary grades. The primary grades do the same nowadays, and the high schools have long imitated the college graduations.

But the theory actually works in reverse: instead of dignifying the lower "graduations," it merely degrades the graduation from college, which used to be a solemn and unique occasion. If everybody gets a cap and gown and diploma — from kindergarten right up through the Ph. D. — then nobody's cap and gown and diploma has much significance. It all becomes an empty ritual, important mainly for demonstrating the virtuosity of parents with a camera.

This has happened even more blatantly in the field of honorary degrees. A generation or so ago, an honorary degree was an honor; today it is more likely to be a publicity stunt for the college, or for some more commercial enterprise: Bob Hope, after all, was not long ago made an honorary "Doctor of Laws" for telling jokes in Moscow.

I trust this is not mere stuffiness on my part. It matters little to me personally who gets an honorary degree or a diploma, who wears a mortarboard or a dunce cap. But it does matter to me that standards of excellence have become blurred and blotted by our excess of democratic fervor.

The traditional cap and gown was something students had to work hard for, through sixteen years of schooling. It symbolized both a termination and a commencement; in Europe, where the custom originated, it represented a recognition that the student was ready to accept both the responsibilities and the privileges of the adult world.

Putting these ludicrous costumes on kindergarten children is unconsciously an insult to, and a repudiation of, the value of higher education. It is on a par with awarding an honorary degree to a building contractor who has provided the new gym at cost, or making a Doctor of Laws out of a performer who recites the jokes other men have written for him.

Without firm standards of excellence, without special recognition for higher levels of achievement, a democratic society becomes a perversion and a corruption of its original purposes. Perhaps it is time to ask whether much of our love of "equality" is not merely the embrace of mediocrity.

Why Americans "Undress" in Public

IT IS TOO SIMPLE to say that we Americans are just a "friendly" sort of people. There must be something more behind our compulsive need to undress ourselves — verbally — in front of perfect strangers.

This has happened to me countless times during my travels around the country, and it happened to me again as I was lolling on the front porch of a resort hotel a few days ago. A man sat down in the chair next to me, and within five minutes I was told that he lived in Columbus, sold insurance, had four children, belonged to the Elks, was born in Delaware, had attended the University of Ohio, thought his wife was getting too plump, didn't like his son-in-law, and wanted me to be sure to look him up any time I happened to be passing through Columbus.

He didn't know me from Adam Smith, nor did I give his confidences the slightest encouragement beyond perfunctory politeness. I have met this same man by the hundreds, on trains and planes, in hotel lobbies and lunch counters — and the same autobiographical material starts pouring forth, like a gusher that has been repressed for years.

This is a peculiarly American habit, and it must spring from some hidden insecurites in our social life. The Italians, after all, are a warm and friendly people; but neither in Italy nor anywhere else in Europe have I witnessed this same relentless urge to Tell All in ten minutes' acquaintance.

Perhaps we have a need to identify ourselves, to give ourselves some sense of permanence in this shifting and highly mobile social scene. About one fifth of all Americans move every year, and maybe this nomadic form of existence creates tensions that can be relieved only by reciting the story of one's life wherever one goes. Or perhaps there remains, beneath all the frantic activity and surface joviality and Joining the Club, a feeling of lonesomeness, a wistful desire to be understood and appreciated, even by a passing figure who may never be seen again.

I do not find this need repugnant, but merely pathetic. It points to some lack of emotional equilibrium, some hunger that is not satisfied by the family and the job and the club and the old school pennant.

Europeans are convinced we are a nation of self-engrossed egotists, continually talking about ourselves to indifferent strangers. I think it is the opposite of egotism — it is, if anything, a quest for reassurance that our life has some meaning and some point.

Why Do Platforms Often Lower Speakers?

IN MY VAST and exhausting experience as a speaker on the banquet circuit, I have noticed, time and again, the curious split personality of men who are called upon to speak officially in public.

It is not that most of these men are shy or tongue-tied or

stupid — but when they rise to give a report or make a few brief remarks of introduction, their whole personality undergoes a violent change for the worse. Privately, they may be charming and witty and intelligent; but as soon as the mantle of speakerdom descends upon them, they become dull and pompous and long-winded. Some of them, of course, are nervous; but many of the greatest actors in the world are nervous when they first step out in front of the curtain. It is more than a matter of stage fright.

It is, I think, a deep-seated feeling that our ordinary self is somehow not "good enough" for public display. The actor, after all, can hide confidently within the role he is playing — while the ordinary banquet or meeting speaker has no role he can step into.

And so he wraps himself up in a senatorial toga of solemnity. He tries to elevate his stature by speaking in a stilted manner that is quite alien to his natural speech. He is attempting to "rise to the occasion," but in so doing he only succeeds in lowering the temperature of the whole audience.

We have all seen how a child can gaily and charmingly sing a song to himself while he is playing. Yet the same child, if forced to perform for adults, becomes formal and forced and loses the spontaneity that is the essence of his delightfulness. He feels he must meet some higher standard than self-enjoyment, must assume some "presence" to cope with the expectations of his audience. And in doing this, of course, he wholly misses the mark.

There is no use in advising a man to "just be yourself" on the rostrum if he doesn't like what he sees when he looks into himself. The first lesson in public speaking is a true self-appreciation, which knows both one's abilities and one's limitations.

Nobody likes a person who is perfect, and limitations can

be as winning to an audience as abilities can be. If we don't expect too much of ourselves, if we are willing to offer ourselves for whatever we may be worth, we will soon find that audiences can accept and enjoy us. What they cannot accept is a false face or a pompous front.

Thief Robbed of Faith in Criminals

THERE IS A STANDARD in every profession, a code in every craft. I ran into a criminal the other morning who was "shocked" at the crimes going on today.

He is an old-fashioned criminal I used to see occasionally when I was a reporter nearly twenty years ago. A quiet, round-faced man who was a first-class burglar and safe-cracker, but otherwise a quite decent sort of chap.

"I don't know what's got into young fellows these days." He shook his head mournfully as we had a cup of coffee together. "They're monsters, not human beings. I wouldn't spit on the best of them. In my day, a thief was a thief. He did his job and went home and tried to enjoy himself the same way other men would. He didn't like violence, he didn't hate anybody, and he wasn't trying to prove anything. Now I see these punks all over the streets, and they're enough to make an honest thief's stomach turn. They don't have any brains, and they don't have any heart either. All they can do is hit and shoot and curse.

"They're not even good thieves," he reflected, as a Master Tailor might mourn the passing of the age of craftsmanship. "With a couple of drinks, they'll knock off a cabdriver for ten bucks in change. What do you writing fellows call them — 'psychopaths'?"

"How do you account for the difference?" I asked him.

"Who knows?" He shrugged. "Something has gone out of them. They don't love anything, and they even seem to hate themselves. They don't have families or hobbies, as we used to. They don't even seem to want to be successful — just noticed — and that's the surest way to get caught."

"Then you think they want to get caught?" I suggested.

"Sure," he said. "They want to prove how tough they can be, even walking to the chair. What's the point of 'punishing' punks like that? You've got to straighten out their mental kinks when they're small, or you can't do anything with them at all.

"The old bunch I used to know are mostly dead," he sighed. "Ah, they were fine fellows, some of them, a pleasure to talk with. It's a funny age we're living in, when a professional thief can't bring himself to associate with the scum running around these days. That's the real reason, if you want to know, why I went straight."

Why Education in U.S. Is a Joke

THE ILLINOIS STATE Chamber of Commerce has spoken out for stiffer college standards. All six Illinois state universities, said a spokesman for the Chamber, should raise their entrance requirements. I couldn't agree more heartily. But I also know that there is a vast difference between our public statements and our private attitudes.

Suppose the son of some substantial member of the Chamber were unable to meet these higher entrance requirements? The father would then, most likely, move heaven and earth to get the boy into college — if not in Illinois, then in some other state with more relaxed standards.

Most American parents are split personalities about education. They want the colleges to teach better, and the students to learn more — but they indignantly reject the thought that perhaps their own children do not belong in college. Yet the plain fact is that many do not. Thousands of young men and women are attending college today with no plan and no purpose, beyond getting a diploma. The faculty knows it, and the students know it. Only the proud papas turn their eyes away from this bleak reality.

In my travels around American universities, I have seen hundreds of boys who wondered what they were doing at institutions of higher learning. They weren't learning much, and most of them would be happier working at some manual, mechanical, or commercial job. Yet college has become such an absurd badge of prestige in our society that fathers who have made their mark are ashamed if their sons do not go to college, however meaningless it may be to them.

Until we recognize that college is a privilege that must be earned, and not a right that can be demanded upon payment of a tuition fee, we will continue to flood the nation's universities with misfits and malcontents.

And until prosperous parents will face the fact that the ability to pay bears absolutely no relationship to the ability to learn, we will continue to spend huge sums, both publicly and privately, in turning out graduates who have wasted four years for the dubious distinction of putting a square hat on a square head.

If the colleges could select applicants for learning as carefully and discriminatingly as the papas select applicants for jobs, American education could become the envy of the world, instead of the tasteless joke that most educators privately confess it to be.

Noise—The Silencer of Thought

WE COMMONLY THINK of narcotics or liquor as being "opiates" for those troubled personalities who have a constant need to escape from reality. A much more prevalent, and just as deadly, modern opiate is *noise*. The noise addicts number in the tens of millions, and while their habit is socially acceptable, it is no less spiritually devitalizing than dope or drink.

These people are more obvious in the summer, when every beach and park and picnic ground is dotted with portable radios, all of them blaring out the latest musical inanity. And the addicts are not really listening — they are merely using this sound to kill off any inner stirrings of thought.

The new tiny transistor radios have a zombie-like quality about them: I have seen dozens of men walking along the street holding this device in their hands, close to their ears, their jaws slack and their eyes glazed — moving in an almost catatonic trance. There might be some excuse if they were listening to a ball game, or to some special program that captured their interest — but most of them are just listening in a void.

The capacity to be alone with oneself, and with one's thoughts, at least part of the time, is a mark of maturity. But for millions silence is a curse that must not be endured. The music — or what passes for music — induces in them a hypnotic state that shuts out the need for reflection or self-scrutiny.

Such dependence on mechanical opiates can be a more brutalizing factor in modern life than the more obvious vices. The man who drinks excessively will soon lose his job and his family; there is an incentive for him to take the cure. But the man who deadens his spirit with sound waves can go through a lifetime without ever developing a thought or reaction that raises him above the level of the beasts.

Music is for listening to; it is a creative, positive thing, designed to make us more fully alive, to evoke a wider response to the world, to expand our sense of beauty and increase our delight. When it is used for precisely the reverse of this — as a drug to stultify the spirit and inflame the passions — it ceases to be music and becomes a hideous enslavement, like the sirens' songs which turned men into swine unless they stopped up their ears or, like Ulysses, tied themselves to the mast to keep from swimming to their doom.

A Dope Who's a Dope About Dope

MY FRIEND J. Spastic Twitchell awoke at 7.45, feeling, as the English put it, "fragile." He brushed his teeth, gargled, and popped a couple of aspirins into his mouth. Those early morning headaches were getting intolerable.

On his way to the office, he stopped at a water fountain and gulped down a pep-up pill. "Going to need a lot of energy today — staff meeting and all," he murmured to himself.

At lunch, while downing his tomato juice, he fortified himself with a large white pill. "Don't know how I'd get through the afternoon without this little old tranquilizer." He smiled vacuously.

He had already gone through a full pack of cigarettes by lunch time. "Just can't seem to work without them." He shrugged. "They give me a release of nervous energy I've got to have these days."

By four, he had gone through a half beaker of martinis, consumed two more aspirins (a new kind, with a super-empirin base), and was halfway along a fresh pack of cigarettes. Another benzedrine geared him into high for the staff meeting.

At 5.30, on his way home, he stopped off at the local pub for his customary pick-me-up. He picked himself up at 6.45 and weaved his way in the general direction of his house.

"Rough day," he told his wife as she greeted him, "but another dollar, as they say. This rat race gets nuttier all the time." They seated themselves in the living room for their usual libation before dinner, and he tossed down another tranquilizer with the drinks. "Now I'm really starting to relax," he said, ambling into the dining room.

For two hours after dinner, he stupefied himself in front of the television set, sitting there with jaw agape and eyes getting redder. At 10.30 the Twitchells prepared to retire.

As he crawled into bed, he was holding a glass of water in one hand and a yellow pill in another. "This Nembutal should knock me out," he said. "In twenty minutes, I'll be sleeping the sleep of the just."

He riffled through the newspaper, back to front, and his eye was caught by a headline on page one. He turned to his wife and chortled: "I see that the police just seized a huge cache of heroin. One of the biggest operators in the country. It's sure good to know that they're on the job — cracking down on those dope addicts!"

He fell asleep with an eminently respectable, self-satisfied smile on his lips.

What's Happened to Responsibility?

THAT OLD-FASHIONED virtue known as "responsibility" seems to be passing out of style. It is being supplanted by something known as "provocativeness." Commentators and critics and columnists have adopted the dubious credo of show business: "It doesn't matter what you say about me, so long as you mention me."

This is a despicable and degrading attitude for anyone charged with the task of influencing public opinion. A man who is given power, and assumes no responsibility along with it, is as dangerous as a hand grenade in a nursery.

Ignorance, arrogance and brashness are riding high in the field of mass communications. The men who boast that they never read a book are busy telling the public what to think about literature; the men whose personal horizons are limited by a suburban patch of lawn are smugly informing Europeans and Asiatics how they should behave themselves.

It is easy to be diverting, in a shallow sense, if you ignore the facts of history. It is simple to shock or startle readers and listeners if you appeal to the credulous, the discontented, the self-righteous.

Such commentators — and their number is growing — seem to operate on the theory that if they wildly shoot buckshot into the air, they are bound to hit something sooner or later. That nine times out of ten they hit the wrong target does not seem to shake their self-esteem. Nobody reads a retraction, anyway.

In the past, when a man assumed the task of informing and persuading the public, he prepared himself for the job. Whatever the rightness or wrongness of his views, he at least had a grasp of public affairs, of philosophy, of psychology, of the humane arts. Nowadays, a man considers himself equipped to comment simply because he is an "average fellow" — as though mediocrity in itself were some sort of special virtue. He calls his ignorance "open-mindedness," his inhibitions "morality," his lack of culture "simplicity," his provincialism "patriotism," and his irresponsibility "courage."

What makes these men precisely so dangerous is not that they are frauds, but that they are painfully sincere; that they combine a high earnestness of manner with a low level of comprehension; that under their compulsive need to be provocative is a hatred of all the ideas they do not understand, and a fear of all the emotions they have long repressed.

Bigness a Curse of Our Society

ONE OF OUR SITTERS has been working all summer as a checker in a supermarket. I asked her how she liked her job, and she said, "Fine — but I'm shocked at all the people who try to steal."

The store is in a respectable neighborhood, and most of the patrons are ordinary middle-class families in comfortable circumstances. Yet, she disclosed, every day some adult customers try to walk off with groceries they have not paid for. "How do they get the nerve?" she exclaimed. "Even if I wanted to, I'd be scared. But they just calmly try, and if you call them on it, they pretend it all was a big mistake on their part."

This prevalence of thievery on the part of otherwise respectable citizens is another symptom, I am convinced, of the curse of bigness in our society. People who would not dream of taking anything from a neighbor, or from a small shopkeeper whom they know personally, have no such scruples in stealing from a huge, impersonal corporation.

Telephone companies, insurance companies, transportation firms, chain stores — all these are victimized daily by men and women who have the implicit philosophy that "these outfits are so big and rich that it won't hurt them at all."

Everyone knows that the main reason auto insurance rates

are so high is that motorists — perhaps the majority of them — connive with garages to pad their bills, or conspire with other motorists to turn in false reports on accidents. And not many months ago a trucking company was indicted for defrauding the telephone company of thousands of dollars on long-distance calls, by using a special code that enabled the main office to transmit messages to its drivers.

None of this is possible in a small, self-contained community, where economic activity is seen to be a direct result of personal endeavor. But in our increasingly mechanized society, where there is no sense of identity among producer, seller, and consumer, the moral code has become split — we behave one way toward those we know and another way toward those we don't know.

This is a graver and deeper threat to our social order than all the "isms" in the book. And, like most dangers, it is one we have brought upon ourselves by racing too fast toward an unknown goal.

Provocative—or Just Ill-Mannered?

READING ABOUT those disk jockeys and TV interviewers who confuse bad manners with honesty, and irresponsibility with frankness, I should like to examine today the word "provocative."

It comes, of course, from the root "provoke." To provoke meant, originally, just "to call forth." It also means "to incite to anger, to stir up, to incense."

We need men, in print, on the air, and in public positions, who are provocative. The question is: what do they provoke? Do they arouse emotions and stir up anger? Or do they provoke thought and intelligent discussion? Are they provocative for its own sake, for the sake of publicity and exhibitionism, or are they provocative in a responsible and meaningful way?

Anyone can be provocative in the first sense. Anyone can stand in front of a microphone and ask rude questions, make outrageously impertinent judgments, and probe into sensitive spots that should only be examined by trained, professional hands. All this takes is a big mouth, an empty head, and a coating of brass. But to be provocative in the original sense of "calling forth" is an entirely different matter, requiring superior skills and more polished techniques.

To be provocative in the best sense of the word is to open a door on a person's mind, not to slam it on his fingers. It is to reveal the hidden mainsprings of our motives, and trace the sources of our behavior, not for sensationalism or shock value, but because the more we know about ourselves the more easily we are able to control our destinies.

And we must be able to relate this knowledge to some view of society in general, to some standards of conduct, some ideal of the good life. This implies a firm sense of responsibility and a sound grasp of philosophic discipline.

The man who shouts "Fire!" in a crowded theater is being "provocative" — he is provoking the audience to fear and panic. Even when there *is* a fire, he is doing a dangerous thing. And when there is no fire, he is a positive menace to society. Such provocations are too often merely a cheap substitute for talent, for insight, and for taste.

Why Are We Afraid to Grow Old?

SPEAKING ABOUT age, as I was not long ago, it always embarrasses me when people want to be praised for looking young. I never know quite what to say when someone makes an obvious play for a "youthful" compliment.

"You might not believe it," murmured a woman at a party last week, "but I have a twenty-eight-year-old daughter and three grandchildren."

I believed it. But I was supposed to exclaim. "Well, who would have thought it!" or "I didn't think you were a day over forty." She looked fifty-five, easy.

Or somebody else will say, "I'm nearly sixty, you know," and the addressed is supposed to widen his eyes, draw in his breath, and respond jocularly, "You look like a kid!" Anybody nearly sixty who looks like a kid is seriously retarded in some significant way.

Some mothers of grownup daughters are particularly vulnerable to the "you-look-more-like-sisters-than-mother-and-daughter" routine. If I were a young lady, the last thing in the world I'd want would be a mother who looked like my sister. Something unhealthy about such cases, and many such mothers, beneath their sleek charm, are subconsciously competing with their daughters, to their mutual frustration.

It cannot be said too often (although I am trying) that our indiscriminate worship of youth is in large measure responsible for the waywardness and willfulness of American youngsters today. Young people do not respect age because age does not respect itself. Older people are not interested in becoming wiser, but only in feeling younger. A woman who wants to look like her daughter can scarcely blame the daughter for acting vain and self-centered and contemptuous toward ancient truths.

Juvenile delinquency, on a wide scale, is peculiarly an American problem; not merely because of our easy access to wealth, but also because throughout most of Europe and Asia parents behave like parents and oldsters like oldsters.

This does not mean — as some readers will interpret it — that people past middle age must fall into dusty decay; but it *does* mean that our values and our activities must change with the years, so that we provide stability and evoke respect in the rising generation.

Most of us seem desperately afraid of growing old, and even of admitting to it. Can we, then, blame our children if they blithely assume that the world belongs to them, and that our pathetic efforts at discipline are only a show of resentment because the times have passed us by?

Oh, to Find a Way to Beat the Bores

I HAVE, PAINFULLY and slowly, learned over the years to suffer fools gladly — well, if not gladly, at least passively. But how is it possible to suffer gladly in the presence of a bore?

It takes exquisite politeness and the tact of a saint. Irwin Edman once told his students about a Chinese sage, bedridden with an incurable illness, who was visited at great length by a well-intentioned but extremely dull friend.

One afternoon, unable to bear the boredom any longer, the Chinese sage, famous for his incomparable courtesy, said quietly: "Will you please excuse me for a moment while I turn to the wall and draw my last breath?"

Few of us have the opportunity to make an exit line with

such superb finesse. We squirm and sweat, we stare wildly into space hoping for rescue, we nod in agreement when we are scarcely listening, and we finally invent a rush appointment or a toothache or even a trip to the bathroom for a brief respite.

Among all the thousands of how-to-do-it books, I have never run across even one that gave a decent formula for coping with the relentless bore. Yet this is one of mankind's pressing and permanent needs.

I don't mean to give the supercilious impression that I am easily or often bored, or that only high-level conversation holds my interest. I am glad to talk to anybody who has a little lightness, a little sense of proportion, a little sensitivity to the moods of others.

We are all bores to somebody, some time or other. Nobody can be unfailingly interesting. I have found myself boring people — but I am immediately aware of it, feel pangs of guilt, and I change either subjects or partners.

But the true bore is not merely a person who bores others; he is a person who is perpetually unaware that he is boring, and would not believe it if you told him. His insight is nil, and far from feeling any guilt at the thought that he might be boring his company, he revels in his dreary anecdotes and often fancies himself quite the life of the party.

In one of his plays, Shaw advises: "If you are a bore, strive to be a rascal also, so that you may not discredit virtue." For surely, the most oppressive (and the most common) bore is the respectable, virtuous person whose only fault, as Barrie said of a certain lady "is that she is intolerable." When boredom is allied with virtue, it makes us flee willingly into the arms of vice.

Women, Beauty Is Only Voice Deep

THERE WERE three women seated at the speakers' table when I arrived for my talk. All were impeccably turned out. It was evident that they had spent many hours on preparing their hair, their faces and their costumes. And all three had wretched voices. As they rose to make announcements or reports, the ear was immediately offended by their rasping, screeching and whining. They sounded like horses trying unsuccessfully to imitate human speech.

Year after year, I become more puzzled by this phenomenon. American women are surely among the most attractive in the world. They spend billions on beauty preparations, new clothes and other "aids to charm." Yet they stubbornly ignore what should be a woman's prime asset — her voice.

Ironically enough, a plain woman cannot become beautiful, no matter how much she spends; she is pretty much stuck with the basic material God gave her. Yet nearly every woman can improve her voice without much trouble — simply by listening closely to the way it sounds and taking a few simple remedial measures.

It is significant that old King Lear, with his dying breath, remembered one thing about his daughter Cordelia: "Her voice was ever soft, gentle, and low, an excellent thing in woman."

And it is equally significant that men, on the whole, are attracted or repelled by women's voices more than by any other single attribute. Most men will scarcely notice what a woman is wearing, or how her hair is done — but a harsh, shrill or high-pitched voice will embarrass and annoy them.

This odd discrepancy is most striking in Europe. American

women's voices are recognizable in a restaurant, for instance, before one can even make out the language they are speaking. Their tones are nasal, their cadence is craggy, and their general impact is that of a pneumatic drill that has suddenly run amuck.

Few people, except trained speakers or actors, ever bother to listen to their own voices. If they did (a tape recorder placed under the dinner table makes a shocking corrective), they would realize that a grating and unpleasant voice more than offsets the glamorous effect of hairdos, make-up, and that darling new dress they picked up for practically nothing.

Variety (of Guests) Is Life of Party

THERE IS SOME mysterious "chemical" element involved in giving a good party. Some parties, which look wonderful on paper, never get off the ground, while others, which the hosts approach with fear and trembling, are huge successes.

No one, to my knowledge, has ever solved this mystery; but I am convinced that one of the most important (and overlooked) factors is variety in the guest list.

If all the guests are too much alike, the party will generally be dull. Personalities, like colors, need their *complementaries* to set them off to striking effect. The best party we ever gave included "Muggsy" Spanier, the hot trumpeter, and a titled Englishman doing research in astrophysics. They fascinated each other, and all the other guests as well.

I was speaking about this to a woman at dinner last night. She confided that the most disastrous party she and her husband had ever given consisted of the four most brilliant couples they could muster. "We picked them carefully," she said with sad wisdom, "and it was the fiasco of the year."

I asked her why, and she had a sensible and searching explanation.

"Everybody was too brilliant," she sighed. "There were no listeners that night — everybody was a talker. Their colors didn't complement each other — they just clashed. After that experience, we've always invited a dullish couple or two as 'audience' for the bright ones."

Brilliance in jewels is enhanced by placing them on a dull velvet background, as every jeweler knows. The same is true of people at a party: the articulate and witty guests require a subdued background for their performances. If everybody is a star, the glitter is harsh and blinding.

Most of the insipid "gracious hostess" books advise selecting guests who have interests in common. But this can make for a deadly evening. One poet at a party is refreshing; four poets sound like a Greek chorus. One doctor may be amusing; four doctors will most likely huddle in a corner for a postmortem.

Picking people who "go together" at a party, I am convinced, is as rare and delicate a talent as decorating a room. And, indeed, it is much the same thing — for nothing can decorate a room more gaily than a handful of animated guests, or can drape it in gloom more quickly than a company who sit and wonder why on earth they came out this rainy night.

We're Afraid to Say "I Don't Know"

ABOUT THIRTY YEARS ago, when the famous English lawyer and author, A. P. Herbert, was standing (we say "running") for Parliament, he stated his platform on the most important subjects of national concern. Under the heading "Agricul-ture," he simply said: "I know nothing whatsoever about agriculture."

Can we imagine a political candidate in America making this same bald admission? A candidate here is supposed to have opinions on *every* subject, whether he knows anything about it or not.

And not only in politics, but in every area of our national life, we seem to feel a nervous compulsion to have opinions — immediate and decisive — on a dozen subjects we cannot possibly grasp on short notice.

After my lectures, people in the audience invariably ask me what I think about the space race, and why I haven't com-mented upon it in the column. I always give the same answer — which they find unsatisfactory: "My scientific knowledge is small and my military knowledge is nil, and besides the public hasn't been given enough facts, so how can I have an opinion that is worth anything?"

Of course, many decisions can't wait until we have *all* the facts, for then we would never form a program of action. But deciding and acting before we have given ourselves time to study and reflect is as bad as — if not worse than — inde-cision.

This pressure to have opinions on everything from the new-est novel to the latest turn in foreign policy has bred, I am convinced, a great deal of unconscious insincerity. We are afraid to say we don't know, or haven't made up our minds, or have never even thought about the question. So we find ourselves making up our reactions as we go along, out of an old fund of prejudices and clichés, and becoming self-hyp-notized by the glow of our own rhetoric.

America is turning into a nation of garrulous curbstone experts on Russia, the atomic bomb, abstract art, socialized medicine, and — you name it. Only the most naïve among us, or the most profound, will reply, "I don't know enough to form an opinion that has any value."

Our politicians merely reflect this general trend. They are ashamed to confess that they haven't mastered every aspect of public policy which is why they say so many idiotic things and then insist they were "misquoted." It would be far better for them, and all of us, to remain unquoted when we have nothing quotable to say.

Happiness Canned and Catalogued

A FEW WEEKS ago, I mentioned the man I overheard at lunch telling his friend that freshly squeezed orange juice doesn't taste "natural" to him any more, after drinking so much of the frozen and canned varieties.

Shortly afterward, I read a magazine article on high-fidelity that recounted the story about an avid hi-fi fan who had the finest equipment and best record collection in town, but who had never attended a concert in a symphony hall. Finally a friend lured him to a concert. At the end of the program the friend asked, "How did you like it?" The reply was: "I'd say it was weak in the bass and peaked around four thousand cycles."

This sort of thing is happening throughout our society. We are living on synthetics and reproductions and facsimiles — and when we come across the original, it seems dull and distorted and inaccurate to us.

Young people, for instance, get their ideas of romance from the films and story books, and then they are disappointed when life does not live up to its fictional representation. When the artifact does not truly resemble nature, then we blame nature for not being more "artistic."

Most of our experiences in modern society are obtained secondhand, and we seem to prefer them that way. I recently heard about the man in New York who went out on his terrace to watch an eclipse. He called to his twelve-year-old boy to join him.

"No, Dad," the boy said. "I'm staying in the house — they're showing the eclipse on television in a few minutes."

We seem to be swiftly losing contact with the primary sources of experience and sensation. When I was a boy I used to collect stamps — and most of the fun consisted in badgering relatives and friends and swapping with the other kids. My collection was small, but intensely personal.

Today, any boy with a few dollars can purchase a magnificently large stamp collection, in which all the work has been done by somebody else. It has become a *possession*, rather than a *pursuit*.

Our forefathers wisely spoke of the "pursuit" of happiness, for they knew that running after it is most of the fun. Today we want our happiness canned, collected, catalogued, focused and funneled, reproduced and gift-packaged for us. This seems to be the highest aim of our "individualism."

When the record sounds more "natural" than the concert, when the eclipse on the screen is more interesting than the eclipse in the sky, we have lost a precious part of our human heritage.

3

OF CHILDREN
AND PARENTS

Kids Are Not Miniature Adults

WE HAD TO RETURN a pair of cowboy boots we bought for
Michael last month, because he began hobbling when he wore
them — but he wouldn't tell us they hurt. "I was afraid you'd
take them away," he said.

When we took them back to the store the manager
promptly gave us a refund, and then cussed out the shoe
company that made the boots. "They make boots for adults,"
he said, "and just make the same ones smaller for children.
They don't realize, or don't care, that children's feet aren't
just smaller than ours — they're different."

As we left, I thought that this comment applies to more
than shoe companies, and to more than feet. Most of us fall
into the fallacy of believing that children are just "miniature"
adults.

Of course they are not. A child doesn't have a "small
amount" of reason, where a grownup has a lot. The whole
mental and emotional apparatus of a child is different from
that of an adult, and to treat him like a sawed-off version of
adulthood is disastrously wrong.

A tadpole is going to be a frog some day, but a tadpole is a lot different from a grown frog: with different needs, different growth patterns, and different tendencies. These are quite obvious to the naturalist.

A child, however, fools us, because he "looks" like a shrunken version of an adult. This external appearance is largely an illusion. Even the foot is shaped differently, and calls for special kinds of shoes — so we can imagine how vastly the brain and the whole complex nervous system must differ from its final form.

Parents who call their young boy "little man" and who try to "reason" with him in a one-syllable version of adult logic are beating their heads against the wall of nature's structure. A child responds to imagination, to tenderness, to humor, even to an appeal to his budding sense of fairness — but not, until much later, to anything that could be called "logical."

There is a difference in quality, and not merely in quantity, between children and grownups. The forces of fantasy control the childish mind, and it takes long years before they are disciplined. If we try to curb them ourselves, and too soon, the child's imaginative faculties will dry up and wither away. Nothing is sadder than a prematurely old child.

From the sole of the foot to the crown of the head, a child is only a rough prefiguration of what he is going to become. It is as wrong to force the mind or emotions into adult patterns, as to force the foot into the wrong-shaped boot. And, ultimately, just as crippling.

They Separate Fantasy and Reality

WHEN AN EDUCATOR or psychologist suggests that children are frightened, and then brutalized, by programs of violence and sadism on television, someone is sure to bring up the old-fashioned fairy tale. "Have you read the Grimm Brothers?" they will ask. "What could be more scarifying than those bloodthirsty fairy tales? And yet children have been reading and enjoying them for many generations."

But it is a serious mistake to compare the two. I learned this while taking Michael to the children's theater on Saturdays. He was not a bit upset by the fierce giant in *Jack the Giant Killer*, or by the evil witch in *Hansel and Gretel*. But when he watched a gangster film on a friend's TV he couldn't sleep all night.

A child maintains a firm dividing line between fantasy and reality. He may pretend to believe in giants and witches and ghosts, but he never confuses them with "real people." The world of reality, he feels, is safe and orderly and kind. When, however, this world of reality is shown in a cruel and barbarous light, he becomes truly frightened. Then, because this fear must be at all costs repressed, he adopts a casual and hard-boiled attitude toward robbing and beating and killing.

The old-fashioned fairy tale kept this distinction in hand at all times. Evil comes from *outside* the human realm; from creatures that are non-human or sub-human or supra-human. Yet in the end, humanity always triumphs. As the psychiatrists might say, it represents a victory of the ego over the dark irrational forces of the id.

In the modern TV tales, this difference between the specifically human and the non-human is blurred. Good men and bad men belong to the same order of being; and even though a shallow moral may be tacked on at the end of the program, the child is (at the best) confused and (at the worst) paralyzed by this sadistic behavior on the part of presumably mature human beings.

I am not suggesting, by any means, that children should be

sheltered from the knowledge of good and evil within the human order; but such knowledge should be carefully and lovingly directed by the parents and by teachers, and should not come via the lurid exaggerations of "shocker" programs.

A child loves the thrill of pretending his father is a lion and will eat him up, for he knows his father is not and will not; but when "real" people, not lions or giants or witches, are shown as sadistic villains, then the pose of brutality becomes his only means of fending off fear.

Do Babies Know What's Good for Them?

SMALL CHILDREN don't have any knowledge — so we imagine they don't have any wisdom. Small children haven't had much experience — so we imagine they don't know what is best for them.

But there is a kind of wisdom implanted in the blood and the bone and the brain, and parents would do well to respect it. For children, like all young animals, often have a surprising instinct for their own best welfare.

Some parents worry, for instance, because a child likes to sleep with a night light on, or with a door open so that he can hear noises. The parent often attributes this to "nervousness" or even "phobia" on the child's part.

Recent experiments at Indiana University's psychology department indicate that sleepers relax better subjected to a little noise and light. Grown men and women, volunteers in the experiment, did not sleep as well in complete darkness and quiet.

In a black and soundproofed room, these volunteers had "increased muscular and circulatory activity, and decreased respiration." The psychologist explained they were less relaxed because they were "expecting something to happen."

The child who demands a little light may be more sensible than the parent who pointlessly denies it. Similarly, the child who goes on a "food jag" and eats only one kind of food for several weeks may be unconsciously satisfying some nutritional need lacking in his daily diet. It has been found, for example, that some children who persistently nibbled on chalk were suffering from a calcium deficiency — they were attracted to chalk just as deer are irresistably drawn to salt licks.

Hasty readers may come away with the impression that I am urging them to permit children to do as they like, or suggesting that every whim should be indulged. Not at all. But the average parent engages in a great deal of unnecessary anxiety about a small child's "habits" without taking the trouble to learn the origin or the need expressed by the habit.

Children, I am absolutely convinced, have an inner logic of their own, and much that seems irrational or capricious to us makes good sense in terms of their development and the way they are coping with life. The chief task of a parent is to supervise less and to investigate more; to learn to differentiate between the *child* and the *stage*.

Even tiny babies know more about themselves than we commonly give them credit for. If respect for the individual began in the cradle, we would have more creative individualism in the adult world.

Defines Evil as an Absence of Love

THE HARDEST THING for a parent to explain to a small child is not the facts of sex — which children can accept calmly — but the fact of evil in the world.

It is hard because the child must be given a nice sense of balance between innocence and suspicion. He must be taught that some people behave badly, but also that he can confidently trust most adults.

When Michael first learned what pirates did, or "bad guys" in Westerns, or bank robbers, he was astonished. He had thought that only children were "naughty." It puzzled him extremely that adults also had to be punished for their misdeeds.

Here it is easy for parents to go wrong, to implant in their children a deep fear of strangers. It is equally easy to err in the other direction — to pretend that evil does not exist, that the child will be protected in his cocoon of innocence.

The most effective method I have found in explaining such matters to my children is to define evil as an absence of love, as a negative thing, a privation, a lack of some natural development in the personality.

And it is psychologically true that adults who grow up in the ways of wickedness have somewhere along the line been deprived of an essential love element. All of us have "naughty" drives within us, but the right kind of love in childhood enables us to cope with and control these drives in our social behavior.

Some parents, I explained to Michael, are not able to love their children in the right way. Perhaps the parents are sick, in body or mind, or possibly they themselves did not benefit from their own parents.

He can understand this surprisingly well. And it enables him to maintain an equilibrium: an alertness to avoid evil when he sees it, combined with a sympathy for those who have to act that way. It gives him, I hope, a toughness of mind and a tenderness of heart, which is the best possible combination for a human being.

Children should not be sheltered from the sense of evil, and allowed to grow up in a goody-goody world of make-believe virtues; but neither should they be made rigid and suspicious and fearful of strange and wayward behavior. Awareness and trust must go hand in hand. The real "facts of life" do not mean the facts of sex, but the facts of love — which can master all other facts, both good and bad.

Sees Teen-Agers as Pygmy Adults

SPEAKING OF new words, as I was recently, it is hard to believe that only thirty years ago there was no such animal as a "teenager." Not only the idea, but even the word, had not yet been invented.

A generation ago, you were a *child* until you became a man or a woman, and you lived in a child's world, not in the hazy and ill-defined half-world in which boys and girls exist today.

Overexposure to new forms of stimulation has produced a race of pygmy adults today called "teen-agers," and I feel sorry for them. They are chronological half-castes, who belong in neither world — they are too knowing for the pleasant myths of childhood and too immature for the harsh realities of adulthood.

We have done this dreadful thing to them ourselves: robbed them of their innocence and provided them with few substitute gratifications. Little wonder, then, that so many of them are resentful and rebellious, confused and contrary.

To be adolescent is difficult enough, in biological and social ways. But to add to these natural problems the tantalizing view of cars and sex and fast money — through all the modern media of entertainment and advertising — is to place a nearly intolerable strain on their psyches.

At sixteen, my greatest passion was for a racer bike, without brakes. It no more occurred to me to get the family car at that raw age than to marry Vilma Banky. Indeed, marrying Vilma would have been easier than obtaining my dad's permission to borrow our Graham-Paige.

Yet it is foolish and unrealistic to blame modern teen-agers for such drives and desires. They are not responsible for the frantic speed-up of the growing process: they did not invent radio, talkies, television, sexy and sadistic comic books, and all the rest.

Nor did they seek to blur the necessary distinction between the child's world and the adult's. We ourselves have pushed them too far and too fast, putting the boys in long pants before they could toddle, furnishing nail polish for little girls, exposing them to pleasures and stimulations and material possessions they neither wanted, needed, nor cared much about at first.

Our child-centered society is a shock and a scandal to the rest of the civilized world, and it would take a social pathologist to discover the deep reasons for it. But juvenile discontent, and the whole problem of the troubled "teen-ager," is merely a symptom of our own frantic tempo of living, our own delusion that material objects make for happiness, our own overemphasis on bigness and boldness, on speed and excitement and "getting the most" out of life without putting the most into it.

Child's Major Need: Basic Trust

IN ALL THE LENGTHY, heated (and generally futile) discussions I have ever heard about child-rearing, there is one phrase that rarely gets mentioned — although I think it is perhaps the most essential.

Parents and educators and child guidance experts can go on for days threshing around such weighty topics as "discipline," "permissiveness," "cooperation," "authority" — and never reach the heart of a good parent-child relationship.

The term I have in mind is "basic trust." If the child has basic trust, the different strategies and techniques of child-rearing don't matter very much; they are just superficial items of style and temperament.

All the children I have seen who were "difficult" — to use the broadest possible term that covers a multitude of problems — lacked a basic trust, first in their parents, and secondly, in the world at large.

They are, at bottom, fearful and resentful. They feel that something has been denied them (without knowing what), and that something will be taken away from them (again, without knowing what). They are miserable whether you treat them with kindness or with severity.

It is not so much how parents handle their children that counts; it is how they genuinely *feel* toward their children. Children can stand an enormous amount of improper treatment so long as they can sense good vibrations from their parents; and no amount of "correct technique" can help if the parents' unconscious feelings are unstable or inconsistent.

This is why I am impatient and more than a little contemptuous toward those books and courses that aim at teaching the "skills" of child-rearing. The true skills cannot be taught, for the child does not respond to what he hears on the rational level, but only to what he grasps on the emotional level.

A woman who unconsciously rejects her femininity, who resents motherhood, or who tries to get those satisfactions from her children that she should be getting from her husband — such a woman could take twenty years of "child psychology" and be no better a parent. Maybe worse.

It is not child psychology we need so much as adult psychology. We subject the child to an intense scrutiny when in most cases it is the parents who need an X-ray into the secret places of their hearts. When a child lacks basic trust, why should he listen to an alien voice?

Silent Language Speaks Volumes

By the time he was two and a half, Michael could tell how I was feeling before I said a word. An expression on my face, the slump of my back, the way I fingered a cigarette — all these revealed more to him than the words he could not understand.

Ours is such a verbal society — so many millions of words are spewed out at us daily — that we forget what the anthropologist Edward Hall calls "the silent language."

The silent language is the way we communicate by our manners and behavior. It is the unspoken give-and-take of human relationships — and often the most important part.

According to Hall, we communicate in *space* and *time*, as well as in words. The office worker's jealous defense of his desk is a communication in time, telling others exactly what he thinks of his privacy and position, and what he would like others to think of them.

Likewise, the way in which we keep others waiting for an appointment, or are kept waiting by them, signifies our feelings of superiority, equality, or inferiority. The informal rules of punctuality are communications in time.

It is a serious mistake, I think, to assume that what we *tell* our children is what they automatically believe — if they can see that our expressions and gestures and general attitude do not agree with our spoken words. To a child, reality lies in the total existence, not in a verbal formula.

The parent who preaches truth and tolerance, and who is sneaky in his behavior and bigoted in his beliefs, soon finds that the child is imitating his basic attitudes rather than his verbal decorations.

Our true emotions can be more successfully hidden from adults than from children, for most adults can be hypnotized and deluded by the word; but children immediately pierce beneath the rhetoric: they promptly know when a parent doesn't like a visitor, even though the visitor may never know it — and, indeed, the parent may be unaware of it himself until the child blurts out the candid fact.

People who dislike others give themselves away a dozen times a day, through the silent language. Children are notorious for being able to spot phonies; this does not mean that a child cannot be fooled — but he cannot be fooled by the spoken word.

"Why are you annoyed, Daddy?" Michael will sometimes ask. I start to reply that I am not annoyed, and suddenly realize that he is right.

Let Children Pick Own Friends

"I CAN'T UNDERSTAND why Michael prefers that Valerie girl," said the woman across the breakfast table, "when Anne is so much nicer in every way."

Here is a little boy not yet four — and his mother is already concerned about the girls who interest him in nursery school. (Needless to say, those are not their real names.)

It is difficult for parents to understand why a child prefers one playmate to another, and it is hard to resist pointing out to the child why one playmate is superior to another. But children, I am convinced, must be given a chance to make their own choices and to find out their own mistakes — if they are mistakes. The child who is continually protected from "unsuitable" playmates is likely to grow up with a permanently crippled sense of judgment about people.

By the time they are teen-agers, through a process of trial-and-error, they will have developed a capactiy to make sensible choices. When an adolescent runs around with a "wrong crowd," it is usually because he or she is rebelling against the hot parental breath on the neck.

Besides, young children have a need to find their opposites in playmates — to find someone who represents a part of themselves that has been repressed at home.

What I mean by this is that a child who has been drilled in good surface manners will often seek out an unruly companion, and then can vicariously enjoy his companion's defiance of the adult world. He becomes attached to this companion as the "hidden half" of his nature.

We are all bundles of conflicting drives and emotions, and what attracts us to others is not so much a similarity in temperament and training as a dramatic difference in backgrounds. The shy woman who marries an aggressive man finds a forbidden pleasure in identifying herself with bold traits she has been trained to repress in her own nature.

It is a grievous mistake, I think, to "pick" friends for one's children. Michael doubtless finds in Valerie certain piquant qualities he longs for in himself, and only by exploring these fully may he then come to a better appreciation of what Anne has to offer. If you don't allow them to make little mistakes at four, they may make ghastly ones at fourteen.

Parents to Blame for Dirty Words

A MOTHER visiting us recently was mortified when her three-year-old son shouted at Michael, "For crissake, don't do that!" She reprimanded the boy, and fluttered, "I can't imagine where he picks up that kind of talk."

He picks it up exactly where all children pick it up — mostly at home. The reason we blame school or other children in the neighborhood is that we aren't able to hear ourselves talk.

I was driving the children to the zoo Saturday morning, when a car suddenly pulled out of an alley and cut ahead of me. Michael, jolted back in his seat, yelled "You dirty buster!" at the offending motorist.

Starting to reprove him, I quickly caught myself in time. He had, of course, heard the same sort of comment from his dear father — only it wasn't quite "buster."

Most of us are tone-deaf toward our own speech, both the words and the tone. The whiner does not hear herself whining, the bellower does not recognize a bellow, and the habitual users of naughty words are not even aware they are using them. The words have long since ceased to mean anything, and are simply explosive emotional sounds.

Much of what is called "dirty language" is not really obscenity — if we define obscenity as having an obscene *intention*. We do not use these words to signify something dirty, but as a substitute for physical action when we are frustrated or baffled or exasperated. They are a way of defying convention, of rebelling against what Justice Holmes called "the plain ordinary cussedness of the universe." Most people who use foul language from time to time would be shocked and disbelieving if a tape recorder were played back to them.

Just as no one recognizes the cadence and timbre of his voice when he hears it played back, so no one would recognize that his everyday speech is sloppy, slangy, and half-inarticulate most of the time. We rarely speak a full grammatical sentence in our daily conversations.

Children, as everyone knows, are devilishly quick to seize upon these defects and transfer them to their own speech. And they pick the "bad" words because they recognize intuitively that we use them to express our own hostility and frustration.

Since the child himself is so full of aggressions he is not allowed to exhibit, the words give him an emotional gratification and a way of striking back at repressive adult authority. But we ourselves have provided him with the weapons.

Why Kids Lose Interest in Fads

"THERE'S NOT A hula hoop to be seen this summer," remarked a friend as we passed some children playing in the park. "Kids certainly tire of those things fast."

It is easy for us to laugh at childish fads, but we should not be contemptuous of them — for this is how a child learns. All play is a serious form of education. When a child discards a once-loved toy, what does it mean? That he is "fickle," that he is "tired" of it? Not at all; it means that he has exhausted its possibilities for teaching him anything. The hula hoop was popular only as long as it presented a problem and a challenge. When the child eventually mastered its secret, he promptly lost interest in it.

This is true of all games children play. They are seeking to manipulate the physical world they live in, and as soon as they can easily handle one aspect of it, they quickly pass on to another.

Instead of deploring such fads, we should rejoice in them. The child who continues to play the same game, long after he has mastered it, is in trouble: he is giving up adventure and is yearning for security.

The reason, of course, that games such as baseball and tennis continue to interest people is that they can never be wholly mastered. There is always something more to learn, even for the expert. A perfect player (if such existed) would no longer care to play.

If parents could be taught to look upon play as an important part of education, they would not be so impatient when the child refuses to "stop that silly playing" and come in to eat.

What a child learns in school depends to a large extent upon the play habits he has formed before school. If he is encouraged to experiment, if he is presented with challenges, if his curiosity is stimulated, then he will approach the problems of reading and writing and counting in a similar spirit.

All grown-up work, if it is to be satisfying, must contain a large element of play. Men speak of their business as "the game," and this metaphor has the phychological ring of truth to it. One who has not learned how to play with zest cannot easily learn how to work with zest.

This is why the word "playboy" is such a contradiction in terms. The man who does not enjoy some kind of work does not really enjoy any kind of play, for they are obverse sides of the same coin. The playboy, paradoxically enough, is a man who never learned how to play as a boy.

A Primer of Education for Parents

SCHOOL IS A PLACE where children go to learn how to read, write and count. It cannot be much more than that, and when it tries, it often becomes much less than that.

A school cannot build character; it cannot guarantee success; it cannot teach popularity; it cannot automatically make a child happy.

Most of our frantic talk about "good schools" is a cheap and cowardly evasion of our own parental responsibility.

Where the child goes to school is not nearly so important as what he learns at home — the moral, spiritual, social and emotional climate of the family.

By the time a child goes to school, his basic attitudes have already been formed; school can do little to change them.

Many parents want the school to rectify their own mistakes in the past, and to do the job that parents were meant to do.

When the school makes a halfhearted attempt to do this, it usually falls down on its basic job of education.

When I was a boy, a child went to the school in the district in which he lived; parents did not shop for schools, did not move long distances to find a "better" school for the child.

If the school was at least average, the parents were satisfied; they did not expect, or demand, a superior institution for an ordinary child.

This was a much healthier attitude than exists today, when we load down the school with functions and duties it cannot possibly perform well.

All the outstanding children I have ever known grew up in homes where their intellectual and moral qualities were encouraged; the school they went to made little difference.

This is not to say that school standards should not be improved; but it *is* to say that parents should spend less time at PTA meetings and more time in the home; less energy in devising school programs and more energy devising family programs; less concern with a child's grades and more concern with his emotional needs.

The only thing that makes better children is better parents — not better schools, or better anything else in the material world.

Parents need a Primer of Education more than their children do.

School Exams Fail to Pass Test

WHEN I WAS A REPORTER, nearly twenty years ago, I used to enjoy doing interviews, and I must admit that I did them well. My technique was simple and effective.

I would sit down with the interviewee and chat, usually over lunch if possible. After about an hour, the interviewee would usually ask: "When do you start interviewing me?" and I would reply, "It's all over." Had I pulled out a pencil and a sheet of paper and begun firing formal questions, I would have received tight and cautious and carefully tailored answers.

Almost everybody tenses up under such conditions, and the results are most unsatisfactory. Doctors have learned, especially in treating children, that the best examination is made casually, while the child scarcely knows what is taking place.

I bring all this up to point out the parallel with school tests.

In my view, they should be abandoned. Pupils should be judged on their week-to-week work, and testing should be a regular part of the ordinary assignment, not a great emotional crisis twice a year.

Pupils who score highest in tests are not necessarily the best students — they are merely the ones who are least nervous under pressure. All that is being tested is their imperturbability, not their intelligence or their knowledge. Many bright pupils freeze up under the emotional impact of a formal test, forget what they have learned, and sit in a stupor for hours, even though they have the material well in hand. At the same time, many dumb pupils cram their craniums with facts the night before a test and simply sit down and reel off this mnemonic tape-recording without the faintest idea of what it really means.

Our whole examination system is antiquated and unreliable. It is devised to make life easier for the testers, who can grind out mechanical grades without knowing or caring much about the minds behind the answers.

Evaluation of a student should be a continuous process, part of the warp and woof of daily classroom work, and should not depend so heavily upon a couple of peak performances under intense and artificial pressure. The interviewee, the patient, and the pupil all give their finest responses when they are unaware of making a special response.

Children Maturing Far Too Quickly

Michael, who has yet to take his entrance exams for kindergarten, strolled into my study yesterday and announced: "I'd like a red and white sports car."

"Oh, you would," I retorted wittily, "and when do you want it?" He smiled blandly. "When I start college."

One of the consequential changes between the rising generation and my own declining generation is the expanding idea of time and space. As a boy, I rarely looked ahead more than a few weeks, and a trip a hundred miles away seemed adventurous and remote. Nowadays, the tempo of living has been so speeded up that even small children, who can scarcely grasp the ideas of time and space, are quite blasé about huge distances, both in years and in miles.

In grade school I occasionally thought about my future career, but I did not make plans for college, as so many youngsters do today. I was content to live pretty much in the present, and the future was vague and imponderable. My plans were keyed to getting a racer bike, not a sports car; to making the high school tennis team, not the college boards.

Today, before a little girl is through lisping she is critically evaluating the colors of different lipsticks. And they all start dating at an age when, in my time, the sexes still detested each other's company.

Technology, of course, is responsible for this accelerated pace. Children are now exposed to a thousand visual and verbal stimulations that were absent a generation ago.

I went to a children's movie each Saturday morning, and was allowed to hear two radio programs, for kids only. I lived in a world that was sharply separated from adulthood.

Such separation has all but disappeared today. Especially since the advent of television, children move in the same social and cultural world as their parents do — in the orbit of sleek cars, refreshing brands of beers, and toothpaste to make you more kissable.

The horizon of youth has expanded so tremendously that

it is easy to see why youngsters now project their fancies and fantasies for years ahead. Childhood to them is merely an irksome period of waiting for the day when they can step across the glamorous threshold of adulthood. The more we have given them, the more dissatisfied they have become with a child's estate.

"Sure," I promised weakly, "I'll buy you a sports car for college." Knowing that next year he'll ask for a rocket ship.

Do Our Children Really Change?

CHANGE IS EXCITING, but repetition is just as wonderful in its own way. The change of seasons would not be so impressive if it were not part of nature's cycle of repetition.

Observing a child grow up is an engrossing experience — partly because the child is a unique individual, but also because the child repeats the same patterns that reawaken our own childhood memories.

Carolyn has sent me a column called "Campus Quips" from her school newspaper. She and another girl write the column, and it is amusing and interesting — but (and I hope her feelings will not be hurt) it is exactly like all the campus columns I remember as a youth. Nothing has changed in the quarter century since I edited my school newspaper. The same jokes are still making the rounds; the same sly digs at faculty members; the same impish reflections on homework and vacations and study periods and gym classes.

This is not plagiarism, however; it is originality that simply does not know it is following a time-worn formula. Each generation thinks it makes these discoveries, and cannot believe that its parents had the same jokes and the same attitudes.

We can see it beginning even in very small children. How do they learn to adopt the identical tricks for staying awake later at night? Where does a child of two pick up the technique for calling for water, for milk, for toileting, for another story, for a second glass of water? It's almost as if someone gave each infant a *Handbook for Handling Parents* at birth.

"The more things change, the more they are the same," goes an old French saying. This is surely true in the life development of children. Today's youth grow up at a faster tempo, and know more *things* than we did, but their similarities to us are greater than their differences.

Those who despair of the younger generation see only the superficial differences and not the deeper similarities. The basic structure of the personality changes very little — the humor and trust and candor and skepticism, and the whole mixed bag of emotions that make human beings so fascinating and unpredictable and predicatable at the same time.

Of course, changes in the culture do affect the personality; but it is easier to see change than to note persistence. There is a heritage in civilization that is hardy and resistant, and the same old jokes in school papers give witness to the encouraging fact that our radical children of today will, as always, become the traditionalists of tomorrow.

Why Our Children Don't Trust Us

STEKEL, that brilliant and erratic psychiatrist, said near the end of his life: "When I look back upon the long series of nervous diseases that I have observed, I see that invariably the parents have failed to practice what they preached to their children."

This comment, more than anything else, seems to me to sum up the chief reason for the resentment, the restlessness, the rebellion of so many American youths today. We are living in a culture which shows all the symptoms of a split personality. And our children do not know which part of us to believe, to trust, to follow.

On the one hand, we preach the Judeo-Christian system of ethics: to treat our fellow men decently, to extend mercy, to behave with honor, to place the welfare of our community above our own self-interest.

On the other hand, we secretly (and sometimes openly) respect the qualities of cunning, shrewdness, self-seeking, duplicity, and the aggressive accumulation of material goods.

On Sundays we worship the God of our fathers; on weekdays we make supplication before the idols of the market place. We send our children to Sunday school in the morning; and in the afternoon we bribe a policeman to refrain from giving us a ticket for speeding.

Children take in more with their eyes than with their ears. They recognize that our homilies about honesty do not always jibe with our personal practices, at home, in the office, or on the road.

If we tell them to value the quality of "sharing," and then we boast about our "sharp deal," they intuitively know that we are not handling our lives the way we tell them to handle their toys.

What Erik Erikson in his magnificent book *Childhood and Society* calls "basic trust" is the most important legacy we can leave a child. But when the child cannot trust us, when he witnesses the gross disparity between our preachments and our practices, then he feels baffled and cheated, and runs wild because he has no guidelines he can cling to.

When parents talk about "discipline," they mean a rigid set of rules to prevent the child from misbehaving. But the only discipline worthy of the name lies in providing a solid framework of ideals — not for the child to live up to, but for the parents to live within.

You can beat a child until he is black and you are blue, but it cannot make him any better than the examples he sees around him every day.

A Sharp Ear and a Loving Heart

WE ALL KNOW that some persons are physically tone-deaf; to them, a sour note is no different from a sweet one. I am convinced that many others are *emotionally* tone-deaf, which is a harder condition to recognize.

On the beach yesterday, I rebuked Michael for some minor naughtiness and he snarled at me, "You dummy daddy, you!" The family on the next blanket looked surprised and shocked when I ignored his insult; no doubt they believe that I am a "weak" parent.

But I fancy myself as having an acute ear for the emotional tone of a child's reaction. Michael's remark meant nothing except an impulsive explosion of resentment; and ignoring this discharge was the best way of handling his feeling.

At other times I will whack his bottom for less than that: when he is genuinely insolent or willfully mean. And a child has such an inborn sense of fairness that he knows when he deserves punishment and when he does not.

This is why so much talk about "discipline" is confusing nonsense. A child should be disciplined not so much for what he *does* as for what he *means*. Unless we understand the dynamics of his behavior, then we are deaf to the emotional overtones of his remarks and his actions.

You can see this more easily with a child's crying. Some parents are forever unable to distinguish one type of cry from another. But the parent with a sharp ear soon learns to differentiate, even at a distance, the various cries of his child.

There is the cry of real pain, the cry of frustration, the cry of irritation, the cry of fear, the cry of sleepiness and hunger, the cry of mere attention-demanding.

A tone-deaf parent treats all these cries as much the same thing, which is a disastrous breakdown in communication. A parent with good emotional hearing will comfort one cry, ignore another, rebuke a third, and jolly the child out of a fourth.

Likewise, there are times when the child must be permitted a discharge of anger against the parent; if he is always stepped on for such defiance, he will repress his expression but intensify his anger. There are other times when the child is begging to be punished for his willful behavior — and no handbook on discipline can enable you to tell the difference between the two.

Rules and regulations, therefore, are crude and unreliable guides to parenthood. Only the cultivation of a sharp ear and the sensitivity of a loving heart can inform us when to smile, when to shrug, and when to slap.

The Child Needs Incentives, Too

I AM CONSTANTLY surprised at the number of parents who train their children negatively, rather than positively, without ever realizing what they are doing to cripple the child's confidence.

In the park yesterday, I heard a mother keep saying to her young son: "No, you're too little for that slide — you're too weak to lift that rock — you're too small to walk the fence."

The point she should have made was that soon the boy would be bigger and stronger and older — and able to do these things. Michael keeps looking forward to "when I'm a big boy," and he understands, at least vaguely, the concept of growth and development.

When I spoke of this to a woman at dinner, she reflected, and then said, "Do you know, I believe I was about twelve years old before I realized that I wasn't always going to be a child! I guess I always thought that childhood was something permanent — that the world was divided between big people and little people."

We recognize the importance of incentives for adults, but we often fail to apply the same psychology to children — who need it just as much, if not more.

Emotional studies of delinquents have shown that most of them secretly feel weak and small and defenseless, and strike back at the world in a kind of desperate fury. It is usually the runtiest and skinniest boy in a gang who exhibits the most daring, for he is actually fighting against his own inner sense of helplessness.

Even a child of two or three can be imbued with the idea that someday he will be able to do what the bigger children are doing; that everybody was once a baby and grew into adulthood; that life is a constant process of growth.

A child needs to be taught to look forward at the future; "Next summer you can go into the water by yourself," not "Little boys like you can't go in the water alone." The first statement holds forth a bright promise; the second merely creates frustration and resentment.

I am firmly convinced that the child who is given confidence in his increasing powers, who is provided with incentives for development (and thus for self-control), will not grow up into a troubled and troublemaking youngster with a nagging need to test his powers against the authority of the grown-up world. Only the people who feel little need to act big.

Down-to-Earth Look at High Grades

As A PUPIL, I never got the highest grades, because I was forever asking embarrassing questions, and refusing to be satisfied with evasive answers. The pupils who got the best grades were by no means the smartest — they were docile, accepting, studious, neat and unimaginative. And I secretly despised them.

Now comes a report from the admissions committee at Harvard, which says exactly what I have been insisting upon the last twenty-six years. This is the juicy heart of the report:

> We are aware that high test scores and top class ranking in secondary schools are not . . . very reliable evidence of real quality, intellectual or otherwise . . .
> We are concerned lest we overvalue the conformist pupil of high verbal facility who has always kept his nose clean, done what was expected of him and gone blinkered down the middle of the road, grinding out top grades as he went . . .
> Passion, fire, warmth, goodness, feeling, color, humanity, eccentric individuality — we value these and do not want to see them give way to meek competence.

This is an admirable statement of a sensible position, but it is a position that needs to be adopted long before the pupils get to college. For the nation's high schools, generally speaking, resent and repress any passion and individuality on the part of their pupils.

Some of the dumbest girls I ever knew in school won the highest marks, simply because they memorized what was in the book, wrote in a neat script, did their homework dutifully — and then forgot everything they had "learned" as soon as the diploma was put into their moist little hands.

Whereas the really bright boys I attended school with — and we had some corkers in my class — rarely received more than passable grades because they invariably upset the teachers' apple cart by arguing, deriding, questioning the book, and rejecting the stock answers.

There are few incentives for intellectual curiosity in the public school system. The bright students soon become bored, and quickly learn to go through their paces with a minimum of effort.

If they don't, they are labeled "troublemakers." To the average teacher a "troublemaker" is any pupil who disturbs the bland tedium of a classroom by taking a passionate interest in a subject that goes beyond the book. Our standards are low not because the average students won't study but because the superior students are crushed by conformity.

Schools Can't Teach Character

WITH ALL GOOD WILL toward the splendid young woman who was recently named the nation's "Teacher of the Year," I must sadly dissent from her suggestion that the schools should "put more emphasis on teaching morals and spiritual values." This fervent Iowa teacher, who doubtless is superb with her second-grade kiddies, told a conference of educators that the public schools should do more about "character building."

If there is one thing that is unteachable, it is character. If there is one thing a child cannot be given in a classroom it is an active sense of moral and spiritual values. Character is a plant that must be nurtured from birth. By the time a child is old enough to attend school, the basic structure of his character has already formed. A school can help him go in the direction he already wants to go; it cannot alter the direction.

Moral and spiritual values are gained by example — by watching what the parents do, not by listening to what they say. It is a steady, unconscious, day-by-day process.

Urging the schools to assist in directing and reforming character is an impossible imposition they are not equipped to handle. Their primary job is to teach the child reading, writing and comparable skills. When they try to do more than this, they usually end up doing less than this.

Parents should not be allowed to get off the hook of personal responsibility quite so easily. They cannot continue to throw the child at the school and expect the school to turn a selfish and undisciplined brat into a model of deportment. Even a trained psychiatrist could not do this against the odds of some home environments.

Children who will listen responsively to talks about moral and spiritual values don't need the talks; and those who most need it won't listen. Their conduct is shaped by the way their parents behave to them, and to each other; not by the sweet sentiments of classroom moralists.

Character is built just as a building is built — from the substructure up. If the foundation is shaky, the building will tilt or collapse. In the entire history of mankind, education has never improved the character of a single person who wasn't already looking for improvement.

A Child—and the Reality of Death

MICHAEL AND I went for a swim and found some dead fish lying on the beach. He picked one up by the tail and asked me if it was real.

"Yes, it's a real fish," I said.

"Then why doesn't it swim around like the fish at the 'quarium?" he wanted to know.

"Because it's dead," I explained.

"Is it a toy?" he persisted.

This went on for quite a while, until I realized the total impossibility of explaining the concept of death to a young child. Either something is alive, or it isn't "real." And if it isn't real, then it's a "toy."

Many bad jokes are made about teaching children the so-called "facts of life." But I think it is much harder, and more important, to teach them the fact of death.

The sexual habits of human beings can be readily grasped by children, for they unconsciously feel these stirrings within them. But the idea that everyone will die — Mother and Daddy and the child himself — is so vast and mysterious in its final simplicity that not even many adults truly recognize the fact.

Because death in our society is mistakenly thought to be a "morbid" subject, children are not prepared to accept the fact of death. Death is something that happens to other people, but the child believes that he will somehow live forever. The end of his personal consciousness seems inconceivable.

Selfish and self-centered adults are those who have grown up pushing away the fact of death, rather than accepting it calmly as a natural phenomenon. They believe they can buy immunity against death by amassing wealth or consolidating power or drenching themselves in pleasure.

To know — at the emotional level, and not just with the top of the mind — that everybody dies is the beginning of learning how to live properly, with courage and grace and a measure of good will toward all mutable creatures.

And it is also to see that one's own life is part of a vast pattern of living, in which the social organism constantly strives to better itself and become more like the idea that exists in the mind of its Creator. Because we, as a culture, try to prettify and ward off the ultimate reality of death, we have not learned how to be realistic in our approach to life — or to our children.

Strange Habits of Parents at the Zoo

ON MY REGULAR Saturday morning excursions to the Zoo with Michael, I have plenty of opportunity to observe the strange habits of parents while Michael is engaged in cryptic communication wth the ducks. These parents have presumably taken their children to the Zoo to enjoy themselves — the only flaw being that the parents and the children have widely differing concepts of "enjoyment."

"C'mon and see the bears," the parents push. "Let's look at the elephant," they cajole. "All ready for the train ride!" they shout with false joviality.

But the children may not care about the bears. They may

care (as Michael does) to spend a half-hour talking with the ducks, skipping the mammals altogether. Perhaps the elephant bores them, and they would rather stare in fascination at the snakes or the octopuses (octopi? octopods?). They are not out to make the grand tour and Improve Their Minds; they just want to see what they want to see.

But a distressing majority of parents will not permit this. They have taken the trouble to go to the Zoo, and by all that's holy, they are going to cram that Zoo down the child's throat, giraffe and all.

This kind of planned, scheduled, timetable, get-it-all-in "fun" is death to the spirit of a child, who would be much better off if let alone at home to wander around aimlessly exercising his own imagination and wallowing in his own fantasies.

I saw this same kind of parental stupidity in its most hysterical form when I took my daughter to visit Disneyland in California this summer. Mothers and fathers were rushing around frantically, nearly pulling their children's arms out of the sockets in order to take in as many attractions as possible before sundown.

The child's needs and desires are rarely consulted or respected on these planned outings. We wrongly believe that a child is impressed with *quantity*, when the plain fact is that a youngster cannot and should not absorb too much at any one time. This is how children become spoiled and prematurely bored with pleasures.

Childhood is a time for the leisurely contemplation of the ducks, for a long, full flavoring of something as simple and miraculous as a squirrel scurrying along the branches of a tree. Three rides on the merry-go-round will not make him happier; it will only make him sick.

We've visited the Zoo a dozen times, and Michael still

hasn't worked up any interest in the lions. Who cares? It's *his* Saturday, isn't it?

Punishment Isn't Discipline

THE STUDY OF WORDS is useless unless it leads to the study of the ideas that the words stand for. When I am concerned about the proper use of words it is not because of snobbism or superiority, but because their improper use leads to poor ways of thinking.

Take the word "discipline" that we hear so much about nowadays in connection with the rearing of children. If you know something about word derivations, you know that "discipline" and "disciple" come from the same Latin root — *discipulus*, which means "to learn, to follow."

The disciples of Jesus were those who followed his teachings and adopted the discipline of Christianity. There was no idea of punishment or chastisement connected with the word "discipline."

When we forget this, or do not know this, then we use the word "discipline" in a wholly misleading sense. We think of discipline for the child as consisting of a strict set of rules, followed by punishment for their infraction.

But genuine discipline means leading the child by example, giving him a firm pattern of conduct to follow, as Jesus gave the disciples. It means bringing out the best in them, not hammering down the worst in them.

In connection with this distorted view of discipline, it is interesting to note that we speak of "old-fashioned" discipline, meaning the severity of the nineteenth-century family. But this was very new-fashioned, if we take a long view of human history.

As George Sheviakov recently observed, spanking as a means of discipline is unknown among the so-called primitive peoples. "It is the civilized man's method," he tells us, and goes on to say, "Perhaps we civilized people resort to spanking because we are too much in a hurry about many little things. And hurry is not a child's way of living."

I am not rigidly against spanking, so long as we recognize that it is a poor substitute for real discipline, and reveals a weakness on the part of the parent more than a willfullness on the part of the child. We may do it for exasperation, but not as a matter of principle.

Our task is to make our children into disciples of the good life, by our own actions toward them and toward other people. This is the only effective discipline in the long run. But it is more arduous, and takes longer, than simply "laying down the law." Before a child (or a nation) can accept the law, it has to learn why the law has been created for its own welfare.

Child Doesn't "Belong" to Parents

I FELT A STAB of pain and envy this morning, and then I quickly chided myself for being a fool. But it still hurt.

Michael has found a little girl friend across the hall, and he wants to be with her much of the time. This morning I took him over and as soon as he set foot on the threshold, he slammed the door in my face. That was it. Daddy is an old square. Mummy is somebody to run to when you're hurt or hungry. But for fun, give him Kathie any time.

You start to lose them almost as soon as you get them. And it's good, in a way. A child should be outgoing and social, not forever clinging to its parents. One part of me is delighted that Michael is that way. But another part of me, deep below

the reasonable level, is resentful. Here we give him everything, make all sorts of sacrifices, rearrange our lives completely — and off he waltzes with a little flirt he only met a
few weeks ago.

This is where many parents, I believe, start to go off the
track. They assume that a child "belongs" to them, like a
thing. But a person is not a thing, and can never be a possession. A child is given by God into the custody of parents. It
is their task to develop him into the best kind of human being
they are capable of. This is their whole reward — and it had
better be enough.

If they play their cards right, the child will like and respect them as it grows older. But they must never *demand*
devotion or loyalty or sacrifice from the child. His love will
go to his children, not back to the parents.

Our aim should be to develop personalities who will love
and fend for their own young, not personalities who live under
the heavy obligation to please their parents. And a great deal
of neurotic conflict in later life, I am convinced, arises because
young people acquire a sense of guilt about their parents.
They are made to feel "unworthy" and "ungrateful" if they
do not put the parents first.

The wisest parents ask only that the child become a decent
human being. If this goal can be reached, then the child will
give the proper respect to his parents, because it is the "right
thing" to do, not because he is "indebted" to them.

I went to work feeling blue because Michael slammed the
door in my face. But I should have had the sense to close it
myself, gracefully.

Frustration Can Be Good for Child

FREUD IS REPORTED to have said, "I am not a Freudian," just as Marx is supposed to have remarked, "I am not a Marxian."

What both these men meant, of course, was that their theories became exaggerated and perverted at the hands of their ardent followers. The people who champion a cause often do it more harm than the enemies of the cause.

I thought of this today while reading an article about "frustration" in which the author assumes that it is always a bad thing. He warns us that children must not be "frustrated," using the word as if it were some sin or crime. Yet Freud, who was a balanced and sensible (and highly moral) man knew that some frustrations are necessary and some are harmful. It is our job as parents and as adults to learn to distinguish between the two.

"Frustrated," in its original sense, before the psychologists made it popular, simply meant "baffled or defeated." Now, it is a good thing for a child to be occasionally baffled or defeated. It is one of the means by which character is built.

Everybody is frustrated in something or other throughout life. The way we gain maturity is by learning to cope with frustration, to accept it, and to transform it into a positive source of energy.

We must not frustrate a child's efforts to develop his emotional and mental capacities, but we are called upon daily to frustrate those demands which will only make him spoiled and querulous and resentful of loving authority.

Parents who are too strict and parents who are too lax are both failing in their duty — which is to give freedom to the child's real needs and to frustrate only his illegitimate needs.

It is often hard to tell the difference — but who ever said that parenthood was easy?

Intellectual laziness is often at the root of both these attitudes. Strict parents are like judges who decide that all criminals are unworthy and should be given long sentences; and lax parents are like judges who decide that all criminals should be given another chance. But the judge is supposed to judge individual cases, not to make arbitrary rules.

"Frustration" is a neutral word, like "sex." It can be either good or bad, helpful or harmful. It must not be used by psychologists as a verbal bogy man to scare parents into letting their children become unfrustrated little monsters.

Unlike Adults, Animals Don't Nag

MICHAEL GOES to bed nightly with five or six toy animals in his crib. He loves them dearly — even the tattered toy giraffe, which represents an animal he has never seen in real life.

A young child's early affection for animals is so commonplace that we take it for granted. His first books are generally about animals, not about people; and Michael could name some thirty species before he could distinguish between a man and a woman.

I think if we can begin to understand this almost instinctive turning to animals, we can understand many of the child's earliest fears and needs. He lives on the fringe of the adult world, which is both frightening and fascinating to him.

Somehow, the young child seems to sense that animals, also, do not belong to the grown-up world; they, too, are on the outside, beyond reason and beyond morality. As René Guillot, the French psychologist, has observed, "Animals do not worry about doing and becoming, they are content just to be; to the child, the animals are his peers and with them he can feel at home."

We adults are forever concerned, on the other hand, with doing and becoming. We want the child to grow up — often too fast. We are impatient with his lack of coordination, his failure to grasp wrong from right, his faltering sense of time and place and propriety.

A toy animal (and, later, a real animal) is content just to be, and to let the child just be. The lamb does not want to become a lion, the teddy bear does not pass judgment or make a fuss. There is a basic *undemandingness* about animals that is enormously satisfying and reassuring to the child's mind.

When a mother says, with humor that barely masks her vexation, "My little boy thinks more of that dirty old toy rabbit than he does of me," she is simply stating a need that is deep in every child — the need to be accepted as he is and to be loved without being reformed. Of course, parents cannot wholly do this. We must help our children develop into something more than animals, which means instilling in them the social and moral virtues; all growth is a painful process.

But, at the same time, if we push, if we nag, if we deny them their instinctual outlets, we only drive them further into the company of animals, and what began as play may turn into dangerous fantasy.

4

OF THE
SOCIAL ANIMAL

Our Cities Have Become Uncivil

WILL THOSE in the class who know where the word "pagan" comes from, please raise their hands? I thought so.

A "pagan" was originally a peasant, a rustic, who had not yet been reached by the civilizing influence of Christianity. It was a term applied by ancient city people to the country folk around them.

This will come as a rude shock to many persons today, who like to think of the city as a den of iniquity, and of the country as the true site of all the cardinal and theological virtues.

Small towns, generally speaking, are positively smug about their superiority to the city, in terms of moral and religious qualities. They may be right in our time, but they are wrong in assuming that the city was always the locus of wickedness. St. Paul preached only in cities, and all the early Christians were urban dwellers.

I mention this embarrassing fact merely to point out the difference between what cities *ought to be* and what they have become. They are designed to spread their influence over the countryside, for man is a *civic* animal; but we have allowed our cities to become uncivil.

It is important for us to distinguish between the original purpose of cities and their subsequent perversion, or else we shall fall into the mistake of provincialism, of assuming that our little hamlet sets the standard of goodness and righteousness.

There is a Latin saying, *optima pessimo corruptio*, which means that "the worst is a corruption of the best." A city today is almost the worst place to live, in terms of decency and stability, because it is a corruption of the best. Places that were never designed to be very good cannot become very bad either; neither can people. The Devil, we must remember, began as an angel.

The urban dweller, of course, has a great deal of unjustified contempt for his rural brother. But this is no excuse for the ruralite to retaliate by insisting that only the country is God's country — as if a skyscraper or a subway is not as much an effect of God as a sunset or a sea of daffodils.

Our Society Lacks a Moral Sense

"How CAN WE deal on equal terms with those Chinese?" asked the man at dinner. "Human life is cheap there. What do a million people more or less mean to them?"

This may have been true in the whole Orient of the past; it is less true today than ever before. But, ominously enough, it is becoming truer in the Western world — especially in the United States.

Human life valuable here? I fail to see the evidence. We have more homicides than any other country in the world.

Our auto fatality rate alone indicates the cheapness in which we hold human life. And our incidence of armed robberies, in which death is always possible, is greater than all of Europe combined.

More depressing than these facts is the atmosphere in which young people are growing up. What upsets me about the film and TV diet of modern children is the anesthetic effect it has upon their sense of shock.

Violence, cruelty, hate and destruction have become the order of the day. Human suffering is ignored; death is an incident, not a disaster; aggressiveness has become a cardinal virtue, and mercy is a sucker's word.

Criminals and delinquents in our society have little sense of wickedness in snuffing out a life. The great sin is getting caught. Hoodlums may lament their stupidity, but rarely their viciousness.

A few years ago, a joint study was made of delinquents in Great Britain and in the United States. Boys being held by the police were asked by psychiatric social workers: "Why are you here?"

The British boys almost always answered, "Because I stole," or "Because I did wrong," displaying some vestigial glimmer of conscience.

The American boys, almost uniformly, answered, "Because the cops railroaded me," or "Because I didn't plan my getaway well enough," or "Because somebody ratted on me."

This is alarming testimony to the decline of a moral sense in our society. A thief, whatever his other faults, at least used to admit he was a thief; now he engages in defensive double-talk — "I just happened to get caught," or "Everybody's crooked in one way or another."

Human life was cheap in China because the population so

vastly exceeded the food supply. But human life is held cheap here for no such compelling reason. There is more than enough for everybody — what is lacking is not space or food supply, but a basic respect for our fellow creatures' right to exist.

Telling the Cops from the Robbers

A NEWS BRIEF out of New York recently may have escaped your attention: it disclosed that Nassau County plans to pin name tags on its 2000-man police force, to help the public identify policemen.

When I read this, I thought of a true incident someone told me a few months ago. A young woman and her escort had been held up by two robbers in a parked car. When the police came to question her, they asked what the robbers looked like, and the woman said she couldn't see their faces. Well, then, the police wanted to know, what did the robbers *sound* like?

"They sounded like hoodlums," the woman said. Pressed by the policemen to give them a better idea, she blurted out, "I'll tell you honestly — they talked just like you fellows!"

Anyone who has ever been interrogated by a big-city policeman must know just what she meant. With a few pleasant exceptions — such as ruddy traffic cops from the Auld Sod — the urban policeman is as brittle, as curt, and as side-of-the-mouthish as the public's conception of a hoodlum.

I do not share the average citizen's feeling that most policemen are crooked; I think the percentage of honesty is surprisingly high, considering the available temptations when placed next to the low rate of pay and the high rate of risk.

But there is no doubt that most American policemen are uncivil, and regard the public as only a necessary nuisance. It is a mistake to think that the average policeman considers himself "on the side of" the honest public, as allied against the crooks.

The police mentality looks upon the public as an extraneous element in the daily conflict between cops and robbers. The square Johns are simply a factor that must be considered (especially if they have political influence), but they do not really count in the game, which is a private one with its own rules and its own curious code of conduct.

What is important is getting a high score, and making the captain's record book look good, which in turn makes the commissioner's record look good, and thus indirectly helps City Hall to keep its hold on the voters.

In all this, the public is generally treated like bleacher spectators, with a minimum of courtesy and regard, and a maximum of irritated impatience. It's hard to tell the cops from the robbers without a tag.

Boredom Is Driving Us to Ruin

ACCORDING to recent surveys the average American family watches television six hours a day, seven days a week. You will hardly get any family to admit it, but that is because everyone feels obscurely guilty about this modern form of addiction.

Boredom is the only explanation. The pandemic disease among so-called civilized countries today is *boredom:* a lack of goals and purposes beyond the immediate and the material; an incapacity to entertain oneself; an unwillingness to converse, to learn, to grow in spiritual and emotional dimensions.

In his fascinating book, *Mirage of Health,* Dr. René Dubos of the Rockefeller Institute classifies boredom as a major modern disease, remarking that "it is not easy to define or to recognize, and its onset is insidious."

He continues: "Boredom often masquerades in the passive forms of entertainment, in the dreary hours of aimless driving, in anonymous holidays which have lost their meaning because they are no longer holy, as well as in the attitude of the persons who 'couldn't care less' about the events of the world around them."

The chief manifestations of boredom, Dr. Dubos points out, go from the various forms of escapism — such as addiction to drugs or alcohol — to suicide, "which relieves the victim of the need to care about anything."

Recent statistics published by the World Health Organization disclose that the highest rates of drug addiction, alcoholism, suicide and death from violence occur in countries which enjoy material wealth and have the most effective social legislation and political stability.

For the last ten years the United States, Switzerland, Denmark and Australia head the list. The lowest rates of both suicide and homicide exist in countries where life is harder and more uncertain — Spain, Scotland and Israel.

The one factor we have not yet fully considered in the frightening rise of juvenile delinquency in this country is boredom — the boredom of youngsters with nothing to do — no aims, no horizons, no values, no challenge for their abilities and energies. It is an arresting fact that there were fewer homicides and suicides — as well as less crime generally — during the Great Depression than there are right now.

Material prosperity poses its own severe problems. "Production" is not enough. A high income is not only meaning-less, but dangerous, unless accompanied by a high level of genuinely creative activity.

What Is Happiness in Marriage?

A COLLEGE STUDENT asked me, during a bull session on campus last week, "How many happy marriages do you think there are in our country?"

Of course, it is an impossible question to answer, even on a rough percentage basis. But the question itself interested me more than the lack of an adequate answer.

Most people don't know that the idea of "happiness" in a personal sense is a relatively new one — no older than the French Revolution. The idea that happiness as such should be the controlling or dominating factor in human life rarely occurred to the ancients or to the medievals.

Along with the vague concept of "progress," happiness is a product of the last two centuries, when man began to feel he had overcome the forces of nature and when the idea of the individual personality became more important than the family, the tribe, the city, or the nation.

People in the past were not supposed to aim at happiness as an ultimate goal; they may have hoped for it as a by-product, but they did not judge the worth of their lives by this stand-ard. Marriages then held together not because the couples were "happier," but because they weren't looking for happi-ness in marriage.

We can see this even as late as our grandparents' time. Di-vorces were infrequent not merely because the laws were stricter and morality more severe. The couples themselves were content if they rubbed along together, had enough to live by, reared decent families, and died with a sense of communal accomplishment.

We today ask a great deal more of marriage — just as we ask a great deal more of life generally. The average married couple is not satisfied short of "happiness," however this happiness may be defined — and its definition usually includes some idea of romantic love that was irrelevant to marriage in past ages.

I can see good in both attitudes. The past was more realistic, and we are more ambitious. Our grandparents didn't expect too much out of marriage, and were satisfied with mere "adjustment." We expect a great deal — perhaps too much — and are unwilling to settle for less.

We have a much different idea of the *individual* than they did, and this accounts for the restlessness and instability of modern marriage. We want marriage to be more than an enonomic and social contract (which I think it should be) but we have not yet matured enough to realize that "happiness" cannot be *found in* someone else — it must be *built with* someone else. We have not yet grown up to our vast emotional wants.

Suburbanite Sealed Off from Reality

"I'M LIVING like a country squire," said the man who had just bought a large house with extensive grounds in an exclusive suburb. "This is the way the gentry used to live."

He is deluding himself. He is living in exactly the opposite way. The old-time gentry saw almost nobody but the "lower classes." This man sees almost nobody but his own class. All his close neighbors are similar to him, in background, station and convictions. He belongs to a country club of his peers, and spends his days shuttling between his office, his club in town, and his club in the suburbs. He is effectively sealed off from reality.

The real gentry, in the nineteenth century and before, lived in country houses with no peers around them for many miles. Except for occasional parties or hunts, their daily lives were spent among the common people of their districts.

They mingled with the farmers, the craftsmen, the laborers, the shopkeepers. They understood the problems of these people, their feelings, their frustrations, their special funds of sense and nonsense both.

In a way, our modern society is much more stratified than during the "aristocratic" periods of life. The rich man is almost totally divorced from the actual making of things and the growing of things; and, conversely, the poor man feels no bond of any kind connecting him with his "superiors."

Democracy, in a way, is less democratic than feudalism. Social intercourse between the classes is limited to the service trades; there is little reciprocal understanding of problems, and therefore little sympathy for them. Organized "charity" is a poor substitute for personal charity.

Of course the feudal system had grave drawbacks; and democracy, as Aristotle said, is at any rate the *least bad* of all possible systems. But let us not delude ourselves that we do not live in a sharply defined class structure. It is less formalized than before, but just as real.

It is this artificial separation of classes (which is not so prevalent in an agrarian society) that provides the entering wedge for Marxism. Isolation always perverts; when a man lives only among his own sort, he soon begins to believe that his sort are the best sort. This attitude breeds both the arrogance of the conservative and the bitterness of the radical. The country squire and the suburban executive are worlds apart — as the squire and the hostler were not.

Time Is Relative to All Our Affairs

EVERY new role in life requires a new sense of timing, and I feel sorriest for those persons who cannot easily make such adjustments. For "time" is not only relative in the Einsteinian sense, it is relative to all the ordinary affairs of mankind.

I was thinking of this Sunday afternoon, when I was baby-sitting for a few hours. The children wanted to go out and play in the snow, so I dressed them — sweaters, leggings, overshoes, hooded jackets, scarves and mittens.

It took me nearly a half hour to complete this arduous process — and in ten minutes they were back in the house again, complaining of the cold. The whole process then had to be reversed.

Contrariwise, the day before I took them out sledding in the park for "a half hour" after lunch. I stood on the hill an hour and a half, trembling with cold, while they tumbled in the snow. I practically had to lasso them to their sleds to get them home again.

"Time" with children is very different from time without them. Unless we understand this, and make allowances for it, we will either go crazy or drive the children crazy. They live only in the present; past and future mean nothing to them.

And marriage, generally, requires an exquisite sense of timing. As a single person, time is relative to one's needs and demands; as a married partner, time is a joint venture — the husband may be an hour late getting home, while dinner grows cold; the wife may be an hour late dressing for a party, while her mate grows hot under the collar.

Time does not belong to us alone; we share it with those we love, those we work for, those we play with. It is an elastic concept: we must, as we grow older, be willing to be bored for someone else's sake. And it can be as fatal to be stingy with our time as with our money.

I have often seen mothers pulling their small children along downtown streets, while shopping. But nobody should take a child shopping unless she is prepared to be generous with time. A child has no sense of urgency, and to pull him along hectically is merely to make him stubborn, anxious and resentful. In such cases, the mother is more childish than the child.

Each area of human activity has its own special tempo. This tempo must be respected, if any harmony is desired. You can't play the "Minute Waltz" in thirty seconds and still have it sound like Chopin — but most of us keep trying.

Some Figures—and Food for Thought

Notes on our High Standard of Living:

Do you know that crime and delinquency cost more than *six times* the entire cost of all public education in the United States?

That for each dollar spent for schools we spend $2.96 for military purposes, $1.60 for new automobiles, and $1.75 for amusements?

That we spend more money for comic books than for all the textbooks used in our elementary and high schools?

That, although research can help conquer blindness, only

about $3 million a year is spent on eye research, but $12 million a year on unprescribed eye lotion, washes, mascaras, eyebrow pencil and eye shadow?

That last year Americans spent a staggering $1.5 *billion* on travel abroad, but the nation spent only a paltry $10 million on mental health research — which is the most pressing and widespread medical problem of our time?

That, according to the American Heart Association, only $25 million went into heart research last year — which is less than we spent for buying decks of playing cards?

That, in our country today, there are some 3 million excessive drinkers and 750,000 alcoholics — which are more than all the polio, cancer and tuberculosis cases put together; yet we spent $200 million on prevention of cancer and TB, while the American public spent more than $9 *billion* on alcohol?

That each year we spend about $2.5 billion in hospitals — but nearly twice as much for tobacco?

That, although doctors' fees are high, the nation's total medical bill is only one-third as much as we spend for alcoholic drinks?

That, although drug bills are high, we spent $1 *billion* a year more for items involved in personal care, such as hair lotions and toilet waters?

That each year we spend about $3 billion for health care — and more than four times as much on recreation?

That we have no right to speak glowingly about our "high standard of living" until we are able to spend our money as wisely as we are able to make it; that the ultimate test of a civilization is not its power or its riches, but its sense of values; and that every flourishing empire of the past collapsed because it began paying more attention to the incidentals than to the essentials of a good life?

Creators of Delinquent Hate

A MAGAZINE called *Presidio*, which is written and published by the prisoners at Iowa's state penitentiary at Fort Madison recently observed: "One characteristic seen often in prisoners and seldom noticed in outsiders is that of violently hating something."

This short and simple sentence offers the best clue to what creates juvenile delinquents — who then go on to become adult criminals. Hate is the motivation. Hatred of society, which is a projection of hatred of one's family and environment — and, deep down, hatred of oneself.

What good can it possibly do to punish boys who hate? This simply gives them something more to hate — the police, the judges, the prison guards, and everybody involved in this "conspiracy" to punish.

The time, if ever, to "get tough" with a boy is before he has learned to hate. True discipline can be based only on love, understanding and respect.

Getting tough with a troubled, angry, hostile boy just turns him more inward upon himself, and breaks the last remaining emotional link of communication between him and the outside world.

Juvenile delinquents are acting out their hate (and their fear), for reasons they themselves do not comprehend. They cannot tell you, in so many words, why they do the things they do, because they are driven by forces beyond the surface of consciousness.

Obviously, the penal approach to this problem has proved an utter failure. Boys become deformed, not reformed, in most reform schools: they pick up the worst things from the worst elements, because they are looking for ways to be more effectively bad.

And even those few who may be helped soon revert to their old patterns of conduct if they are tossed back into the same environment, the same bleak housing or brutal father or boring life.

Society needs to move a gigantic task force into this area. We need to deploy as much skill and energy and concerted effort in wiping out the slums and all they stand for as we do in time of war, when we know that no price is too high to pay for victory. Not by training our guns, but by training our knowledge and sympathy on this problem, can we make a future that is safe for our children.

The Top Commands a Heavy Price

WATCHING a newly famous actress behave (or, rather, misbehave) at a luncheon last week, I thought of Goethe's remark that "it is important to know as much as possible about what you want most of all, because sooner or later you are so likely to obtain it."

What this actress had wanted most of all was eminence in her field. She worked hard and achieved it — but she is not happy, and she is making miserable the people around her. She is not happy, or truly fulfilled, because she did not know as much as possible about what she wanted most of all. She only knew that she wanted stardom, and she worked for that ceaselessly and remorselessly. How she would handle it, what kind of person she might become en route, are questions that never puckered her pretty little face.

Coping with success is as much a problem as arriving there.

There is an old Spanish proverb: "'Take what you want,' says God, 'and pay for it.'" What one must pay, what one should pay, for what one wants is an essential component in the career-drive; but a component rarely thought about until it is too late.

To her, theatrical stardom meant fame and adulation, money and the thrilling sense of being desirable in the eyes of the world. She did not know that it also — unless handled with great personal skill — means loneliness and fear and brittleness and bone-deep fatigue.

Grasping for the top rung also means accepting the dizzy height with no net to break the fall. It means coming to terms with oneself as a person, retaining a firm sense of values, a humor, a perspective, a basic knowledge that there is nowhere to go from the top but down.

The world is full of people who desperately want something more than anything else in their lives, and who foolishly believe that they will remain the same sort of person after they get it that they were while still working for it. Nothing could be further from the truth.

How many men have achieved their heart's desire in a sweetheart, only to learn that they couldn't handle her as a wife? This is perhaps the greatest and most common tragedy in marriage; that we may know what we want, but we do not know that both we and the object change after possession.

Unless we can adjust to that change, unless we can draw up an emotional balance sheet as we go from desire to fulfillment, we remain like the actress holding in her hand a bubble she cannot enjoy and dare not burst.

Paradoxes You Meet Around You

PARADOXES OF Everyday Life:

The man who is too shy to stand up and talk at a meeting is the same man who stands talking too long, once he does get up; nervousness makes him overly diffident in the beginning and overly garrulous in the end.

The woman who is too indulgent toward her children is the same woman who treats them too harshly when she at last loses her patience; repressed feelings exact a heavy price when the lid is finally lifted.

The employer who is magnanimous about large matters concerning his employees' welfare is often the same man who is insufferably petty about small matters; in this way he reassures himself that he is still the boss and not the victim of his own benevolence.

The entertainer with the scintillating personality in front of an audience is usually the same one whose personality is flat and colorless in the seclusion of his own home; for most entertainers are like mirrors — perfectly blank except when reflecting some object in front of them.

The patriot who waves the flag most furiously is often the same one who despises the patriotism of other nations; not realizing that his emotion is more the hate of aliens than the love of country.

The moralist who publicly assails the sins of the flesh is generally unaware that he is prone to the private sins of the spirit: smugness, self-righteousness, a sense of superiority, and all such deeper moral vices which Jesus found more repellent among the "respectable" than the human weakness of the woman taken in adultery.

The young person who consciously tries to make the best impression is the same one who makes the worst impression; for nothing eventually defeats its own end so much as the inordinate desire to look well in other people's eyes.

The lovers who stay up until all hours talking and mooning about are often the same couple who have nothing to say to each other across the dinner table after they are married; for a romance that is hectic and intense tends to burn itself out in its own consummation.

The waiter — to strike a light note — who hovers above your table impatiently waiting for the order before you have scrutinized the menu is the same waiter who is nowhere to be seen when you have long finished your meal and are tapping the table top impatiently for the check.

And finally, the writer who is conscious of the paradoxes in human nature is the same one who cannot resolve the paradoxes in his own nature, and uses his insight as a substitute for a solution.

The Conventional Is the Natural

THERE SEEMS to be a great confusion in many minds — especially young minds — about what is "conventional" and what is "natural." Some persons actually think that these are opposites.

Let me suggest that they ponder the following paradox: in human behavior, the conventional *is* the natural. To have conventions is as natural for mankind as it is for bears to have caves and birds to have nests.

Rebellious youngsters are fond of dismissing certain forms and manners by saying with a sneer, "That's just a convention." But everything specifically human is a convention. It is conventional that we use the alphabet for speech — everyone has just decided that "a" will sound like "a" and "b" like "b." There is nothing in nature that dictates this to us.

Without these conventions, society could not operate. Man is a conventional animal, because he lives by symbols — and all symbols are conventional. A red traffic light says "Stop!" because we mean it to; otherwise it could just as well say "Eat!" or "Sleep!"

Now, no one denies that different societies have different conventions; that these conventions change from generation to generation; or that some conventions have meaning and force and charm, while others are simply outworn fossils of the past.

It is our task as human beings to distinguish the useful from the useless conventions. But it would be inhuman of us to discard conventions — even if we could — with the cry "Let's be natural." Mankind needs its symbols as much as the bears need the cave and the birds the nest.

To shake hands with a stranger may be an absurd formality; it might be better to rub noses, or bow three times from the waist. But we need some form to signify courtesy and friendship, to allay the fear of others, and to put them at their ease.

Clothes are a convention; this does not mean, however, that nudity is "natural." Even in tropical climes, people wear some clothes as protection against insects and the elements. Our specifically human nature gives us the power and sense to make and wear clothes.

People who imagine they are being more "natural" by ignoring or flouting the conventions of their society are simply setting up a new convention of their own: that rudeness for its own sake makes one a better human being.

Tough: Being Your Own Policeman

WHEN YOU ASK a man to be his own judge, jury and jailer, you are asking too much of him. Nobody can be objective in his own cause.

It is for this reason that professional societies have set up their own bodies to guide their members and to chide them when they have broken the rules of the profession.

But what if these societies turn into mutual protection agencies, who are interested mainly in shielding their members from the consequences of their misdeeds? Then who is in charge of the custodians?

This, I think, is largely what has happened to such powerful and stubborn groups as bar associations and medical societies — and explains, in part, the widespread public resentment against doctors and lawyers.

Everyone knows that it is virtually impossible to get a bar association to take punitive action against a lawyer, or a medical society to reprimand a doctor.

These groups are in business to protect their members more than to protect the public from the folly or fraudulence of legal and medical practitioners. It requires a scandalous crime of the first magnitude before such groups will take action against a fellow professional.

Ironically enough, it is these groups that declaim most stridently against "government powers." But government rushes in only to fill a vacuum. If an organization does not police itself adequately — as, for instance, the Stock Exchange did not in the 1920's — then it paves the way for government intervention.

The way to maintain what we call "free enterprise" is for

private organizations to enforce their regulations so stringently and impartially that there is no excuse for the government to step in.

Doctors simply will not testify against others doctors in lawsuits, nor will the average medical society pay much heed to a patient's complaint. And bar associations are notoriously reluctant to disbar or even suspend a member unless he has murdered a judge downtown at high noon, in the presence of the entire Committee on Ethical Practices.

To be a "professional" means to profess, to take a vow, that the welfare of the client or the patient is paramount, and that profit must take second place. A profession differs from a mere "occupation" in that the latter is done mainly for money; this is why we confer more status upon professional men.

But this status must be earned, maintained, and zealously guarded. At present, the guardians have lost much public confidence and respect.

How Small Is a Small Minority?

How SMALL should a "small minority" be? I, for one, am getting terribly tired of hearing people defend their crafts or businesses or professions by insisting that only a "small minority" are dishonest or negligent.

Nobody has ever suggested that a majority of people in any activity are bad. Even a city with a high crime rate can say that only a "small minority" — less than 1 per cent of the population — are involved in crimes.

This kind of defense is meaningless. If auto or TV repairmen are under fire for questionable practices, their trade associations immediately issue self-righteous statements to the effect that "the great majority of our members are honest, decent, competent and fair."

They behave as if somebody had accused 90 per cent, or even 50 per cent, of their members of dishonesty. But what if only 10 per cent pad their bills for poor service? This is still a shockingly high rate, even though 10 per cent represents only a "small minority."

How large a minority should the public be expected to tolerate before it indicts the entire craft or industry or profession for gross failure to police its members and punish those who persistently violate ethical standards?

You will not easily get an answer to this question, because it is a specific question, and the men who make the defense prefer to deal in vague generalities and high-minded platitudes which fool nobody but civics teachers.

If slum landlords are found to be willfully abusing their ownership, and cruelly exploiting their poor and ignorant tenants, we are promptly told they are only a fraction — another "small minority" — of landlords.

Of course they are. But these are precisely the ones who give a black eye to the entire group — for any group is generally judged by the most obvious and the most flagrant of its members.

The public may be unfair in stigmatizing an entire group for the faults of a few — but I suggest it is the duty of each group to examine the amount of violation it is willing to put up with. To plead a "small minority" is as slyly hypocritical as the plea of Lincoln's mythical client, who murdered his father and mother and threw himself on the mercy of the court on the ground that he was an orphan.

Why Are We So Afraid of Russia?

I DON'T KNOW if you're getting as tired of the Russians as I am, but sometimes it seems as if every activity in America would collapse and disintegrate if we didn't have the "Russian threat" to point to.

Why do we need more science in the schools? Look at Russia. Why should we keep our streets clean, avoid forest fires, have TB checkups, attend neighborhood meetings, buy a new car this year? All because of that menacing Union of Socialist Soviet Republics.

Didn't we get anything done before the bolshevist threat appeared on the horizon thirty years ago? Are we so lacking in initiative, energy, imagination and civic zeal that every activity must be keyed to some warning that Russia will outstrip us, outproduce, outschool us, outlive us?

Now comes a letter from Douglas MacArthur, on behalf of the 1960 Olympic Businessmen's Committee. The letter begins: "You have repeatedly read of the determined and unrelenting efforts of Soviet Russia to defeat the United States in all sports in the 1960 Olympic Games. We believe you will want to join with us right now to prepare to repel this threat . . ."

What have pole vaulting, broad jumping and discus throwing got to do with the political and economic systems of our two countries? These sports existed long before Soviet Russia and they will persist long after that particular tyranny has been ground into dust.

If we train a crack Olympics team it should be for sport and not for diplomatic gloating; indeed, the whole purpose of sport is to judge a man on his individual merit, without considering whether he comes from Yonkers, Yalta or the Upper Yukon.

But every public speaker, every writer, every promoter of a cause, feels he must frighten us into action by rattling the Russian skeleton over our bedsteads. I cannot believe that the rabid nationalism generated by this tactic is any better than the rabid nationalism provoked by the Soviet leaders. The more "anti" Russian we try to be, the more like the Russians we become.

Let us begin to lead our lives, individually and collectively, for positive reasons, because virtue and wisdom point the way, and not because the Russians have done this or have not done that. Let us win the Olympic Games as an example of our fitness, not as a grim maneuver in the perpetual chess game of world politics.

Better Communications—for What?

THIS YEAR the Big Word is "communication." It seems as if almost every magazine article, every seminar, every research paper, is concerned with "communication" in one aspect or another.

Yet most of this talk leaves out a rather essential element; it doesn't tell us *what* is supposed to be communicated, over our enormous network of TV, radio, movies and tape recordings.

Electronics is a marvelous science, but it lacks a content. And what we need today, most of all, is a content as noble as the machines we have devised for "communicating" to hundreds of millions of people across the continents — and perhaps to new worlds.

A hundred years ago, that sourly prophetic agitator, Thoreau, saw what was beginning to happen. In his classic work, *Walden*, he observed with his usual asperity: "We are in great haste to construct a magnetic telegraph from Maine to Texas; but Maine and Texas, it may be, have nothing important to communicate — like the man who was earnest to be introduced to a distinguished deaf woman, but when he was presented, and one end of her ear trumpet was put into his hand, had nothing to say.

"We are eager to tunnel under the Atlantic and bring the Old World some weeks nearer to the New; but perchance the first news that will leap through into the broad, flapping American ear will be that the Princess Adelaide has the whooping cough."

The earliest, and still best, form of communication is one man talking to another, or talking to a small group who can talk back to him. Most modern communication is talking *at* people — and what it says is too often scarcely worth saying.

If we should unexpectedly find human life elsewhere in the universe through our Interstellar Electronic Communicator, what message will we send the inhabitants? That filter cigarettes will relax them? That Elsa Maxwell snubbed the Duchess of Windsor? That movies are better than ever?

The blind beggar Homer, singing his saga of the *Iliad* through the towns of ancient Greece, still lives and inspires us, for he had something permanent and valuable to say. Will the monstrous Univac of Communication transmit to the people of another galaxy that we down here are "all shook up"?

Big Bargain: Cost of Being Crooked

EVERY ITEM has risen steeply in the cost of living — except the cost of being crooked.

Most fines, for both criminal and civil offenses, are still at their laughably low 1940 level. The cost of being honest has more than doubled, but the lawbreaker has not felt the dwindling value of money.

Every day the newspapers report stories of swindlers and thieves who have made off with vast sums — and are subsequently fined $500 or $1000, and perhaps given a year in jail.

I do not believe that long prison sentences do anything but embitter men, but I am convinced that large punitive fines can be effective deterrents to crimes.

A slum owner who persistently defies the law and exploits his wretchedly poor tenants is required to pay some piddling fine while he retains his swollen profits from human misery.

Frauds and fleecers take billions from the public annually, but the law is powerless to do more than assess some trivial fine that was not even adequate a dozen years ago.

A psychopathic drunkard who breaks into a shop and steals a carton of merchandise in order to buy more booze and drown himself in oblivion is sent to prison for a considerable number of years — but the sleek and bloated criminal who uses craft instead of force, and can afford a cunning lawyer, generally is tapped on the wrist with a feathery fine.

We live in a money culture, and money is the only language such men understand; but our justice seems to be in inverse ratio to the magnitude of the offense. The aim of the thief is to be a bigger thief, because size brings relative immunity from punishment.

All our efforts at reform and rehabilitation will prove futile so long as youngsters can plainly see that a man is disgraced not for being a crook, but for being a failure as a crook. Society's worship of success has extended itself to the enemies of society, and irony can go no further than this.

What we require is a brisk overhauling of our criminal statutes, bringing the fines into more sensible proportion to the value of the dollar today, as well as to the gravity and scope of the offense.

Fines have been doubled for illegal parking, but the upper reaches of lawbreaking have scarcely been touched by the magistrate's hand.

Is Greed or Pride Our National Sin?

I SEE THE SAME symptoms that Billy Graham does, but somehow I make a different diagnosis.

Speaking in Charlotte, N. C., the evangelist indicted Americans for being "engaged in a mad race, trampling over each other, cheating each other, lying, stealing, anything to get another dollar."

He said this represented the sin of "covetousness," which outranks murder and immorality as our nation's greatest sin. We are guilty of being "greedy and covetous," both as a people and as individuals, he asserted.

I happen to think that our principal sin is pride, not greed. We are the most generous people in the world, the most softhearted, the most willing to share our bounty with the less fortunate. This generosity of spirit is our saving grace.

Our insane and ruthless pursuit of the buck, to the exclusion of almost all other values, does not rise from covetousness, but from a deep need to Be Somebody. And the only Somebody in our country is the Man of Substance.

In other times, and other cultures, to be Somebody meant different things: it meant to come from Good Stock, or to have Honor and Courage, or to possess Wisdom. Nobility of descent, and the moral and intellectual virtues, counted for almost everything in past societies.

Democracy, in throwing overboard the traditions of aristocracy, also threw overboard any distinctions which make one man superior to another — except money. The rising mercantile middle classes that took over shortly after this country was formed (largely by such natural aristocrats as Jefferson) had no permanent standard except affluence.

What Billy Graham sees as "greed" in our mad competition for material goods is really a perverted way of trying to obtain *status*, of attempting to achieve superiority by amassing the only value we respect — the value of property. The money itself is only a means.

This is certainly a sin (and a terribly shortsighted one), but it is the sin of pride. We want to be looked up to, not because we are morally better or intellectually higher or more civicly responsible, but simply because we have been able to smash our way to commercial success.

When we evolve (or return to) more humanistic values, when a man will be respected for what he *is* rather than for what he *has*, then our folly of today will be seen not as greed but as a pitiful clutching for prestige.

Is the U.S. an "Imperial" Power?

DURING A three-day trip through Canada last month, I was interested, amused and annoyed to hear a half-dozen persons

I met refer to the United States as an "imperial power." We in the States do not commonly think of ourselves as "imperial." The Russians are, of course; so were the Nazis, and the British until recent decades. But peace-loving America? Hardly. Yet this is how we are seen by the rest of the world. And not merely by the people of Turkestan or Timbuktu. By our closest neighbors, the frank and friendly Canadians, who are similar to us in origin, language, outlook and interests.

We think of an "imperial" power as one which wants to extend its frontiers or capture colonial territory; and the United States, of course is perfectly content with what it has. We are not land-grabbers, and we cannot understand how other nations can misinterpret our innocent and warm-hearted purposes. But somehow they do. Either we are not as innocent as we like to think, or else we have failed dismally in communicating our aims even to our English-speaking next-door neighbors.

In Canada, there was as much alarm that America might "start" the next war as that Russia might. Our attitude toward China is widely regarded as being stiff-necked and unrealistic; our strained relations with Russia are seen as the fault of both "imperial" powers.

I writhed under the accusation, because, whatever our defects in foreign policy, I could not swallow the concept that America falls under the same cloud as Russia. After all, we believe in Freedom.

To Canadians, however, what we believe, or say we believe, is less significant than how we behave in the world arena. They regard us as bristling and belligerent, smug and self-righteous — and quite capable of plunging the world into war over an abstraction.

They point out caustically that we praise Freedom but at the same time ally ourselves with any repressive government that we can woo out of the Russian orbit; that we invoke Principle and Morality when the Russians misbehave, but pride ourselves on being Practical when we play the same game of devious power politics.

Whether these Canadian critics are right or wrong is only half the question. What disturbs me, and should disturb all of us, is the obvious fact that the image of America in the eyes of the world is nothing like the image we see reflected in our own looking glasses. Do we need a new mirror, or has the rest of the world gone blind?

All You Have to Do Is Explain

I WAS IN a strange restaurant yesterday, waiting for my luncheon order, when the waitress came over and said smilingly: "There's a foul-up in the kitchen; one of the cooks took ill this morning; can I get you a newspaper to read?"

With these rare and wonderful words, she won me for life. As I am sure she has won hundreds of friends for her employer over the years. For she understands that impatience thrives on ignorance. Most of us don't mind waiting (most of the time) so long as we know *why* we are waiting. It is the feeling of being neglected that breeds dissatisfaction in patrons, not the mere fact of a delay.

A former airline stewardess of my acquaintance has confirmed this psychological fact. "Whenever we had a delay," she said, "I would explain to the passengers exactly why, and I'd make them feel they were sharing in the workings of the organization. It's surprising how this knowledge converted them from angry patrons to members of the team." Too often, alas, airline passengers are merely told "there will be a delay," and no other information is forthcoming. This is infuriating and frustrating — and creates a mass of ill will.

Knowledge is a great healer of emotional scars. The dentist who carefully explains to his patient (as mine does) precisely what is being done, and why all these laborious procedures have to be gone through, has made the patient a *participant* in the work, and not merely an *object* that is worked upon. His technique removes fears and anxieties as well as decay.

Everybody has a natural affinity for belonging. We are willing to share in the problems of a service organization that is having trouble — if we can be made to feel that we are an important part of the operation, and that our good will is an asset earnestly desired by the company. What we resent is being treated as an anonymous mass, too stupid to be told what is going on, and forced to wait until the demi-gods in the inner office decide to push the proper buttons.

There is a huge reservoir of cooperation in the public that has rarely been tapped. Service organizations may be financially astute, but they are psychologically shallow in not recognizing that the best service consists in giving their customers the facts when things go wrong.

The "Average" Is Not the "Normal"

FLIPPING THROUGH a magazine in the barbershop yesterday, I came across an article on eyesight, which made an interesting statement — that only 2 per cent of people have "normal" vision.

We tend to forget the difference between "normal" and "average." Often, we use them as if they were synonymous — which is a dangerous and misleading thing to do. The "average" person, for instance, has about three colds a year. This does not make a cold "normal" for human beings. A cold, or any other infection, is always an abnormal condition, no matter how many people have it at the same time.

The peril in such research as the Kinsey Report is that it tells us (if its facts are correct) what is "average" in sexual behavior; it does not tell us what is "normal." But people immediately assume that an average is a norm — and use this to justify their own behavior. Children who blackmail their parents with the familiar phrase, "All the other kids are . . ." have cunningly learned how to transfer an average to a norm.

Nobody would suggest that because only 2 per cent of the people have "normal" eyesight, therefore we should not strive for better, or for perfect, sight. Nobody would use this average as an excuse for weak eyes or poor visual habits.

Likewise, if only 10 per cent of the people tell the truth, and the other 90 per cent tell lies with considerable frequency — do we condone telling lies, or do we try to instill in our children a high regard for truth?

Our shocking auto accident rate indicates that the "average" driver is a menace to life on the highway — reckless, thoughtless, and often incompetent. Yet the whole task of driver education is to turn the average motorist into the "normal" driver who controls both his vehicle and his emotions behind the wheel.

Human beings, unlike lower animals, have goals that are not merely physical. A biologist, such as Kinsey, can tell us how we behave; he cannot tell us how we *should* behave, for a human being is more than an animal mechanism. And, until we understand the proper norms for the human being, we shall continue to let false averages dominate our thinking and our conduct.

City Drivers Are Rebels at Heart

THE SO-CALLED "transportation problem" in American communities has, I think, little to do with transportation — and this is why it is not being solved. The problem is a psychological one more than a physical one.

Why do individuals drive their cars downtown every day, into a highly congested neighborhood, where parking space is negligible and parking rates are insufferably high? Common sense and reason would dictate that most of these persons should take public transportation. A car is a cumbersome and expensive nuisance in a downtown area. Yet most persons continue to drive, even though the crush gets more lunatic every week.

It is a matter of status, which is psychological. Buses, subway trains, elevateds and streetcars have a "mass" odor about them which is repellent to most Americans. They feel like cattle trapped in these vehicles, and their deepest emotions of individuality are outraged. It is true that much public transportation is slow, ill-planned, and generally uncomfortable. On the other hand, even when these physical defects have been remedied, the average American still prefers the botheration of driving his own car.

Even on the inter-city level, this psychological feeling has been more responsible for the decline of the railroads than any other factor. Passengers were treated shabbily for so many years that they finally engaged in wholesale rebellion and transferred their allegiance to the courteous airlines, even when "time" was not important.

The grim traffic situation in American cities will not be alleviated by building more and larger highways and more parking facilities; these only encourage a larger number of motorists to drive downtown.

What we require, more than anything else, is a mass-transportation system that can make passengers feel like human beings, not like so many porkers being pushed up a ramp to the slaughterhouse. Schedules, routes and connections must be arranged for the convenience of the riders, not for the company, the traffic engineers or the drivers.

One of the direct consequences of our high standard of living is the public's reluctance to huddle in the cold waiting for a bus, or stand sardine-tight in a crowded vehicle, or be treated with neglect and contempt by transit companies. Driving downtown, in defiance of all good sense, is the only way we can show our resentment at such treatment.

Tollway Tremors Have Got Sydney

As a MOTORIST, I appreciate the speed and safety of those new expressways, tollways, throughways, and freeways that are unwinding all over the American landscape these days.

But, as a middle-aged man whose eye and brain are not as quick on the reflex as his foot is on the pedal, I find myself getting befuddled and panicky on these supermonster roads. I am suffering from a new mid-twentieth century disease called "Tollway Tremors."

The other evening, for instance, I drove out to a distant suburb to make a speech and almost wound up near the Grand Canyon. As I approached the juncture of a new tollway and an older superhighway from my expressway, I saw dozens of grinning green signs beckoning me into as many diverse lanes.

I felt for a moment as if I were being sucked up by some

man-eating plant. "Rockford," beckoned one sign, "Aurora," said another. A third invited me to visit Toledo. And yet another winked me seductively up to Milwaukee.

Along with these were another dozen signs, wholesaling travel information incredibly faster than I could absorb it at sixty miles an hour — and I couldn't slow down or I would surely be rammed from the rear.

"Make Two Right Turns To Go Left," said one. "Take Right Lane Into Cloverleaf to East-West Tollway," proclaimed another. "Toll Booth 1 Mile Ahead," warned a third. There were arrows, branching lines, dividing barriers, and at least four vertical layers of traffic intertwining like some fantastic vehicular maypole dance.

Not long ago, I made a premature turning on Chicago's Calumet Skyway — or was it Tollway, Throughway or Expressway? — and found myself in Gary when I really meant to be forty miles west of it. Sartre's ominous play *No Exit* has a nightmarish application to modern traffic — once you're on the high road there is no getting off for twenty-two long, bitter, frustrating miles.

No doubt as I become more used to it all I'll be able to fight off the mounting sense of panic as I am swiftly confronted with a dozen choices all at once. But right now Tollway Tremors has me in its grip, and if the speaker of the evening is late for your next club meeting, I just want you to know why. He's cruising down U.S. 294, near Cape Hatteras.

Fallacy in Worship of Numbers

A RADIO PROGRAM in my city was recently booted off the air by the station, because a "survey" showed that the program didn't command as large an audience as the station had hoped for.

A great deal has been said about the validity of such surveys, pro and con. Many people feel that the samples taken are too small, and that the answers are not reliable. My own objection has been that these surveys do not — and do not pretend to — deal in depth. They are two-dimensional. Even if they answer the question "How many?" they do not answer the equally important question "How strongly?"

Mere numbers are not as important as we sometimes think. A fire or explosion may attract a thousand people, who have dismissed the incident the next day; an art exhibit may attract fifty persons, who may feel strongly enough about the pictures to buy and to tell their friends about them.

"Effective attention" is what counts in persuading people. You can get anybody to look at anything that is shocking enough; but you do not thereby command their interest or loyalty beyond a brief span.

One of the reasons given for the closing down of *Collier's* Magazine — despite a circulation of several million — was the lack of effective attention that its readers paid to the contents. They read the magazine as a habit, but it did not move them — nor did it, apparently, appeal to the people who motivate others.

The *Saturday Evening Post*, recognizing that psychology is more important than statistics, is now campaigning on the basis that its readers are "Influentials" — that is, they act and they act on others in shaping the large body of public belief and behavior. This is a healthful trend away from the worship of mere numbers for their own sake. It is a lesson not yet learned by radio and TV — which is why most of their programs appeal to the lowest common denominator.

The program tossed off the air may have had a comparatively small audience in numbers, but those who listened were fanatical partisans, and their influence was much greater than twice the number who listen tepidly to some giveaway show. Over the long haul (which, unhappily, sponsors often don't care about) it is depth and not mere scope of appeal that gives a program and a product real significance to the public.

Magic Won't Solve School Crisis

A schizophrenic, as everyone who goes to movie thrillers knows by now, is a split personality. The left side of his head doesn't know what the right side is thinking. It seems to me that our nation, as a whole, is suffering from social schizophrenia. I was talking yesterday with a friend who happens to be president of the school board in a thriving suburban community.

"All the parents in our town want bigger and better schools," he shook his head dolefully. "Yet when we want to float a bond issue, or raise taxes slightly for that purpose, they vote us down."

Nowhere more clearly than on the issue of education can this social schizophrenia be diagnosed. Parents spend much of their time talking about their children's schooling — without knowing what a good education should consist of, and what it would cost to make it better.

In his recent book, *America as a Civilization*, Max Lerner brought up the startling fact that between 1932 and 1950 — a period when the student enrollment doubled in the U.S. — the percentage of national income spent on universities from both public and private sources was cut in half — from 1 per cent to ½ per cent. Yet everybody is going to college these days, and head football coaches get as much as $60,000 a year, while the average faculty pay is $5300 a year, and even the average college president's pay is only $11,000 a year.

Much the same situation obtains on the lower levels of education, where we need not only new buildings but new salary scales, new library books, new scholastic equipment, and new morale for a sadly battered profession. Somehow we seem to believe in magic — to believe that if we attend enough PTA meetings, or complain about teaching methods, or urge our children to study harder, then the school system will suddenly and mysteriously transform itself into a magnificent institution of learning.

We don't apply this kind of magical thinking to our businesses, or our marriages, or even our sports. We know that, in these, a considerable investment must be made, in time, in money, in energy, in realistic planning that has a sense of direction and a goal.

When parents are alarmed about a school fire, they rush to mass meetings and vote to have the schools made fire-resistant, but they are reluctant to spend the money to have the faculty made poverty-resistant, or the pupils made ignorance-resistant. This is schizophrenia.

Crime a Symptom of World Unrest

WHAT WORRIES me more, in the long run (if there is a long run), than the rumbles of war across the world is an ominous paragraph I read in a British legal journal last month. It provided the disquieting information that the prison population in England is now the highest it has ever been. Last year there was an increase of 50,000 indictable offenses known to the police — a 15 per cent rise over the previous year. More than five thousand prisoners are sleeping three to a cell, because British jails cannot accommodate all the inmates. And most menacing is the fact that the number of prisoners under twenty-one years of age has risen *by 40 per cent in the last two years*. Thus, the bulk of the increase in British crime is coming from the teen-agers.

England has long been one of the most law-abiding countries in the world, with a deeply ingrained respect for law and order, an honest police force, and a wholly uncorrupt system of judicial machinery. If the structure of Western morality is cracking in England, what can prevent the swift decay of our civilization?

I don't think young people can grow up with a respect for law when they plainly see that there is no effective law in the great world of nations, which live by the rule of the jungle.

Nations take what they can when they feel strong enough to do so. They preach pious platitudes at home, but in the arena of world affairs they acknowledge only power and ratify only success. Even the U.S., which covets nobody else's territory, has collaborated with evil regimes, has supported despots, has swept morality under the rug.

We cannot be naïve enough to suppose that young people do not feel all this. In our half century, two world wars and the threat of a third have embittered youngsters about such abstractions as "law" and "justice" and "democracy." They have seen the big, the strong, the rich, too often get away literally with murder. We have been so busy gazing across the sea at the Russians that we have failed to recognize how expediency and opportunism have wrecked our Judaic-Christian concept of the good life. When nations behave like willful children, how can we expect our children to behave decently?

Crime is not merely a result of a bad home life, of slums or schooling. Its rapid increase is always a symptom of deep disturbances in the great world, of a system of ethics that is preparing to topple.

Make Sailboat Symbol of Your Job

DOWN AT THE boathouse, over the weekend, I was watching some teen-agers get their sailboat ready for a race. They had been working furiously since early morning. These youngsters are contemptuous of the motorboat people. "What fun is there in a stinkpot?" they snort. "You just turn on the ignition and it goes."

What they are saying, in effect, is that you get the maximum pleasure when you put in the maximum work. Sailing is a labor compared to powerboating, but it has many more joys. Yet the same youngsters seem incapable of carrying this idea over from their hobby to their vocations. They know that a sport is more fun when it involves hard work; but they refuse to believe that a job is more fun when it offers a challenge.

In their choice of vocations, most of them are looking for a snap; they want to turn on the ignition and loll on the deck while the money comes in. What they despise at the boathouse, they desire at the office; they make a serious business out of their pleasure, but they don't understand how to get pleasure out of a serious business.

I am not making the Pollyanna-ish assertion that every hard job is worthwhile; but I am making the realistic assertion that every worthwhile job is hard. Duty and pleasure are not opposites, as so many shallow people think, but rather are linked together in an unbreakable dialectic. The powerboat people, with relatively few duties toward their boat, cannot achieve the sublime height of pleasure experienced by the sailboat people after hours of scrubbing and sanding and polishing.

In life, as in sailing, the difficult and worthwhile and re-warding tasks often demand the same degree of tediousness. The concert pianist, who finds an ecstasy in a Schubert sonata, continues practicing for many hours a day, even after his success has been assured. But what two-finger piano-pecker can match his satisfaction?

In our racket society, youngsters are often beguiled by the illusions of soft living and quick returns; what they fail to see is the boredom that rots away the spirit of persons who live without challenge and without goals. Easy Street soon turns into an emotional slum.

Down at the boathouse, the bright teen-agers know this. What they need to learn is that knowledge is amphibious, and runs on dry land as well as on water.

Accidents Happen to Other People

I SPENT LAST weekend at a resort hotel in Pennsylvania, where I was guest speaker for a national convention. The weekend was marred by two announcements from the floor by the convention chairman. On Saturday he announced that a couple driving from Indiana had been seriously hurt in an auto crash en route to the meeting. On Sunday he announced that a couple driving from Buffalo had been injured even more seriously.

This unhappy news subdued the gaiety of the group, most of whom knew the injured members. But, strangely enough, none of the men seemed to construe this as a warning to himself.

Standing in the lobby, listening to the newcomers who were checking in at the registration desk, I heard the same remarks from all the motorists: "Made it from Akron in three and a half hours." "Just pulled in from New Haven in under five hours." "We left Chicago at noon and got here in time for dinner — in exactly seven hours."

These were bright and successful men, grown men, most of them in their forties. Yet, neither their intelligence, their abilities, nor their age prevented them from bragging like adolescents. Everyone knows by now that there is a direct ratio between speed and auto fatalities. Everyone knows that hurrying in a car creates tension and makes for carelessness. And everyone knows, too, that going eighty gets you to your destination not very much sooner than going sixty.

I don't mean to sound superior toward these men, because I am not. That is the whole tragedy. Behind the typewriter, I am prudent and mature in my driving attitude; but behind the wheel I am as likely to hit eighty as the next man. More than once I have driven up to the country for the weekend, burst in the door, and proudly boasted to the family, "Well, I made it tonight in four and a half hours, even with heavy traffic."

Why I tried to make it in that time, I couldn't tell you. I was going up to relax. I had nothing special to do that night. It is, I suppose, just some dangerous vestige of boyhood bravado.

None of the convention guests who heard the two announcements applied the warning to himself. It was an unrelated fact. Accidents are what happen to other people, because they are rash or unlucky. Accidents don't happen to us competent drivers who make it from New Haven in five hours. Little wonder our wives look at us with pitying glances when we start to play the Big Man.

5

OF THE FINE
AND VULGAR ARTS

Family Chronicle Easiest to Write

A FEW WEEKS ago, I received a card from the editor of the
Catholic Digest Magazine, sadly seconding a recent column of
mine about religious writing in which I pointed out that it
was the hardest form of literary endeavor, and that piety and
good feelings are no substitute for talent.

I can think of two other fields of writing that are equally
difficult: crime, and the theater. Both of these are special
interests of mine, and I suppose I must have read hundreds of
books on each subject — yet no more than two or three
were at all worthwhile.

Just as it seems to a religious person that his ideas and feelings could easily be transmitted to paper by the sheer force
of his convictions, so it seems to stage folk that their personal
experiences and the vagaries of their careers would make exciting reading.

But not one such book in a hundred has the slightest merit,
beyond the merely anecdotal. I have read biographies of
actors and actresses, directors and producers, which were

nothing more than patchworks of big names and little stories, tedious itineraries and dreary recitals of honors and awards.

On my desk at this moment is sitting the newest of this breed: *A Life in the Theater* by the distinguished British director Tyrone Guthrie. It is a worthy, and quite dull book, replete with such lines as "We did tremendous business in Toronto," and "Ruth Gordon and I had become fast friends." That sort of thing.

True crime books — as contrasted with crime fiction, which is delightful — are another trap for the unwary writer. Dozens of retired detectives and police officials have laboriously copied out their experiences — which, in print, invariably seem heavy, tawdry and pedestrian. I have just finished such an account, by a recently retired head of Scotland Yard's criminal unit; and I swear that a more exciting book of memoirs could be written by a window washer.

Surprisingly, the genre that comes most easily to writers, and the one that can hold readers even if ineptly written, is the chronicle of family life. Domesticity, seen from the right angle, is the most fascinating of subjects, for each family has its own peculiar charm.

It is no accident that Shakespeare's four greatest plays center around a prince and his mother, a king and his three daughters, a wife's ambition for her weak husband, and a husband's insane jealousy of his beautiful wife.

Most Autobiographies Are Atrocious

WHAT SEEMS THE easiest sort of book for any person to write? Naturally — his autobiography. And what, actually, is the hardest book for anyone to write? His autobiography.

Hardly anyone you meet does not think, secretly or openly, that his life would make a fascinating book "if only I had the gift of words." Among the ordinary, this remains merely a wistful belief; among the celebrated, it amounts to an obsession. Only the very strongest of famous personages can resist writing his autobiography.

I have just finished reading another depressing one, which set off this chain of thought. It is a quite bad book, although the author has been a professional writer and editor for all his adult life. And it is (like most autobiographies) shallow, embarrassing, self-deceiving and utterly pointless.

Even the greatest writers have faltered and failed in this peculiarly difficult task. Mark Twain's worst serious book was his *Autobiography*, which grossly displayed all his faults and none of his genius. His biographers, although inferior to him as writers, did a much better job on his life than he did.

In our own time, that splendid writer G. K. Chesterton attempted his autobiography, with disappointing results; his biography, by Maisie Ward, is an incomparably superior job. Chesterton's angle of vision, which was marvelously acute when applied to the outside world, was terribly obtuse when turned within.

Not more than a half-dozen worthwhile autobiographies have been penned in the fifteen hundred years since St. Augustine gave us his *Confessions*. After Cellini and Rousseau, after John Stuart Mill and Benjamin Franklin, what do we have? Mostly gossip, vanity, mawkish recollections, dreary anecdotes, self-justification, libel, half-truths and untruths.

It used to be, at any rate, that only genuinely famous persons undertook this task: eminent authors, generals, statesmen, scientists, divines, whose personal contributions provided at least a footnote to history.

Today all that is changed: we find the bookshop tables heaped high with autobiographies (mostly ghosted) by movie actors, comedians, dress designers, innkeepers, and — the latest atrocity to arrive on my desk — Perle Mesta.

No other field of writing is so beguiling, so treacherous and so doomed as that of autobiography. Literary skill is not enough; psychological insight is not enough; honest intentions are not nearly enough. Where is the surgeon who can perform a successful heart operation upon himself?

A great autobiography is a miracle; even a good one is beyond the grasp of most geniuses. Let us be grateful Shakespeare never tried — there is no reason to believe he would have succeeded.

Artists Crave Praise, Not Criticism

ONLY ONCE in my life have I heard a critic attacked by someone he had "overpraised." I was at a party with a famous violinist, and he derided a music critic for having given him a "rave" review the day before. "I played terribly," he confessed. "It was the worst recital I've given in years. That critic should be fired for not knowing his business. Who wants such praise?" Most authors, artists and performers do. They rip into critics mercilessly when the critics depreciate their work; but they never object when their productions or performances are overvalued, as they often are. They insist that what they want is "objective criticism"; apart from the fact that there's no such animal, they don't want it anyway. They want praise, as much and as often as possible, even when they don't deserve it.

In some fifteen years of drama reviewing, I have received

many notes from actors and actresses thanking me for kind words about their performances. Not once has any of them berated me for a glowing review about a poor performance.

Sometimes, when plays and concerts are good, they receive bad notices, and the performers are outraged. But other times these plays and concerts are bad and receive good notices. Honesty should compel the performers to complain just as vigorously, if they are serious about wanting "objective criticism" — but somehow they never do.

Perhaps an artist or performer cannot be objective about his own work; perhaps he thinks that everything he does is good. But the really top-rank artists I have known are painfully aware when they do less than their best. I have heard musicians curse themselves after a sloppy performance — but they never curse the bestower of unmerited praise.

This is one reason I pay little attention to the complaints about the "severity" of critics. When they are unfairly severe, the artists jump on them; when they are unfairly favorable (because justice does not mean being kind, it means being just), nobody takes issue with them. As a result, most critics attain a reputation for severity.

Only when artists object just as vehemently to undeserved praise as they do to undeserved disparagement will they be able to make out an honest case against the critics. Until then, what they really want is not criticism, good or bad, but simply a massaging of their egos.

An Artist's Personality Is Paramount

"I HAVE MET A NUMBER of writers and other artists," observes a college student, "and they are generally not as pleasant or as pleased with themselves as other people. Can you explain the reason for this?"

The explanation, it seems to me, lies in the nature of the work itself, and of the type of person who is attracted to it. A human being is happiest when he can *objectify* himself in his work; in popular terms, when he can "lose himself" in what he is doing.

It is in the nature of art — and especially literary art — that the person making it is engaging in a highly *subjective* task. He draws the material out of himself, as it were, and is perpetually involved in excavating material from the the depth of his own personality. This is neither a pleasant nor a happy project; it is merely an essential one for the human race — for great art expresses the deepest and most lasting values of mankind.

But the artist himself cannot find an objective contentment in his work; he is not *giving* himself to something outside himself. By the very nature of his craft, he is unable to lose himself in the task itself; his own personality is always paramount.

In a crude way, one might say that the writer is always scratching himself to find where he itches — and the more he scratches, the more he itches. Art is produced in this introspective way, but it does not make a man pleasant to be with or serene within himself. The so-called "artistic temperament" (when it is not pose) comes from this aggravated sense of self.

Genuine contentment is found in performing tasks that take us out of ourselves, for a purpose greater than ourselves. Only when the personality is subordinated to a higher goal do we attain the serenity we are looking for — this is why the beatitude of the saint, whose life is directed toward the highest possible goal, is unattainable by the rest of us.

It is the burden of the artist that he cannot escape this sense of self and achieve the simple and profound happiness of the surgeon in performing a delicate operation, the researcher at the microscope, the sea captain navigating his craft through turbulent waters. All of them, like the Zen archer, become the bow, the arrow and the target.

The artist has other satisfactions that compensate for this — after all, he provides the future with lasting objects of enjoyment. But he himself is no happier than a patient with a constant itch.

You Get Soiled in Hunt for Dirt

SHAKESPEARE'S LINE about the lady protesting too much has been confirmed by modern psychology. We have grown increasingly suspicious of those who aggressively parade their loyalty, their piety or their honesty.

The same holds true, I believe, for the censorious mind. It is one thing to dislike literary dirt; it is quite another to seek actively for it, and often to find it where it does not exist.

I have known individuals who thought they were dedicated to stamping out obscenity — when, actually, they were fascinated by it. Their greatest thrill consisted in finding a "dirty" picture, or a "pornographic" book. They would relentlessly pursue this quest, in the name of decency — but they were really engaging in a lewd activity while at the same time able to pride themselves on their moral superiority.

Thus, they are able to have their emotional cake and eat it: to maintain a good conscience about their "purity," and to indulge in the prurient curiosity they have repressed in themselves.

A famous actress once satirized this attitude when she told an interviewer: "I was disgusted with the dirtiness in *Tobacco Road* — and each time I went back to see the play, I was even more disgusted."

People with normal and decent instincts do not become crusaders against dirt, for they know that obscenity flourishes only when the society itself is sick. The dirt is a symptom, not a cause. It is a symptom of bad emotional housekeeping, of poor parental training, and of grownups failing to practice the virtues they smugly preach to their children.

Honesty in human relations is the only way to diminish this kind of dirt; an honesty that candidly admits man is a delicate balance of animal and spirit; and does not close the blinds to whatever is bestial in us.

Schools, and books, and newspapers, cannot develop the proper reactions of young people in this matter. Only the family, in its intimate setting, is capable of putting sexuality in its proper perspective, neither overplaying its importance nor ignoring its vitality.

Until then, the hunt for dirt is as futile as sweeping out the Augean stables — except for the sweepers, who love the task.

Why Humor and Satire Are Dying

S. J. PERELMAN, perhaps the funniest man writing in America today, recently took a look at contemporary humor and found it unfunny.

What's left of humor, he said, is doomed by "the great, creeping paralysis of television" and by a growing conservatism that restricts the humorist.

"There are more pressure groups and minority groups protesting today," he reflected sadly, "and humor flourishes best in a free atmosphere."

The same might be said of satire. At the airport yesterday, I picked up a new paperbound edition of some of H. L. Mencken's essays, written mostly in the 1920's. Reading them on the plane, it was shocking to see the change in the temper of our times. Mencken was a slashing satirist, and some of what he wrote about American society was unjust or shallow or vicious. But the point is that he wrote it, that millions of people read it — and took it without complaint.

We prate a great deal about "freedom of expression" today, but I doubt whether Mencken could have operated so freely in today's climate of opinion. In the 1920's, he derided the bankers, the clergymen, the doctors, the realtors, the do-gooders, the do-badders, and the do-nothingers. He swung his pole-ax with impartial malice at greed, hypocrisy and stupidity, wherever he happened to think it existed.

Nowadays, however, every group is highly organized and highly sensitized to criticism. Our society has become a multiplicity of pressure groups. Most of them employ expensive press agents to gloss over their foibles and failings.

We preach "individualism," but we have become parts of collectivities. Organizations do our speaking for us; skilled "public relations counselors" tell us what to say. This is an era not only of the ghost-writer, but of the ghost-thinker.

Wit, humor and satire cannot flourish in such an atmosphere; indeed, they can scarcely breathe. When we have to tread carefully to avoid stepping on toes, we have begun to lose the capacity for self-criticism that is an indispensable cleansing agent for civilization. When humor ceases to sting a little, it is no longer a tonic, but only an opiate.

Soft Words Are Hard to Come by

IT IS A CURIOUS commentary on human nature — and on human speech, which reflects our nature — that we have so few words to designate good things, and so many to designate bad.

Flying home the other evening, I heard the pilot announce to the passengers, over the intercom: "There's no weather between here and Chicago."

By "no weather" he meant no bad weather. To aviation people, the mere word "weather" signifies a difficult condition; just as on the ground the mere word "traffic" often means a tieup.

If we think a man is a liar or a drunk or a cheat, we have scores of deprecatory words at our command; the English language (like any language) is rich in scornful epithets. But if we think he is an admirable person, we can only falter and fumble for words . . . and end up calling him "a good guy."

A nice day is just a nice day; everyone calls it that. But an un-nice day is mean, miserable, drab, ghastly, chilling, bitter, inhuman, depressing, and lots more. We are never at a loss to describe our negative feelings.

This explains, I think, why criticism often seems so much more harsh than it really means to be. When a critic likes a book or a play or a piece of music, he can only murmur a few conventionally grateful phrases. The vocabulary of approval is extremely limited, even among talented writers.

All criticism is therefore distortion, in some sense. Positive feelings, which come from the heart, are difficult and embarrassing to articulate; negative feelings (in which fear or anger or contempt have been aroused) pour forth with hardly any conscious manipulation. Not only do we express ourselves more vividly and vehemently in a negative way; but we obtain a greater enjoyment in hearing such criticism.

None of Wilde's or Shaw's or Dorothy Parker's generous comments have ever won wide currency; it is only their wittily devastating attacks that are repeated with relish. No critic has achieved eminence for kindness of heart.

This may be a pity (it is certainly an injustice) but it seems to be an inevitable part of the human condition. The most we can do is reach a private understanding with ourselves that all negative criticism (including our own) shall be discounted at 50 per cent on the emotional dollar.

The Paradox in Men of Great Talent

WHEN CHARLIE CHAPLIN "killed" the little man with the baggy pants, and tried to become a deep thinker and political commentator in the films, he lost touch with the deepest sources of his comic genius. Now, in London, Chaplin has disclosed that he plans to bring back the little man — which is welcome news. In his self-written roles, Chaplin has been embarrassingly half baked.

It is one of the paradoxes of talent that the persons who possess it often hold it so cheaply and desire to be something else. Goethe, the finest writer Germany has produced, was convinced that his poems were not as important as his "theory of colors," which has long since been forgotten.

Isaac Newton, the greatest scientific genius of his era, looked upon his scientific discoveries as a mere pastime, and devoted most of his efforts to becoming a politician and a peer. In his later years, he even thought that his trivial research in biblical studies was more significant than his mathematical work.

The world of letters is replete with similar instances. As everyone knows, both Gilbert and Sullivan resented their successful partnership, and each thought he was meant for more lofty things than operettas. Yet singly neither of them has left a memorable work.

Henry James, the most polished and subtle story writer of his time, kept trying to write dramas — until one opening night in London when he was roundly booed off the stage while taking a curtain call.

Charles Dodgson was annoyed at being best known as "Lewis Carroll," and wrote many mathematical works which he thought were original and lasting. But he was a shallow mathematician, and his "Alice" books will live forever.

At the turn of the century, the world's greatest chess master, Emmanuel Lasker, looked upon his chess ability as a contemptible means of making a living, and regarded his philosophical and sociological papers as his significant life work. They are utterly worthless.

Even Mark Twain, who was enormously successful as a writer, lost several fortunes investing in business deals and dubious inventions, for he felt that his real talent lay in the financial field.

The man with small abilities is usually satisfied with what God has given him; to have a lot, in most cases, means to want much more.

Fine Art Pays Best in the End

WHEN WE SPEAK of the "commercial" theater and of the "artistic" theater, we generally imply that the former makes a great deal of money while the latter languishes into bankruptcy.

But this is taking the very short view. The paradox of the so-called "commercial" theater — or the commercial novel or music or what have you — is that ultimately it doesn't even do as well on commercial terms as the artistic work.

The reason is perfectly simple. A commercial play has only one life. It flares into popularity for a few weeks or months, and then it dies without hope of resurrection. One day everybody is humming the same popular song. It cannot be repeated too often; a million records are sold; but a few weeks later the public will not tolerate it on any terms. And if it is a purely commercial tune, it cannot be, and never will be, revived.

Now this does not happen to genuine works of art. As Shaw pointed out, "the masterpiece begins by fighting for its life against unpopularity, by which I do not mean mere indifference, but positive hatred and furious renunciation of it as an instrument of torture."

Beethoven's *Ninth Symphony*, for instance, did not have anything like the success of the "Intermezzo" in *Cavalleria Rusticana;* some eminent musicians of the time described it as an outrage by a maniac. But in the long run Beethoven makes Mascagni look like an organ grinder, *even as a money maker.*

The Shakespearean plays have earned more for their producers over three hundred years than all the popular Broadway hits rolled into one. Homer's *Iliad* sells only a few thousand copies a year, while *Gone With the Wind* sold millions — but no longer, and never again.

Even popular works of some merit run a comparatively brief course. When the Sherlock Holmes stories were first adapted to the stage, the public clamored to see the production. A few years ago, however, when Basil Rathbone attempted a stage revival, it was a major disaster, losing a great deal more money in a few weeks than the original play had made in a year.

The demand for a "best seller" seems to stop overnight. It is not, by its very nature, a long-term investment. But works which are not constructed with popular success in mind have the power of coming to life again and again, in succeeding generations. Even by a banker's calculations, the commercial is less successful than the artistic.

Novel Has Gone a Long Way—Down

THE POST OFFICE DEPARTMENT has impounded some copies of the old D. H. Lawrence novel, *Lady Chatterley's Lover*, which was recently published in the first unexpurgated American edition.

Meanwhile, the public was buying all the copies available. My local bookseller reported a brisk sale, adding wryly: "The joke is on the public — because it's not really a dirty book at all, by today's standards." *Lady Chatterley's Lover* contains a number of four-letter words and a few frank references to s — x, but otherwise it is as fresh and innocent as the Bobbsey Twins series, compared with many modern novels.

A cousin of mine brought back the Florence edition from

Italy about twenty-five years ago, and I perused it with shocked delight as a teen-ager. When I picked it up again last week, it was ludicrous. The book is almost quaintly dated, and really quite dull.

What I find offensive in modern novels is not their candor about sex (which is, after all, a legitimate area of human experience), but their blindness to other values in life. I would have the same objection to a writer who used a whole novel to describe what the characters ate and drank every day.

Lawrence was coarse, but earthy and wholesome. *Lady Chatterley's Lover* is a straightforward tale of a love affair. The modern novel, on the contrary, wallows in perversion, violence, hate, and squalor — for their own sake, and not for the sake of any redeeming spiritual qualities.

We must not, of course, demand that a novel be "uplifting" — this is a task for ethics and religion, not literature — but we have a right to ask that the novelist present us with a well-rounded portrait of life. And the author who stresses nothing but degradation is as lopsided as the "inspirational" writer who sees only Beauty and Goodness in life.

An author needs a scale of values as much as he requires talent. Lawrence had the talent (which most modern sex novelists do not have), but he was so busy rebelling against the Victorian standard of primness that he fell headlong into the opposite error of deifying sex.

But whatever his faults in this direction, he was a serious artist and a passionate seeker for what he hoped was the truth in human relationships — unlike the sensational and semi-literate scribblers of today, who seek merely to shock us with scabrous case studies of psychopaths.

We have come a long way in the last forty years. Most of it down.

Actors Are Often Two-Faced Critics

BEING ONE OF THAT unhappy breed known as a drama critic —
the man blamed for everything that is wrong in the theater
— I was wickedly pleased to read a self-revealing article last
month in *Actors Equity Bulletin*, the journal of the actors'
union.

Actors had been complaining that theater managers were
not giving them nearly as many free tickets to Broadway plays
as they used to; and a representative of the union interviewed
theater managers to learn the dark reason.

It turns out, the official reported sadly, that actors consti-
tute the most critical audience, behaving in a way that drama
critics would never dare or care to. Many performers who
attend a show free of charge, he said, "and sit next to a person
who has spent $6.60 for a seat . . . comment disparagingly
upon what is going on on the stage. That can ruin theatergo-
ing for the people who overhear it . . .

"Then," the report continued, "there were actors in the
lobby between acts, who would run down both the plays and
the actors on the stage, even though they were guests of the
management."

To add sartorial insult to the verbal injury, the fact that
many performers attended the theater (free) in sweatshirts,
tennis shoes and dungarees didn't make the theater managers
especially eager to invite them again in the future.

Drama critics have long been aware of this two-faced attitude on the part of professional actors. Publicly they upbraid
the critics for saying harsh and unpleasant things about a play;
but privately — and even not so privately — performers
themselves are brutally candid about the deficiencies of a

production or a cast. I have heard actors and actresses on radio and TV interviews blasting the critics for "killing a play" they are appearing in, and then an hour later in some night spot the very same performers are confiding to all around them that the play is vile, the director is an idiot, and the management is beneath contempt.

Even press agents, who are paid (and handsomely) for trumpeting the merits of their production, have admitted to me, on the day the play closed, that the critics were absolutely right, and that everyone connected with the play knew it all along. The critic is usually blamed for saying in print what the professionals in the theater say to each other and to their friends.

Why Actors Prefer the Stage

"WE MURDERED THEM in Cleveland," I overheard an actor saying at the restaurant table next to mine. "We knocked them dead for two weeks."

Phrases don't just happen; they are carefully selected by the unconscious mind to describe the actual hidden feelings in a situation. And performers always speak of "murdering" an audience when they go over well.

For acting is basically a contest between two antagonists — the performer and the audience. The audience comes wanting to be subdued, but ready to turn and sneer if it is not; the performer walks out on the stage like the gladiators of old, to slay or be slain.

When actors are interviewed and they babble away about "the wonderful audiences in your wonderful city," either they are being consciously insincere or else are fooling themselves.

Men and women take up stage careers for many reasons; but the most important, I feel, is neither vanity nor exhibitionism, but a need to acquire the authority on the stage which they feel they lack in real life. The theater transforms dull and drab creatures into magnificent specimens of courage, charm and beauty.

This is why veteran acting coaches stress the importance of "authority" in a performer — that almost mystical ability to walk out of the wings and instantly command the audience's attention and respect.

Without this authority, all the talent in the world is wasted; with it, a little talent can be made to go a long way. In a sense the actor is a kind of lion tamer, forcing the audience to jump through the hoops he has devised for them.

The best performances send a current tingling from the stage down to the seats; this current is suspended hostility, like a truce between two sides in a battle. If the play falters or sags, the lions begin to bare their fangs and snarl.

Rodgers and Hammerstein, in a moment of candor, once referred to the audience as "The Big Black Monster." They meant no contempt, but were simply expressing a psychological fact of stage life. The breathing monster in the dark pit of a theater is a potential enemy to everyone on the stage — and nobody knows it more than the weak or frightened actor.

This is a large part of the allure of the living theater: an element of conflict that is lacking in films, where everything has been predetermined. Actors prefer the stage to the screen, despite the lower pay, because they want to tame the beast and prove nightly that they are heroes.

Real Artists Don't Need a Push

SCARCELY A WEEK passes that I do not receive at least a few letters from men and women (usually women) who think they might be writers if only given a little encouragement and a slight push in the right direction.

"My friends all tell me my letters are so wonderful," the correspondent often writes, "that I am taking the liberty of enclosing a few little pieces, and I hope you have the time to let me know what you think of them."

I always answer such letters politely and evasively, pointing out that I never give literary advice, that there are reputable firms which make a business of doing so, and that I wish the budding writer the best of luck in his choice of a career.

In ninety-nine instances out of a hundred, the material they send me is perfectly awful — from a professional point of view. But they would not believe me if I told them so, and would chalk up my reaction to jealousy or ill-temper or just stupidity.

Apart from the obvious lack of talent in most of these efforts, the dead giveaway is the desire for "encouragement" or a "slight push" in the right direction. With such beginning attitudes, no person can ever become a creative artist of any kind.

If you have the stuff of which artists are made, you cannot be discouraged. You will continue to produce work, not because you like to, but because you must. The artist's compulsion is very much like the addict's.

Nor does an artist require a slight push. He is self-propelling; he cannot be torn away from his mission. He will write, paint or compose, whether his children are starving,

his wife has deserted him, or the world treats him like a lunatic.

I am not saying that these are optimum conditions for the
artist; I am not making the foolish and insolent middle-class
assumption that such scorn and sacrifice are actually "good"
for the artist; I am simply pointing out that these are the
dynamics of his nature.

If Mozart had waited for encouragement, he would have
written nothing but café songs; if Melville had looked for a
slight push, he would have continued a government clerk and
not put a line of *Moby Dick* to paper. Such instances could
be multiplied endlessly.

Writing chatty, amusing letters to friends has no more
relationship to literary talent than trotting a pony has to
winning the Grand Steeplechase. The amateur and the professional may differ in degree of talent; but, more than this,
they differ in persistence, in courage, in zeal, in a spirit that
need not be encouraged and cannot be at all discouraged.

Friend Often Artist's Worst Enemy

ALTHOUGH IT MAY BE grossly overestimated in popular fancy,
there is certainly something to the theory that "opposites
attract." This is true not only in love, but also in literature.

I was recently trapped into listening to a professor of
English give a talk on Shakespeare, and I wondered what in
the world had attracted him to Shakespeare in the first place.

He was everything Shakespeare was not — dry, didactic,
precise, superior, stuffy, cold and humorless. If there was one
man among a million that Shakespeare would not have been

caught dead drinking with in the Mermaid Tavern, it was this professor who "adored" him.

This is not an isolated instance, or I would not bother to mention it. I have seen it again and again — passionless prigs devoting themselves to a study of the passionate poetry of Dylan Thomas; dusty dons involved in the wildly irreverent letters of Lord Byron; dreary scholars dully dissecting the plays of Bernard Shaw.

One reason, I suspect, that true greatness often takes so long to establish itself lies in the kind of disciples a great man acquires. They are most likely to be people who misunderstand him, or distort him for their own purposes, or mistake his follies for his genius. To take one obvious example, most Shakespearean "experts" insist that Shakespeare was essentially "a man of the theater," and that his plays can be fully understood only when seen in theatrical production.

Yet there is overwhelming evidence — both in the plays and in the sonnets — that Shakespeare despised the theater, was ashamed of having to write for it, disliked audiences, held actors in low esteem, and was extremely careless and contemptuous of dramatic rules.

His best and deepest plays, indeed, were written for small and highly specialized audiences, and are almost unactable — for they are filled with the kind of complex language that requires two or three readings to grasp in their beauty, subtlety, and profundity.

But, nevertheless, hundreds of books have been written about Shakespeare's "stagecraft" by men who fail utterly to comprehend the real meaning of his poetry and the real bent of his genius. Were he alive, I am convinced he would laugh these books out of existence.

The attraction of opposites in romance can be painful, and often fatal; the attraction of opposites in literature has just as often obscured and perverted the essential greatness of writers. More artists need to be rescued from their friends than from their enemies.

No Business Like Show Business

A Layman's Lexicon of Show Business:

"Negotiating with" means "we've written to a few big stars about appearing here, and while we haven't had any answers yet (and don't expect to), we feel that this gives us a pretext to use their names for some free publicity."

"Fresh new talent" means some performer who has been struggling and starving for ten years in basement bistros, and has been "discovered" just on the verge of a breakdown from nervous exhaustion.

"All-Star Cast" often means "we have so little faith in the script that we felt it necessary to burden the cast with a half-dozen Names to conceal the lack of a story."

"Lavish Spectacle" usually means the same thing — except this time, instead of Names, the production has been loaded down with garish scenery and flamboyant costumes to camouflage the essential hollowness of the entertainment.

"Pre-Broadway Première" too often means "we'll try it out on the dogs before we dare to take it into the Big City."

"Sure-fire comedy" means the same comedy you've been seeing for the last thirty years, with every touch of originality ruthlessly trimmed out — for in show business, familiarity breeds content.

"Raw human emotions!" means a cast of characters who behave toward each other as inhumanly as it is possible to get away with.

"A gay and naughty French farce" commonly means the

sort of infantile nonsense that the French public grew tired of
two generations ago.

"It is my pleasure and privilege to present . . ." means
exactly nothing.

"Direct from thirty-nine record-breaking weeks" usually
means that the press agent is breaking new records for brash
mendacity. (In some segments of show business, everybody
breaks his predecessor's "record," which is about as statisti-
cally reliable as a Soviet production figure.)

"And now, for the first time, Hollywood dares to . . ."
means that the film is perspiring foolishly over some trite
sexual situation that Chaucer tossed off in a couplet of his
"Canterbury Tales" five hundred years ago.

"Limited Engagement" means precisely that, when stated
by a reputable impresario — otherwise, it means an engagement that will be limited by the number of people who decide
to buy tickets of admission.

We Pay a Heavy Price for Gadgets

VISITING FRIENDS the other evening, I observed their three
children slumped in the "family room" watching television
with a mixture of boredom, cynicism and inexpressible sophis-
tication.

And, for some reason, I vividly remembered the first radio
I ever heard. It was in 1924, and my cousins had daringly
bought a new "crystal set" with two pairs of earphones. We
were excited and dazzled by this experience. Mondays were
"silent nights," when local stations went off the air, and sometimes we could hear a cracked soprano screeching from a
station as far away as St. Paul.

But there is a law of diminishing returns in such devices. The worst thing about a manmade miracle is that it soon comes to be accepted as a commonplace. In a year or so the radio set meant little to us, just as the television set has already become a "normal" part of the world to today's children.

This is a relentless part of the price we pay for our mechanical civilization. The gadget that delighted us last year only bores us this year; the automobile that we are so crazy to drive on our sixteenth birthday has become a parking headache on our twenty-sixth birthday.

This psychological fact — the dwindling returns of pleasure from mechanical objects, so that we constantly require new gadgets to titillate our jaded emotions — is one of the soundest reasons for giving our children the kind of "humanistic" education I mentioned in my recent column on schooling. For it is only in the world of the mind and imagination that we can find the eternally recurring springs of enjoyment. Nobody who has ever taken the trouble to read Shakespeare can tire of his poetry; nobody who has learned how to listen to Beethoven has ever been known to grow weary of his "old" music.

Works of art contain their own source of rejuvenation; and the greater the work, the more "new things" one can find in it year after year. *Hamlet* is an inexhaustible play; you can never get to the "bottom" of it.

Children who grow up with an understanding and an appreciation of this heritage have infinitely more to sustain and console them through life than those children who are given nothing but material objects. It is not a matter of Culture, it is a matter of common sense, that the soaring mind of man is the only instrument that does not become obsolete with time and oppressive with use.

It's the Pause That Counts in Art

ARTUR SCHNABEL was once asked for the "secret" of his superb piano playing. "How do you handle the notes as well as you do?" inquired a student.

"The notes I handle no better than many pianists," Schnabel replied. "But the pauses between the notes — ah, that is where the art resides!"

He was not being funny or mischievous. One of the most astonishing things about the arts is what they leave unsaid, or unwritten, or unplayed, or unpainted.

What distinguishes a great actor from a merely good one? Bearing, poise, diction, depth of feeling? Perhaps more important than any of these, it is knowing how to make a pregnant pause in a speech that moves an audience more than anything that is spoken. Mark Twain understood this well when he commented on a certain performance of Shakespeare: "The pause — that impressive silence, that eloquent silence, that geometrically progressive silence, which oftens achieves a desired effect where no combination of words, however felicitous, could accomplish it."

On the lower level of entertainment, this is what is meant when a comedian is praised for his "timing" — that rarest and finest attribute of verbal humorists. The skilled comedian knows, by intuition as well as by craft, when to pause for a heightened effect; and his brief silences are more important than the jokes themselves. "It isn't so much what he says as the way he says it," is the highest compliment we can pay a comedian.

And this also is where the amateur can be distinguished from the professional. The amateur is always *explicit;* he finishes every sentence, draws every line, and plays every note with the same value. He leaves nothing to the imagination of the audience.

Silence is a positive and compelling force, and not a mere negative. Notice at a dinner, when a silence falls at the table, how the silence becomes an almost palpable thing — and how, the longer the silence endures, the harder it becomes to speak. And couples who retreat into mutual silence when they quarrel find it more difficult to make up than couples who shout and argue with one another.

All art is suggestion and implication. Anybody, with practice, can play the notes in a Schubert sonata — but to play the pauses between the notes — "Ah, that is where the art resides."

No Shortcut to Creative Writing

QUITE OFTEN I receive letters from college students and others, wanting to know my working habits, my literary techniques, my source of inspiration, and my personal recipe for becoming a professional writer.

To ask this sort of question is to disqualify oneself from the beginning. There is no recipe, no formula, no Seven Sure Steps to Selling Your Work. All that sort of thing is a commercial fraud.

Anyone who has read widely in the lives of writers — and painters and composers and all artists — surely must know that working habits and techniques differ as widely as tastes in food, drink and women. Mozart composed in a noisy coffee house; Beethoven required the grandeur of solitude. Goethe created while taking long walks; Proust wrote in a cork-lined bedroom. And so on, through the whole Dictionary of Biography.

Temperament, not talent, determines how a man works. His technique is derived from his unconscious structure, not from any conscious formula. His "inspiration" may come from the stars or the gambling tables, the sugared sonnets of Shakespeare or the didactic lines of St. Thomas Aquinas — and sometimes from all of these together.

Our time, and our society, seems to have a peculiarly strong need to believe in a magic recipe for success in every field of endeavor. Incredible sums are spent annually for canned advice on How to Make Your First Million, How to Write a Three-Act Play, How to Succeed With the Opposite Sex.

As if these three basic drives in human nature — for love, for power, and for self-expression — could ever be taught or explained or codified. The man who makes a million cannot tell you how or why he did it, any more than Keats could tell you how he happened to write immortal odes, or Abélard could impart the "technique" he used with Héloïse.

Of course, there are some primary rules of craftsmanship in any activity; but these rules can be learned by any simpleton in a few hours, and they exist only to be broken by men of original talent.

Oscar Wilde tossed off the lines of his plays as casually as he sipped his absinthe; Bernard Shaw carefully reasoned out every sentence he wrote to the utmost of his capacity before commiting it to print. Each of these men would have given diametrically opposite "advice" to aspiring writers.

And both pieces of advice would have been equally useless, for creation comes out of the dark pit of the soul which no textbook can illuminate.

Why "About" Novels Miss the Mark

IN THAT AMUSING musical comedy of some seasons ago, *Wonderful Town*, Rosalind Russell won a huge laugh from the audience when she attempted to rekindle a conversation that had flickered and died out. "I was reading *Moby Dick* the other day," she began. "You know — it's that book about a whale."

The audience laughed, because only a child or a fool would think that *Moby Dick* was about a whale. The story of Captain Ahab's chase is a tale of human aspiration and despair, and the whale is merely a symbol of the inner meaning.

Good books are not really "about" anything, except incidentally. They are concerned with the passions and perplexities of people — and the people themselves, in their nakedly human aspects, must come first.

And this is why, it seems to me, so many of these recent novels "about" advertising and public relations and the business world utterly miss their mark. I have looked through a half dozen of them this week, and all suffer from the same fatal defect.

The authors (all of whom, by the way, have an intimate knowledge of the background of their stories) seem to have said to themselves: "I'll write a novel exposing — or explaining, or defending — this particular business and that particular milieu."

But they are starting the creative process from the wrong end. You have to start with a living, breathing human being, not with a setting. It's impossible to write a meaningful novel about "advertising" or "Detroit" or "television," for these are all abstractions.

Tolstoy's *War and Peace* is not *about* Napoleon's invasion of Russia; Dostoyevsky's *Crime and Punishment* is not *about* the murder of an old landlady; histories and biographies and mysteries are written this way; novels cannot be.

To ask what a good novel is "about" is as pointless as to inquire what a person is "about." Every novel, of course, has a background; but it must not become foreground; it must not become the excuse for bringing in characters who merely typify the author's aim in exposing or defending this or that business activity.

The act of creation is organic and self-sufficient, just as every person is an end unto himself. When a novel forgets this basic premise, then it becomes a story about a whale, and nothing else.

A Poet Can't Always Spout Gems

A WOMAN I KNOW told me she was bitterly disappointed at a literary dinner last month. She was seated at a table with several eminent poets, and she kept listening in vain for lyrical gems to drop from their lips.

"Plane schedules!" she said. "All through dinner they talked about nothing but plane schedules, and how the new jets would cut their travel time. I was disgusted."

She had no right to be. Keats and Shelley, meeting for dinner, probably spent a good deal of their time discussing the coach service from London to Manchester rather than apostrophizing skylarks or Grecian urns. We forget that creative people are craftsmen as well as artists. When they talk shop, as they often do, they are not floating in the empyrean realm of art, but in the practical realm of work — the painter about brushes, the novelist about royalty payments, the musician about rehearsal hours.

It is only the amateur, the dilettante, the yeasty yearner after culture, who engages in misty and poetical discussions of Art, with a capital A. It is the person who cannot create who is most likely to gush about creativity.

Consider the parallel to motherhood — which is also both an abstract art and a demanding craft. It is the spinster, or the childless woman, who generally writes those airy-fairy poems about the spiritual loveliness of babies and small children. When mothers get together to discuss their creations, they talk quite prosaically about feeding schedules and diaper problems and nailbiting and all the unlovely daily problems of their brood.

Deep within, they love and treasure their creations, but their approach is practical and technical, as it has to be. They know that a child is a miracle (just as a great poem is a miracle), but they also know that the formula must be made, the diapers washed, and the little work of art has to be burped with an expert hand.

If you have heard a string quartet rehearsing Beethoven, as I have, you might imagine that the beauty and the power of the music meant little to the performers. They are involved in technical problems; they joke or curse; they talk about food and fees during their brief breaks; yet their end product is soaring and mystical and heart-breaking.

But it becomes heartbreaking only because it has been back-breaking; only because their shimmering castle in the air has a firm foundation of solid and sustained toil beneath it.

Beatniks: Conformists in Reverse

I HAVE BEEN READING some of the literary effusions of the so-called "beat generation," and they seem to me like so many children wearing false beards and sticking out their tongues at their elders.

Lichtenberg, the ironic German essayist, once said that "to do exactly the opposite is also a form of imitation." The beatnik is just the opposite side of the conformist coin.

The conformist has no inner life. He wants to do what he sees everybody else doing. He denies his instincts and his individuality, and lives only on the thin surface of reality. The beatnik, realizing that the conformist has sacrificed much of his personality for appearance's sake, rushes to the other extreme. He ignores social demands. He does the opposite of what others are doing. He gives full freedom to his instincts, and thus becomes less than a man.

Much in modern society is corrupt and cramping and hypocritical and thoughtless. But the art of *creative rebellion* — as distinct from destructive rebellion — is to discard what is rotten while retaining what is proper, necessary and good.

The beatnik fails to make this distinction. He is so blindly hostile to the values of the past that he childishly repudiates everything that should be redeemed from the past. He is overreacting to a situation, just as a delinquent boy may overreact to a strict and pompous father. This is understandable, and even pathetic. The beatnik is searching for virtue of a sort, and because he does not see much of it in conventional society, he believes he can find it by flouting the conventions.

But the true end of man is to achieve a delicate balance between the demands of his deepest instincts and the requirements of convention. This is why it has always been so hard just to be a human being — just to regulate the clashing between our hot emotions and the cool ordinances of society.

Maturity is not a state, but a process — a continual process of making this adjustment. The conformist represses his instincts and makes society the master of his soul, which is a sin. The beatnik turns his back on society, and makes desire the master of his soul, which is an equally grave sin. Each of them is half a man, and the subtle joining of the two halves is the perpetual task of mankind.

Culture? It Belongs to the People

THE WORD "culture" takes an awful beating in our society — from its friends as much as from its enemies.

To its friends, "culture" is something lofty and spiritual and almost sacred; to its enemies, "culture" is a mess of hifalutin nonsense that is spouted by people who think they are superior to the ordinary run.

Yet the clearest, as well as the shortest, description of the word was given a century ago by Thomas Carlyle, when he said: "The great law of culture is this — Let each become all that we were created capable of being."

The culture-vultures try to be more than they were created capable of being, and so they often sound pretentious and absurd. The culture-haters are content to remain less than they can be, and so they sound barbarous and bigoted. Both, in different ways, are untrue to themselves.

A truly cultured person is one who appreciates Beethoven as well as jazz, who relishes a well-written mystery book as well as a literary masterpiece, who knows that a human being is made up of varying and contradictory tastes and desires, and wants to expand his personality to the widest range.

Most people, I am convinced, were created capable of being much more than they are in everyday life. When they allow themselves to be touched, by a play or a piece of music, you can see how a part of them, beneath the surface, has a deep hunger for something beyond the banalities of their ordinary existence.

But the culture-vultures, and the intellectual snobs, and the self-appointed guardians of the Muses often frighten off the average person from the free development of this appetite.

There is a need for more tolerance on both sides. The barbarian who rejects the unfamiliar just because it is unfamiliar is no worse than the snob who embraces the difficult and obscure simply because it makes him feel superior to the mass. Each attitude, in turn, perpetuates the vicious circle of contempt.

Every human being of average intelligence was created capable of being more than he is. He can appreciate Shakespeare because Shakespeare wrote for him, not for scholars; he can glory in Beethoven, because Beethoven expresses the deepest passions and perplexities of the spirit.

Americans are tremendously interested in "personal development" — and this is all that Carlyle meant by "culture." The term needs to be rescued from the prissy-lipped promoters of afternoon teas and given back to the people, who are looking for greatness, but do not know it.

Creativity Isn't a Matter of Mood

"YOU MUST HAVE FELT depressed when you wrote that column," said a friend the other day. "But I suppose it's hard to keep your immediate feelings out of what you write."

Nothing could be further from the truth. Everything we know about the creative process — from giants like Mozart to pygmies like Harris — indicates that your conscious state of mind has nothing to do with what you write, or paint, or compose.

Mozart wrote most of his gayest melodies while suffering deeply, both physically and mentally. Balzac dashed off his *Droll Stories* while rebuffed in romance, pursued by creditors, laughed at by society, and wrapped in the gloom of loneliness. And, of course, Robert Louis Stevenson was racked with pain when he was turning out his adventure tales and his charming poems for children. Such cases could be multiplied indefinitely in the history of all the arts.

The creative person works *unconsciously* with his mind, which operates even when he is sleeping. By the time he sits down at the typewriter, or approaches the easel, his task has already been completed — all that remains is the physical job at hand.

An admirer once asked Anton Bruckner, the composer: "Master, how, when and where did you think of the divine motif of your *Ninth Symphony?*"

"Well, it was like this." Bruckner smiled, "I walked up the Kahlenberg, and when it got hot I got hungry. I sat down by a little brook and unpacked my cheese. And just as I opened the greasy paper, that darn tune pops into my head!"

Much the same is true in original scientific research. Dozens of scientists have testified that their best ideas came to them while they were sleeping, or fishing, or strolling in the woods — and not while they were consciously grappling with a problem.

Creativity is not a matter of being in the right "mood," as so many amateurs think. The man who waits to get into the right mood will find that the best ideas elude him; just as the man who sits down determined to write a masterpiece often finds that his words are wooden and his sentences stiff.

We have scarcely begun to recognize the enormous power of the unconscious mind, which is the true source of creativity. Newton lying under the apple tree discovered more truth than Newton browsing through books and bending over papers.

Harm in Worship of the Sensational

THE GREATEST IMPEDIMENT to the artist in our society — whether he be a writer, a painter, an actor, or a singer —is our blind worship of the sensational.

We appreciate and applaud whatever looks difficult — and only the artist knows that what looks difficult is usually easy, and what looks easy is usually most difficult.

This is as true for the lowly tap dancer as for the concert pianist who is wildly clapped for playing fast and loud (which any technician can do), but is unnoticed for his slow, quiet passages, which are incredibly hard to perform.

I remember some years ago I was home with a bad cold and had to turn in a column by five o'clock in the afternoon. The "e" key on my typewriter suddenly jammed, and I was faced with the prospect of writing without using the most frequent letter in the alphabet.

Writing the column by hand was out of the question, for I couldn't read back my own scribbling. So I gaily sat down at the typewriter and in a half hour or so contrived a column without using the letter "e" once.

Well, when this appeared in print you would think I had composed the Sermon on the Mount. People were dazzled by my tremendous feat; they couldn't believe I hadn't slaved over it for days, and admiring letters came in from all parts of the country.

Actually, it was a crummy column, which said little and said it badly. I have written thousands of others which were incomparably superior; yet readers who never bothered to drop a note about the others took pens in hand to salute my overpowering genius.

This sort of thing is most discouraging to a serious practitioner of any of the arts. It is also tempting for him to perform tricks, to balance the sausage on his nose, to play the piano with his toes, and take the cash and credit without giving the public the substance of his talent.

Our modern emphasis on sensation is a profoundly corrupting influence, which only the strongest and most dedicated can resist. Nor is it confined merely to "high-brow" arts; the jazz musician has likewise suffered because shallow and spectacular performers have overshadowed the real masters of the art.

Only when we develop a discriminating audience can we hope for a genuinely civilized form of entertainment to replace the glitter and the shriek.

There's Art in Enjoying the Arts

EVERYBODY KNOWS that you don't get much more out of a job than you put into it. Everybody knows that you don't get much more out of a game than you put into it.

But too few people realize that you don't get much more out of a work of art than you put into it. Every work of art must be a collaboration between the creator and the audience.

We can accept the fact that the better you play golf, or the more you understand bridge, the more enjoyment you will receive from it. Work or play (which are aspects of the same drive) depend on active participation for their fullest pleasure. Yet, we expect the poet or the painter or the playwright to do all the artistic work for us — to bring us a poem or a picture or a play that is completely finished and that calls for no exertion on our part.

We resent a "difficult" drama, not understanding that it can be more fun than a simple one. I grant that a work of art should not be difficult for its own sake — but too many audiences desire simplicity for its own sake.

In the preface to his new book of collected plays, Arthur Miller points out the varying reactions of different people to his prize-winning drama, *Death of a Salesman*. Many elderly men wrote to him saying that they saw the play as an allegory of their own lives. Older women saw the suffering wife as the central character in the story. And college-age boys believed that the two sons were really the focus of the plot.

But the comment that stuck in Miller's mind was one he heard in the lobby after the play was over. A man summed up his reaction by remarking to his friend, "I always said that New England territory was no damned good!"

This is what he got out of *Death of a Salesman*. He brought a limited vision and a passive mind to the play — and left in the same condition. If he brought this same passivity to his job or to his golf, he would soon be fired at the office and spurned on the links.

As a people, we enjoy tasks that are challenging, that require imagination and ingenuity. We will not reach our maturity as an audience until we learn to transfer our zest to those often puzzling and provocative creations of the mind known as the arts.

6

OF THE LIFE
OF THE SPIRIT

The Agonizing Honesty of the Bible

LOOKING THROUGH the Old Testament yesterday, in search of
a quotation I had forgotten, I was once more impressed with
one virtue of the Bible that is overlooked both by the book's
defenders and its detractors.

And that is the utter honesty and impartiality of the ancient
Hebrews who compiled the sacred books, who decided which
of the documents should remain within the canon, and which
should be omitted. It would have been easy and pleasant for
them to do what a political party does when compiling a
campaign booklet — to include only material favorable to the
party, and to exclude all prickly criticism. Most books which
propagate a single point of view, which propound a specific
faith, do exactly this: they severely ignore all inconsistencies,
all weaknesses, all adverse comments made by their enemies.

But the Old Testament is seething with evidence of such
human flaws and frailties. Consider the bitter books of the
prophets, such as Isaiah, which attack the Jewish priesthood,
condemn the Israelites for perverting their faith, and warn
that the judgment of God will be hard against them.

Can anyone imagine the Republican National Committee including a scathing denunciation by Adlai Stevenson in its campaign literature? Or vice versa, of course. Yet this is exactly what the editors of the Old Testament permitted to become part of Holy Scripture.

Again, if the book were merely a smooth piece of religious propaganda, the compilers could easily have removed all the offensive passages — the brutal wars, the lustful kings, the dishonest statesmen.

They could have given us a book reviling the enemies of Israel; but instead they candidly weigh the sins of their own people in the same balance as they weigh the Canaanites and the Moabites — and, indeed, they judge the sins of the Israelites more harshly than those of pagans.

Street-corner atheists who jubilantly point to such passages as "proof" that the Bible is a barbarous and inconsistent book are making a defect out of what is really a virtue — the inclusion of much material that does not reflect credit or glory upon the Israelites.

The ancient Hebrew priests believed that their people were "chosen" to bring the light of a Single God to the world; but they did not believe this made them better than others; rather it imposed a heavier responsibility upon them, and made their sins more grievous. No other book ever written has vibrated with more agonizing honesty.

Man Is Nature's Most Unnatural Thing

WHENEVER TIMES ARE tense, and people are anxious and upset, we hear voices raised in praise of "nature." We are told that only if we follow nature, only if we learn to live naturally, will we overcome the tensions and conflicts within us and without us.

This is demonstrably false counsel. For man is the most unatural thing in nature. In a real sense, man is alienated from nature. Unlike all the animals, his destiny is in his own hands; he has the terrible freedom of choice.

Wolves and rabbits can only behave like wolves and rabbits, past, present and future. Their ends are served by deep intincts; but man is cut off from his instinctual life, and, instead, must use the fragile tools of reason and will.

We are hybrid creatures, fully at home neither on land nor in water. Our appetites belong to the animal world, and to reject or distort that part of ourselves is to commit suicide. But as self-conscious creatures (the only ones, for instance, with an idea of death), we are estranged from the rest of nature.

This is the basic cause of our anxiety. Man desperately wants to know his origins and his ultimate end; it is impossible for him to live in the present, as all other creatures do. He is a question-asking animal, and there are no easy, obvious answers to most of his questions.

Therefore, "following nature" is advice that can suit only a part of us; it cannot satisfy the other part, because man is constituted to be forever dissatisfied, forever moving and searching and building and tearing down and examining the roots of his being.

To ask him to do less than this — to live in rhythm with the tides and the seasons — is to make him less than he is. He can never be subdued to acceptance of the present. He cannot divest himself of his human energy; he can only learn to control it and direct it.

Each person, unless he has successfully narcotized himself,

is in restless quest of his identity, both as an individual and as a member of a species. He wants to know what it means to be a person, and exactly who this particular person is. This drive is totally foreign to the rest of nature; to conquer it, we must become either more like gods or more like beasts — and this is the dilemma that produces our anxiety. For man, to live naturally is an unnatural thing.

Ideas Can Be Planted Like Seeds

A FRIEND OF MINE was chagrined because he had been argued down at a party. He had taken the unpopular side in an after-dinner discussion, and he was overwhelmed by the sheer volume and numbers of the opposition.

Hearing his side of it, I believed he was in the right. And I tried to tell him that the loss of one battle means little in the war of ideas.

In this way, the mental world is far different from the physical world. Fire enough cannon balls at a tower and it collapses into rubble; but there is not enough ammunition in the world to demolish an idea that is ultimately destined to stand.

This was brought home to me vividly some time ago, when I ran across a man I had not seen for some years. We had engaged in a lively discussion, but since I was very young and he was very learned, he had demolished my arguments by sheer weight and authority. I felt defeated.

When I met him for the second time, he confessed that he had thought about our argument for a long time; some of the things I said (however ineptly) stuck in his mind, and now he was convinced that there was more truth in my position than in his.

In a sense, it was not I who had changed his mind but the inherent power of the ideas working beneath his consciousness. And the same thing has happened to me in reverse, over the years: ideas I derided and demolished (at the time) finally overthrew me, much as a tiny plant, growing persistently, can crack a rock in the mountainside.

My "fanatical" friends who believe in nonviolent resistance to war, who believe in the absolute moral and social necessity of a world community, have thus far lost every battle they have fought with the "realists." Yet who is to say that their arguments have not planted seeds that will grow to crack the "common sense" of the rest of us?

"Nothing is so powerful," observed Goethe, "as an idea whose time has arrived." The time has not yet arrived for the ideas which will bind mankind as a unity under God; perhaps it never will, and destruction is our destiny. But if we do ever reach that millennium, it will be because of the persistent efforts of such "fanatical" men and women.

That truth is mighty and shall prevail, I have no doubt; but for the next race of men, if not for us. Truth can lose an argument, a nation, even a world — but it carries a creative core that is imperishable, invulnerable, and innocently growing in the very heart of corruption.

It Pays to Check on Your "Virtues"

I WAS HAVING BREAKFAST at home when I announced proudly that I had sent a check for $25 to a little boy we "adopted" in Korea a few years ago.

"Yes," said the woman across the table, "and the day before that, you spent twice as much for a new car coat you didn't need at all."

The rebuke was merited. I had been pleased with my "generosity" — but was it really generosity, or was it a means of buying off my conscience for indulging in a car coat I didn't need when little Joo Sop Chang doesn't have a pair of pants he needs?

We talk a lot about "taking a good hard look at ourselves," and surely we live in the most self-analytical age known to man. But what do we generally take a look at? Our defects and our vices, which we are already acquainted with.

It is much harder, but much more rewarding, to investigate our "virtues." As Erik H. Erikson remarks in his splendid new book, *Young Man Luther*, one must learn to "take an especially honest look at one's honesty."

How many persons pride themselves on being "candid" when their candor is merely a mask for cruelty? How many call themselves "courageous" when their courage is just a form of aggression, and "independent," when their independence is simply contrariness?

And how many, like me, like to call ourselves "generous," when our generosity is only a magic ritual for placating the gods who have been good to us — as it were, a bribe to the future?

We need to look, not at our obvious defects (which most of us pretty well know by the time we are grown up) but at those parts of our nature we are proudest of — for there lurk the deeper devils of egotism; the subtle and self-righteous destroyers of true charity.

The frank friend who tells you a harsh truth "for your own good" often tells it as much for the pleasure he gets as for the benefit it affords you; thus, his motives are muddied, and his frankness has been corrupted by what the Germans properly call *schadenfreude* — the secret enjoyment of others' mishaps.

Taking an honest look at one's failings is easy; we do it every day. But taking an honest look at one's honesty — this is a task for heroes, and for saints.

One Way We Can Conquer Time

IF MICHAEL HAS TO wait from Wednesday to Sunday, he almost has a conniption. Four days, at his age, seem an eternity.

The telescopic quality of time has been marveled at by all philosophers. For time does not proceed at a uniform pace; it accelerates as we get older.

I was reflecting this morning that I have had the same job for twenty years. I arrived here as a bright-eyed young man, and am now limping into baggy-lidded middle-age. And where have the years gone? I couldn't tell you. Like a puff of smoke, they have disappeared into infinity. It is more than startling, it is frightening, to think how quickly a life evaporates before our eyes.

When we are young, time stretches before us in a limitless vista. If we have to wait a day for a party, we are racked with impatience. Graduation will never come. The first car of our own seems a million years away. And the fact that the world will find a place for us, will make room for us as a working member of society, seems a remote improbability.

Then, somehow, in a mysterious but implacable manner, all the parts lock into place: the position is found, the marriage is made, the house is bought, and there we are, tramping along shoulder to shoulder in the ranks of the adult world — tagged, numbered, outfitted, and mortgaged.

But Time itself ("that bloody tyrant," as Shakespeare called it) does not really exist until we have reached middle age. All young people believe themselves to be, in a way, immortal; time exists only for older people.

Then we learn, slowly but undeniably, that nothing belongs to us, completely, finally. The job is ended, the children grow up and move away, even the money (when there is money) buys little that we want. For what we want cannot be bought. And it is then, if ever, that we learn to make our peace with destiny. To accept the fact that our dreams have been half realized, or unrealized; that we did not do what we set out to do; that our goals have receded as we approached them.

There may be a sadness in this prospect, but also a serenity. Illusions lose their power to disturb us; we value life by what it has given us, not by the promise of tomorrow. For only by accepting Time can we, in a measure, learn to conquer it.

Greatest Task—to Discover Self

PEOPLE ARE ALWAYS asking Michael what he wants to "be" when he grows up, and he is always telling them. Right now, he wants to be a welder. Last week it was a garbage collector; the week before, a crane operator.

When Thoreau was nine years old, someone asked him what he would be when he grew up, and he answered promptly: "I'll be myself." And he was, too — the most gloriously independent mind of his time.

How many of us in the adult world can say we are ourselves? How many of us even know what that means? Instead, we are subsumed within our jobs, our social positions, our functions as husbands and voters and homeowners.

To be oneself does not mean to run wild, to ignore obligations, to rebel for its own sake (as the adolescent beatniks seem to think). It means, rather, to see oneself first and foremost as a person, not as a part of a person — not as an American, or a male, but as a living organism composed of body and spirit.

Thoreau had a lifelong passion for asserting his own identity as a person; and this passion made him seem like a fanatic in the eyes of his contemporaries. When he sequestered himself in Walden for two years, it was not (as so many people think) to learn more about Nature, but to learn more about Thoreau.

Most of us live locked tightly within our partial little loyalties, and thus never realize what the fullness of a human being should be like. We approach the world sideways, like a crab, seeing it only from the oblique angle of our particular social status, our native background, our special vocation.

But to be distinctively human means not to have a worm's-eye view, or a crab's-eye view. It means to share with God a panoramic view of the world, including oneself; it means rising above the accidental prison of our personalities, and trying to discover what a human being should really be like.

This is a difficult task, but it is the only worthwhile task in life. Compared to it, making money is frivolous, and having fun is dull. When Michael grows up, I most of all want him to be Michael — whether he is collecting garbage or dividends.

The Only Way Man Can Stay Whole

ONE OF THE LADS waiting on table for the summer in a nearby resort is studying for the ministry, and he is perplexed by some of the "hard" sayings in the Bible.

"For instance, I don't understand," he said to me recently, "what it really means that you have to lose your life in order to find it. Does it mean that you have to die before you can know who and what you are?"

I think that modern psychology throws a great light on ancient spirituality. Most of the old moral and mystical truths have been illuminated by recent delvings into the unconscious make-up of man.

That one must lose oneself to find reality is a biological fact as well as a spiritual one. What Ribot calls the "reflex sense of personality" is abolished in the expert rifleman as he shoots, in the surgeon as he operates.

When a person finds an act, or a vocation, that he deems larger than himself, his whole personality is gathered up to converge upon it. At the moment of full participation, he literally loses himself in a fuller identification with his object.

At these times, he feels a sense of expansion, of exhilaration, of intensified consciousness that takes him beyond himself. He has, in a way, lost himself in order to find himself.

This explains the passion which men devote to hobbies, and also the vital function of work. It is true that most hobbies, and much work, are not worthy of this concentration; but, even at the most trivial, it is healthier than a neurotic obsession with oneself.

We cannot find ourselves until we make effective contact with reality, until our relationships with other persons and with the outside world become a real *transaction*, and not merely a distorted reflection of our own needs and desires.

This means cracking the outer shell of egocentricity, and becoming somehow "reborn." On the religious level, this represents a "conversion"; on the psychological level, it means abandoning the neurotic defenses that separate us from others and prevent us from truly loving and giving more than we expect to get back.

To lose one's life in order to find it is more than a mere paradox of mysticism, and more than a vague spiritual myth. It corresponds to the deepest need of the human being — the need to become aware of one's highest powers by donating these powers to a force outside oneself.

The only power that can adequately satisfy this need is God; but in His absence from their sight it is understandable that some people, to retain their sanity, concentrate on golf or gross sales or any of the other false deities of our time. Man, to stay whole, must worship something outside of himself.

The True Values Are in the Spirit

THE HOUSE YOU WERE born in, and left at an early age, always seems like a palace in retrospect — but it looks more like a hovel if you should ever make the mistake of returning to visit it in later life.

That vast baronial hall has shrunk into a squalid little foyer; the enormous living room is a cramping rectangle of fading wallpaper; and the mile-long approach up the driveway and through the spacious grounds is compressed into a few feet of dirt, weeds and gravel.

If we have had this shattering experience of returning to the ancestral mansion — as many of us have — we can better appreciate the perspective and the scale of values that make a child's life so perplexing.

It is terribly easy for us to forget the overwhelming disparity of *size* between a child's view of the world and ours.

He does not see life with the same eyes, nor measure it in the same terms, and therefore what is "real" and "true" to the adult has a different kind of reality and truth to the child.

The first time I visited a movie house outside my familiar little neighborhood cinema, I might as well have been worshiping at the Cathedral of Chartres. It was the grandest, most brilliant edifice I could have imagined, and I thought that the furnishings were the ultimate in elegant expensiveness.

Of course, a few years later, I could see it for what it "really" was — a shabby and pretentious auditorium, crowded with ugly overstuffed furniture and hung with pictures of monumental tastelessness.

Now, this kind of disillusionment is normal and necessary for the process of growing up. But if the child's sense of external reality keeps changing, he must be provided with a sense of *internal* reality to compensate him for this loss.

Unless he is made to feel that reality exists within the mind and soul, that the only permanent and meaningful values come from the spirit, then he may spend his life seeking to recapture the magnificence of his childhood. He will not be satisfied until he can attain the biggest, the grandest, the most impressive — for he is searching for his lost youth.

I am convinced that greedy and overambitious people have remained infantile in this respect; they have not been taught that true value comes from the inside; and so they embark on a futile lifelong quest to find that larger palace around the bend of the road.

The Whole World Is a Huge Legacy

THE BOY IN THE GARAGE was bickering with his father. "I don't owe the world a thing," he said, as adolescents are wont to. "I didn't ask to be born."

It is true that nobody asks to be born, but it does not follow that we don't owe the world a thing. We have a tremendous debt to the past, which we take for granted, as part of our "rightful" heritage.

The boy in the garage has never taken a good look around him. Everything he enjoys doing is a free gift from the past. His tools, his machinery, his clothes, indeed his health itself —all were invented or developed or fortified by his ancestors.

How many of us could survive at all without this tremendous inheritance we accept so thoughtlessly? Consider the brilliant men, the patient men, the dedicated men, who labored (often without reward) on projects both great and small, from the steam engine to the safety pin.

This boy would be like a beast in the forest if not for better men then he: unclad, unshod, ravaged by disease and riddled with misery.

Not one of us contributes more than one millionth of 1 per cent to the accumulated knowledge and comfort we call "civilization." The farmer inherits his tools from his wisdom of the past; the manufacturer depends upon the kind of brains that were more interested in progress than in profit; the schoolboy benefits from untold man-hours of research and devotion.

The whole world is a gigantic legacy. Imagine having to start afresh each generation: who would invent the wheel, devise the lever, construct the alphabet and the multiplication table? I could not; could you?

We owe reverence to God; but, beyond this, we owe loyalty and gratitude to the past. We were born into a world where most of the basic elements were already waiting for us; we merely combine and rearrange them for our pleasure or profit. Not more than a handful of us in any century leaves something permanent for the future to use.

Ungratefulness to the past is a barbarous trait. The boy in the garage is greedy for all the advantages that ancient minds can confer upon him, but he will not pay any homage to history. He did not ask to be born, but he is asking to die, as a sullen savage, crouched in a motorcar he did not make, behind an engine he cannot control.

The Way to Achieve a Good Life

AMERICA IS A public speaker's paradise. Nowhere else in the world are so many people in so many organizations so indecently eager to hear speakers on every topic from atom smashing to zinnia growing.

As I contemplate my lecture schedule for next season — with a mixture of horror and greed — it occurs to me that this passion for information is a dubious blessing. What are the audiences really getting?

Basically, they want to be told *what to do*. What can we do about Russia or China? What should we do about our schools? How can we get better plays on the stage, better films on the screen, better programs on television?

Yet, advice on what we can do is usually futile — for we will do nothing except applaud the speaker, accept those ideas of his we already agreed with, and reject those ideas that run counter to our prejudices.

What is important in our lives is to be told *what to be*, befor we can learn what to do. And audiences resent being told what to be; that is preaching, it is moralizing, and it is uncomfortable to hear, except in church, when we listen as a matter of good form and promptly forget it.

I once heard a brilliant speaker at a Quaker meeting. He was talking about charity and working for philanthropic organizations. He said that there were three steps each person must take.

The first step is *giving*. That is the easiest. Writing a check makes us feel virtuous and involves little personal participation. This is the lowest rung of charity.

The second step is *doing*. That is harder: it means giving up time and expending effort on tedious and unrewarding tasks. It is a higher rung on the ladders of charity.

The third step is *being*. That is the hardest of all: it means transforming oneself into a kind and loving person, not merely in relation to a project or an organization, but in relation to everyone around us.

Achieving the good life is more a matter of being than of doing or giving. It calls for intense self-scrutiny, a relentless honesty about one's motives, and a persistent feeling that we are no better — and perhaps worse — than those we are trying to help.

This is the only lecture worth listening to, and the only one that could ultimately help us in solving the problems of Russia and China, the schools, the movies and the atom bomb. In this profound psychological sense, charity does begin at home.

When not Knowing Is a Virtue

IT IS TRUE THAT a wise man is one who knows how little he knows — but I am tired of hearing ignorant people defend their ignorance on this ground.

What most people fail to recognize is that you have to earn the right to be wrong; physicians sometimes make incorrect diagnoses, but we do not therefore take our ailments to shoemakers.

As Montaigne remarked long ago: "There is an ABC ignorance that precedes knowledge, and a doctoral ignorance that comes after it."

Newton said he felt like a little boy playing with pebbles on the seashore, and Thomas Aquinas, at the end of his life, declared that his great *Summa* was little more than rubbish.

But these geniuses at least knew what there was to know about their respective fields, and their ignorance began only where human reason ends. They pushed their minds as far as they could go, and only then did they bow before the ultimate mystery of the universe.

Lao-Tse, the Chinese sage, beautifully illustrated this in one of his sayings: "To the ignorant man, a tree is a tree, and a river is a river. To the learned man, a tree is not a tree, and a river is not a river. To the wise man, a tree is a tree, and a river is a river — but they are not the same tree or the same river that the ignorant man sees."

What he meant, of course, is that we progress from a naïve realism to a scientific understanding of things; and then, if we procede far enough, we return, but with a heightened awareness of what it means.

For instance, to a child, love is love, unquestioning and unqualified. As we acquire knowledge, we learn that love may be different things, and that it is a complex and contradictory bundle of emotions. But if we become really wise, we return to the child's concept of love, only on a much higher plane. We are still ignorant of its final meaning, but our ignorance is now doctoral, and not the ABC ignorance of the child.

To know how little we know becomes a virtue only *after* we have tried to learn all we are capable of knowing. The ignorant man is arrogant in his profession of humility; as Einstein once said of a mediocre colleague: "He has no right to be so humble — he is not great enough."

All Is Past, Present, and Future

THE PEOPLE WHO insist that one must "live for the present" are as foolish and lopsided as the people who live wistfully in the past or the people who live hopefully in the future.

Time is seamless. Past, present, and future are woven into the same fabric. The present is continually disappearing into the past, before we can grasp it. And, in a real sense, the future never comes. Time and space are part of the same continuum, Einstein taught us. We must also learn that time itself is indivisible, that every act is a blending of past experience, present situation, and future expectancy.

Living for the present is a senseless philosophy. The man who most perfectly lives for the present is the criminal: he forgets the prison sentence of the past, and he ignores the probable prison sentence of the future. He lives from "score" to "score."

We must not look behind too much, we must not look ahead too far, and we must not fix our gaze too steadily on the immediate. Each of these angles of vision has its own particular dangers. What is necessary, it seems to me, is a delicate combination of the three. Those who focus on the past become apathetic; those who peer exclusively into the future become unrealistic; those who live on a day-to-day basis become incapable of learning from the past and incapable of controlling the future.

The mind likes to break up life into categories — but these categories are illusions. For instance, we think the past is behind us, but it is not; it is very much with us, very much alive, very much a part of everything we do now.

We think the future lies ahead, but its seed is contained in the present. There is no sharp break between the two: the lie we tell today can send us sprawling a year from now; the way we treat our infant determines the way he treats us when he reaches adolescence.

Life is a flow, a stream. The current is everywhere. Like mariners, we must learn the shoals, the rocks, the rapids. No man can navigate only from wave to wave, for the waves are part of a ceaseless pattern in time.

Live for the present? It is impossible; and if it were possible, it would be fatal. To live for the present is the surest way of forfeiting the future to barbarism and bestiality.

Well, How Do You Answer the Hindu?

I COULDN'T ANSWER the Hindu. Maybe you can. Maybe you can make a better defense of so-called Western civilization than I could.

"Since traveling in the Christian world of the West," he said at dinner, "I have been puzzled by my readings in the New Testament. How do you people interpret the words of Jesus?"

"What do you mean?" I asked, afraid of what was coming.

"I mean," he said politely, "how do you reconcile his plain doctrine of nonresistance with your guns and your planes and your wars every few decades? Which Christian nation has ever turned the other cheek? Who among you are willing to return good for evil? How can people who share in the good news of His message continually kill one another, while both sides are praying to Him?"

"Well," I stammered, "after all, that's a doctrine of perfection that Jesus preached. Ordinary mortal men can't always live up to it."

"That I understand," he nodded, "but it should be your goal — and I can only see that you go in the opposite direction. Gandhi was not a Christian, and yet it seems to me he practiced the New Testament more than Westerners do."

"But Gandhi was a saint," I protested. "Surely the mass of Indian people are no better, morally and spiritually, than Westerners are."

"Perhaps not," he said. "All the same, we do not claim to have a special revelation from the Son of God. We do not insist that we follow the Prince of Peace, and then follow the Prince of War."

"Not everybody agrees that Jesus was a pacifist," I objected. "Some people point to his scourging the money-changers out of the temple."

"Ah, but there is a difference between scourging — as you might a disobedient child, out of love for him — and wantonly killing millions of innocent men and women and children, all in the name of God. You are commanded to love your neighbors — and today, in this shrunken world, everybody is a neighbor."

I had one defense left; my Sunday punch, if you'll pardon

the expression. "Don't we have a right, an obligation, to fight against injustice and wickedness and tyranny?" I demanded.

"Yes," he said, "you must fight against it — but in your own minds and souls, for that is where it begins, not in some foreign land. When you have purified yourselves, the example of your goodness will be the most effective weapon in the world — if not for now, then in the future."

Maybe you can answer the Hindu. I could not, in all honesty.

Man—The Marvel of the Universe

REREADING SOME of the brilliant and bitter works of Jonathan Swift last night, I was reminded of the old German saying that "every stick has two ends."

One's view of humanity depends on which end of the stick one chooses to grasp. If you look upon man as a spirit corrupted by flesh, it is hard not to become disgusted and revolted with human behavior. But, if you consider man as an animal infused with a spirit, then it is a constant source of wonder and delight that this animal has attained as much as he has.

Swift took the former view. He plunged from dizzy idealism to degrading cynicism. He saw only the great gap between our pretentions to nobility and our selfish animal passions.

Gulliver's Travels is, of course, not a children's book; it is a savage attack on mankind. Swift was nauseated with our sight, our smell, our sound. That we can rise so high in our thoughts and sink so low in our conduct was, to him, a terrible indictment of our hypocrisy.

Seizing the stick from the other end, however, it becomes perfectly plain that man is the marvel of the universe. He *is* an animal, at one with the shellfish, the buzzard and the hyena. If we can look this natural fact in the face, and accept our animal heritage, it seems biologically incredible that we can even conceive of such things as honor and nobility and love and sacrifice.

We often, or usually, do not live up to our concepts. This is regrettable, but not condemnable. Physically, we are forced to live in the animal world; but the soul, or spirit, or psyche — call it what you will — gives us a set of values that goes far beyond the animal kingdom.

We need not like what people *do* but we must admire what a part of them desires to do; and what a few individuals in every society succeed in doing. We can modify our basic pattern of behavior — something no other animal can achieve.

It is easy to be cynical about the defects in human nature; but deep in every personality is the yearning for goodness and truth and beauty. Holding mankind by this end of the stick, we cannot but have reverence for an act of animal creation that so vastly transcends the lusts of the jungle and the laws of the swamp. Man is a greater miracle than anything else in the universe.

An Honest Prayer for Atomic Age

GOING THROUGH the notes crammed into my desk drawers the other morning, I came across a clipping that I had stored away on the day the United States opened its nuclear detonation season.

The test began with a short prayer intoned over the intercom by the warship's chaplain, and it went as follows:

"Unto us who are privileged to draw aside the curtain into the secrets of Thy universe, teach us that our whole duty is to love Thee our God and to keep the commandments."

Presumably there is at least one commandment that a chaplain on a warship is in no position to invoke. It would seem a trifle awkward to enjoin "Thou shalt not kill" just before the detonation of a bomb with the power of several million tons of TNT, capable of killing a few hundred thousand of His children.

Instead of the pious sonorities of this prayer, I suggest a much more realistic invocation to be given by the Representatives of the Lord whenever they happen to be present on similar fraternal occasions. It would go something like this:

"Unto us who have the pride and presumption to release the most devastating forces of nature, O Lord, be merciful;

"Protect us from cardiac contusion;

"Preserve us from cerebral or coronary air embolism;

"Guard us from the dreadful consequences of respiratory tract hemorrhage;

"Allow us not to suffer from pulmonary edema;

"Save us from the trauma of distended hollow viscera;

"Withhold from us the horrors of hemorrhages in the central nervous system.

"Visit these catastrophes upon our enemies, not upon us, and we promise to love Thee and keep the commandments — all except one, O Lord."

This at least, would be an honest and meaningful prayer. No nonsense, no hypocrisy, no solemn theological jargon to disguise and sanctify the purpose and the power of the bomb.

The Lord, I am sure, would not grant this prayer — but it would not, at any rate, be an insult to His intelligence and an affront to His benevolence. Sometimes I think He must be more discouraged by the blindness of His shepherds than by the folly of His sheep.

True Meaning of Good Samaritan

LANGUAGE CAN BE a magnificent tool for expressing mankind's deepest thoughts and emotions; but, like every tool, it has a cutting edge and a blunt edge. Too often, language becomes vulgarized; the original sharp meaning of a word or a phrase is rubbed away with time, and we are left with only a hollow cliché that has lost all significance.

I thought of this today when I heard a man at luncheon referring to a friend who works in the same office as a "good Samaritan," because the friend had helped him out during an emergency.

But the whole point of the parable of the Good Samaritan in the Bible was exactly the opposite of this — which is why Jesus told the parable to the apostles. The good Samaritan was not a friend; he was a stranger. And he was not merely a stranger — he was a despised and lowly alien. To come from Samaria, in biblical times, was a contemptible joke to all good, loyal, upstanding, patriotic, God-fearing Israelites.

Jesus, you may remember, told the story to a lawyer who wanted to know the meaning of "Love thy neighbor." It was the story of a man who fell among thieves and was stripped, beaten and robbed.

A Jewish priest — one of his countrymen — passed by without offering help. A Levite, one of the holy men who assisted in the care of the sacred scrolls, likewise refused assistance. Only the "inferior" alien from Samaria bound up the man's wounds, took him to an inn, and paid for his stay there.

Our neighbor is anyone who helps us, not merely the man next door or in the next pew or under the same flag. The loving-kindness preached by Jesus cuts across all barriers of race and creed and nation.

Thus, the parable of the good Samaritan is not just an insipid and sentimental be-kind-to-people story. Jesus was too profound and too radical for such cheap and easy moralizing.

It is, rather, a command to serve anyone who is in need, not out of a sense of duty or loyalty, but because we are all brethren — and the lowest and most despised among us may find it easier to enter the Kingdom of Heaven than the priest or the Levite.

This is the meaning of the parable of the good Samaritan. But what good does it do us to use the phrase if we forget what Samaria stood for?

You Can *Argue with Success*

TWO YOUNG MEN, evidently salesmen, were having lunch at the table next to mine, "I couldn't do it" one of them was saying "but Bill gets away with it. And, after all, you can't argue with success."

I have heard this vicious phrase a thousand times, but I have never heard its justification. Why can't you argue with success? It is the only thing worth arguing with.

There is no need to argue with failure. And failure doesn't want to argue; it just wants to be let alone and lick its wounds. But success is too often brassy and argumentative, self-satisfied and superior about itself.

The man who won't argue with success has already been corrupted without knowing it. He accepts the world at face value. He thinks that things are what they seem to be. And he is, at bottom, a traitor to Western civilization and to the whole Judaic-Christian tradition.

It was the duty of decent Germans to argue with the "success" of the Nazi dictatorship. It is the duty of good people everywhere to argue with the "success" of all violence and fraud and greed and inhumanity.

It is only by rebelling against these false conceptions of success that man has raised himself from the jungle. It is only by weighing and judging and evaluating the worth of his leaders that man has overthrown tyrants and deposed despots.

Success is the one thing in the world that *must* be questioned, that cannot be accepted without the proper credentials of morality. From the Mosaic Code to the Sermon on the Mount, the Bible insists that the mighty shall be toppled when their ways are wicked.

And good sense confirms this. It knows that man's end is not power, but peace and justice. And peace is impossible, and justice is a mockery, unless we see that power is put where it belongs — in the hands of men who cherish wisdom and righteousness.

Success, rather than being venerated, must be carefully defined. It should include the whole man, in his spiritual and social life, and not just his capacity for taking, for impressing, for commanding. The truly successful man, by these rigorous standards, is a rare and wonderful creature.

But he is the only creature worth imitating. To imitate, or worship, his shabby counterfeits is to sacrifice the most distinctive part of our humanity.

World Lacks Lovers—of the Truth

A YOUNG MAN at a college where I recently lectured was
trying to bait me during the question period. He seemed cynical and defensive and disbelieving — but he didn't fool me
for a moment.

I knew he was a lover, and this is how lovers behave when
they are young. He was a lover of truth and goodness, and
the one thing he hated above all else was "phoniness."

And he was engaged in a typical lover's quest with me. He
had a deep and desperate desire to believe what I said, to believe that I was sincere and honest. But, at the same time, he
felt compelled to attack me, to probe for soft spots in my nature, to expose me if he could as a pompous fraud and a wind-
bag.

It is easy to dislike or disdain rude young men of this sort,
until you realize that they are lovers. Somewhere along the
line they have been hurt and disillusioned; they feel betrayed
by the world's falsity; and they will not rest until they prove
that everything in the world is phony — or until they find a
truth they can cling to.

Much of what is called "rebellion" in bright young people
— I am not here speaking of the obviously disturbed youngsters — is really a search for faith. Their scorn and their immature cynicism reflect their secret desire for goodness and
their unwillingness to compromise with the shoddy standards of older people who have, weakly and sadly, come to
terms with the Devil.

And these rebels, if understood and treated intelligently,
can become the most creative and effective citizens. I much
prefer them to the sheep who are docile because they are
dumb, who accept what they have been taught without ques-

tion, who are tractable because they lack imagination, and who never do anything bad because they have no passion for either good or evil.

There are not enough lovers in the world. There are too few people who care deeply enough about such sublime abstractions as Truth. Time itself is corrupting: as we get older, we become flabby in the mind and the spirit as well as in the body.

These boys see it happening to us, and they resent it. Their cynicism is just the reverse side of their idealism, put on to conceal their hurt. It should be our task to heal them, and to guide them not to become like us, but to become what we once wanted to be.

The Invisible Wall You Cannot Cross

I GAVE MY LAST commencement address this month — last for the season, that is — and returned home feeling more of a fraud than ever. For what can a man in his forties say to young people just starting their twenties? What words can carry across the wide abyss of the generations?

The most difficult communication is not between countries, or even between the sexes (difficult though that is), but between the ages. An invisible wall looms grimly before us, and our message bounces off the hard surface and is disintegrated into a thousand mocking echoes.

Experience cannot be transmitted. Advice cannot be absorbed. The lessons of the past cannot be projected into the future. At twenty, I would not have paid attention to any old fogey twice my age telling me what the world was like, what I might expect, what I should do.

In my address, I try to build a bridge across the years, but it is futile. They cannot believe that I was once like them; I am a stranger in another land, without an interpreter. To them, I "have it made," which puts me wholly outside the circle of their concerns.

And having it made means somehow that you have found your place in the world, have settled down into a routine, with a house and a family and bills to pay and money to pay them with. You have become a fixed point of reference in the community, while they are still looking for identity and status and, most of all, for a sense of being needed and wanted.

How tell them that nobody in the modern world "has it made"? How explain to them that problems change, they do not dwindle? How impress them with the one fact you have learned — that security is something that can be found only within oneself, not outside oneself?

They want practical, immediate, concrete answers — and they will not listen when told that there are no such answers, that life arranges itself almost more by accident than by design. They are eager to be taught the secret of grasping the golden chalice, and look upon you with unbelieving contempt if you suggest that the chalice is no longer golden by the time you grasp it.

This is why commencement speakers issue nothing but noble platitudes which nobody pays attention to. They know that the truth cannot be communicated, that pain cannot be avoided, that one generation cannot save the next from making its own mistakes. And this is why I feel a fraud — at getting paid for trying a hopeless task.

Blind Alleys on Way to Truth

JUST AS WE CANNOT find happiness by looking for it, so we cannot discover truth by a direct search. We can only approach it in a negative way.

When we are young and eager, we seek for The Truth. We look for answers. But as we get older, if we learn anything, we learn to collect "non-answers."

Truth, as I conceive it, is a tiny dot on a large map. We keep taking wrong roads, and crossing them off the map when we find they are not going where we want them to go.

Education is a process of learning what is wrong. Nobody, for instance, can give a satisfactory definition of "happiness." But, by experience, we can learn the things that do *not* bring happiness.

Much of the impatience and rebellion and cynicism of youth spring from a failure to understand that such concepts as Truth and Happiness cannot be grasped by the intellect. They can only be reached (if ever) by trial and error, by blocking out more and more areas of the map until only a small portion is left unshaded.

This is a laborious and painful process. It is much easier to seize a partial truth and take it for the whole truth. But there can be no short cut to personal exploration; even the truths of religious belief must come from deep emotional experience, not merely from a blind clinging to custom.

This wisdom of elderly people is infuriating to the young, because it is almost always negative — as it has to be. They know that money leads neither to truth nor to happiness; they know that sensual pleasures, as a goal, are vain and empty; they know that fame and honor and all the food of the ego provide no lasting nourishment for the spirit.

They have taken wrong roads and blind alleys; and while they cannot tell you where to go, they can tell you where not to go. But, of course, we will not listen; for each person has his own private map which he must block out for himself, at whatever cost.

The most we can do is continue to collect non-answers, as the scientist keeps making experiment after experiment to rule out the wrong combinations. And we must persist, for, contrary to that diabolical proverb, it is the road to Heaven that is paved with good intentions.

But Can You Sympathize with Joy?

IN GERMAN, the word "sympathy" takes two forms — one form means sympathizing with another person's sorrow; the second form means sympathizing with another person's joy.

To sympathize is to be in harmony with someone else's feelings. But in English, we always use it to mean "feeling sorry for," and the opposite sense of the word is wholly lost.

Yet it is much easier to sympathize with sorrow than to sympathize with joy. We always have a slight feeling of superiority when someone else suffers a tragedy, and it makes us feel good to feel bad about it. But when someone we know is rejoicing, is radiant, is successful, how much sympathy do we then feel? Are we able to harmonize our emotions with his, or do we rather feel a pang of bitterness and envy?

I know a good many unpleasant people who are eager to sympathize with disaster; in fact, some of them spend a lifetime in looking for disaster to sympathize with. When, however, a friend of theirs is riding the crest of good fortune, these unpleasant characters are totally unable to sympathize. Instead, they sneer, they pick flaws, and make dire predictions.

It takes no great moral or spiritual qualities to feel sorry for a person who has fallen from a tremendous height, or has suffered an irreplaceable loss. We can easily put ourselves in his place, and feel sorrow for ourselves, in a vicarious fashion.

A genuinely sympathetic person is a rare and wonderful creature. He not only mourns when we mourn, he rejoices when we rejoice, he is able to identify with us in happiness as well as in misfortune.

Many people delude themselves that they are warm and sympathetic because they cry easily over the death of small children or animals or miners trapped in a slide. Julius Streicher, one of the most bestial of the Nazi leaders, used to weep copiously when one of his nineteen pet canaries died.

The true test of a sympathetic nature, however, comes when a friend or a neighbor or a colleague has risen in eminence and is sitting on top of the world. Then we are not quite so sympathetic; then we look for the world to turn, for reverses to set in, even for a tragedy to strike — so that we can again sympathize with him. On our own terms.

This may be worth reflecting about the next time we pride ourselves on our compassion.

No Need to Act as Agents of God

DISRAELI USED TO SAY that whenever a man did him an injury he would write that man's name on a slip of paper and put it into a little-used drawer of his desk. "Once every few years I would open the drawer," he confided, "and look at the names there. And, you know, it was surprising how many of those men had died, or disappeared, or ruined themselves in trying to hurt others."

The instinct for revenge is strong in all of us, especially

when we are still smarting from some injury. But in the Bible the Lord says, "Vengeance is mine" — which is not only sound ethics but also good psychology.

Vengeance is best left to the Lord; when humans invoke it, they become very much like the thing they hate. The Hatfields may have been at first treated unjustly by the McCoys; but in the end the two clans were indistinguishable one from the other. Injustice was the sole victor.

I have been injured only a couple of times in my adult life, and in both cases I repressed my anger. Those who injured me have long since paid a price, of one sort or another — a price not exacted by me, but by the folly of their own natures.

Few of us are strong enough to turn the other cheek, but most of us can learn simply to turn our backs and walk away. Vicious and deceitful people punish themselves, their families and their friends; there is no need for us to act as agents of the Lord. Nor can most of us love our enemies, but we can ignore them, thus saving us the wear and tear of evil passions. The man who attacks you *wants* to be attacked in turn; this, in a way, justifies his attack and makes him feel better. Psychologically, refusing to return an injury may inflict deeper pain than striking back.

The human race has yet to learn that most of the "moral" injunctions in religious literature contain an emotional truth — the truth that only light can cast out darkness, only kindness can conquer cruelty. If we cannot grasp this truth in our personal relations, how can we hope for the world to act upon it in international relations?

Space Age Is Not a Key to Peace

IT IS A HALF-TRUTH, and a dangerous half-truth, to think that the nations will become closer in spirit as they become closer in space. The world is shrinking but our loyalties are not expanding. Soon, by jet, it will take only a few hours to go from New York to any place on the globe. But the differences between New York and New Delhi do not thereby disappear; indeed, they may become sharpened.

The closeness of England and Ireland did not prevent the brutality and blindness of British policy in Ireland; the proximity of France and Germany did not create neighborliness; nor have the Turks been noted for their kindness toward the Armenians, who live close by.

It is worth remembering that the first act of aggression that was recorded in the Western World was the slaying of one brother by another. Cain and Abel lived less than a stone's throw from each other; and so a stone was thrown.

Rapid transportation and communication will not automatically bind the world into brotherhood. They simply make it easier to be hostile at long range.

Human beings are tied together by ideas and feelings, not by geography. The bitterest battles have been fought between brothers — between the Yorkists and Lancastrians in England's War of the Roses, between the Blues and the Grays in America's Civil War.

It is what I call "scientific sentimentality" to believe that as modern technology makes the world grow smaller, our spirits will somehow grow larger. If we (as nations and as individuals) are motivated by fear and hate, then the closer together we are brought, the more fiercely will we bristle at one another.

This is not a plea for "isolationism" which is impossible today, even if it were desirable. But it is a caution that mere proximity is not a force for peace, and has never been.

The only force for peace lies in the heart and in the mind — that is to say, in love and in reason, not as vague Sunday sentiments, but realistically translated into the behavior of our governments.

How to accomplish this is the only significant task facing mankind; but while there are pressure groups to promote everything from highways to low taxes, there is no concerted effort by the public to comprehend and to attack the one problem whose solution will determine whether we survive or perish as a race.

7

OF WORDS
AND PHRASES

Our Language Has Become Fuzzier

IN NUMEROUS STORIES and headlines, the Starved Rock killer has been referred to as a "fiend." In other stories of crimes by juveniles, the boys have been called "toughs" or "hoodlums." But the Starved Rock murderer is not a "fiend." He is a psychopath and a moron. The boys are not "toughs." They are weak. If we are to call them anything idiomatic, "weaks" is the proper word.

This nomenclature is more important than you may think. What we call these people helps determine what they think of themselves. Many boys are out to get a reputation as "tough." In jail they read their publicity avidly. Their pathetic egos are willing to put up with any punishment so long as they can feel important.

Newspapers, which should be most aware of the power of words, often seem the most insensitive to them. Instead of seeking the precise word, they reach for the easy, the dramatic, the lurid word.

Violent criminals, we know, have weak, twisted and unintelligent personalities. They lack the strength to cope with the realistic conditions of life, they are unsure of their own manhood, and they are "acting out" a fantasy of childhood. Most so-called "sex fiends" are actually impotent. These psychopaths thrive on publicity which describes them with fear and horror. They desperately need a "rep," and the worse the rep the better they feel about it. Each wants to be called a "desperado," when he is really just a "thief."

Such thwarted personalities should be described accurately and clinically, not with melodramatic shock. They should be objects of pity or contempt, not symbols of courage, daring and diabolic power. A skinny, pimply youth of seventeen who feels infinitely vulnerable without a gun in his hand will swagger and sneer in the lockup if he reads of himself as a "menace" or, better still, as a "monster."

We laugh at the Victorians' odd use of words, and yet we are less realistic in many areas than they were. A "cad," after all, described a certain type of man; what do we have to take its place? An unprincipled womanizer used to be called a "libertine"; today we call him a "playboy" or a "Lothario." The image he has of himself is much easier to live with than it used to be.

Language has become fuzzier as our values have become diffused. The word "celebrity" nowadays covers everybody from Jonas Salk to Caryl Chessman — and insecure boys don't much care which kind of "celebrity" they achieve, so long as the headline gratifies their cancerous egos.

Words Get Tired, but Not Retired

THE VOCABULARY of English — and, indeed, of every language in the modern world is increasing enormously each decade. There are thousands of brand-new words in use since I was a boy.

But the old words, at the same time, do not get retired, no matter how tired they may become. We seem to have great difficulty in finding new and meaningful substitutes for words that have entirely lost their impact or precision.

Take, for example, the word "spiritual." It comes from the Latin word meaning "breath," and is akin to the Greek "pneuma," which means the same. The Holy Spirit in the Bible is the breath of life, the vivifying principle of existence.

Yet how weak and flaccid a word this has become over the centuries. And what different connotations it has on different lips and pens. It is used to mean "the supernatural," or "opposed to the material," or "vaguely pious," or "inspirational," or "pertaining to the soul and its afterlife," or a dozen other misty and ill-defined usages.

It is often a term used as a substitute for thought — in funeral orations, political speeches, holiday editorials, and too many sermons.

Yet what are we do? A writer cannot embark upon a lengthy and precise definition of his meaning of the word each time he uses it any more than a philosopher can redefine our nearly meaningless use of "happiness" in public speech or a political scientist can pin down the elusive essence of "liberty."

The birth rate of words is much higher than the mortality rate. We surely need a new word for "spiritual" — one

that will not have all the connotations of spookiness and super-
stition and sentimentality. In all the new words at our command, we have not devised one to take its place.

Language can be roughly divided into working words and
show words. "Spiritual" is a show word, which does not pull
its weight, but actually acts as a drag on thought. It does
not stimulate; it lulls. It does not express; it merely sounds.
What a fate to have overtaken a concept as vast and significant as "breath of life."

Our most important acts and attitudes originate in the
realm of the spirit, and it is there we must look for any basic
and lasting changes in our relationships to one another. But
the word itself has as many diverse and perverse meanings as
"love," and has become just as diffused and weakened in its
effects. Its breath of life has nearly departed.

There's Poetry in Everyday Talk

A FRIEND WAS telling us how he tried to explain the clock to
his smallest son. "Here are the hours, here are the minutes, and
here are the seconds."

The little boy pondered the clock for a moment, and then
asked in puzzlement, "But where are the jiffies?"

A sensible and logical question. We have become so used to
idiomatic language that we scarcely think how confusing it
must be to the literal mind of a child.

Living with a small child makes one constantly aware of
the metaphors we use in everyday speech. If you mention "a
stab in the back," he wants to know what you were stabbed
with; if you refer to a "queer kettle of fish," he wants to see
both the kettle and the fish.

People who pride themselves on realistic "down-to-earth" speech simply don't realize how their everyday expressions are shot through with poetry and metaphor, with tags from Shakespeare and Milton and the Bible. Without these imaginative springboards, we would be reduced to grunts and squeaks.

The most factual people in the English-speaking world every day use such expressions as "in my mind's eye," "more in sorrow than in anger," "the primrose path," "the milk of human kindness," and dozens of others — wholly unaware that such phrases did not exist until Shakespeare invented them for his plays.

And the most pious atheist daily makes use of scores of poetic idioms from the King James Bible — "feet of clay," "all things to all men," "filthy lucre," "a drop in the bucket," "a fly in the ointment," "a voice in the wilderness," "a wolf in sheep's clothing," "the blind leading the blind" — I could fill a whole page of newsprint with similar quotations.

But the strange power of metaphorical language is such that it soon ceases to be "quotation" and becomes an everyday part of speech. This is why professional writers try to avoid such phrases as much as possible — for they want to devise their own metaphors that are fresh and stimulating to the reader.

Nobody can speak "literal" English, which has no force and no grace. Molière's comic character was surprised to learn he had been speaking "prose" all his life — we may be equally surprised to learn we have been speaking poetry.

No Wonder Our Kids Can't Read

A READER IN AKRON sends me a letter she has received from a firm of educational publishers, replying to her complaint about a children's book her daughter is reading in second grade.

The mother objected to the use of "can" for "may" in the conversation used in the text, and wanted to know why an educational book should inflict this error upon small children. The answer is most illuminating:

> Our writers and editors think it advisable to observe, throughout the Basic Readers, the normal patterns of everyday speech. Particularly when a child is first mastering the reading process, they feel that the words he finds in print should be familiar and follow patterns of his daily conversation . . .
>
> It has been the observation of grammarians for a long time that in cultivated English "can" has been replacing "may" . . . If our primary grade books use only "may," we feel the children would get only an artificial usage of the word and most of the pupils would eventually use "can" in spite of the textbook.
>
> Of course, these questions have different aspects at high school level. There, one can teach students how our language has developed, and can discuss with them what standard of usage they wish to adopt.

Here in a few concise paragraphs, are summed up all the vices of so-called "progressive" education. The word "may" is to be junked, because most children incorrectly use "can." The aim of the book is to make the children feel at home with their lack of grammar, rather than teaching them the important distinction between these two words.

Then, after the children have been speaking ungrammatically for a dozen years, they will be told the difference, and asked to vote on the way they care to speak English!

Of course words and usages change, but if we use "can" in all cases where "may" is correct, how then do we distinguish between the two? If a child asks "Can I climb that fence?" is he asking for permission or for a vote of confidence in his ability? True communication breaks down when words are used so sloppily.

According to the editor of the book company, if children customarily use "can" for "may" and "ain't" for "isn't" and "would of" for "would have," we should go along with these barbarisms until they have become such settled habits that the child is condemned to perpetual illiteracy. This is a doctrine of "democracy" in its most debased and perverted form.

Little wonder that our children cannot read, write or speak like cultivated human beings, when even "educational" publishers pander to the soft corruption of the language.

Language Is Too Rich to Cheapen

WHAT SCHOLARS CALL (after taking a deep breath) the "pejoration" of language is taking place all around us at a frightening rate. Pejoration means "to make worse."

How are we making our language worse? By cheapening and debasing words, so that they no longer mean what they once did, and still should. Like "divine," which once referred to God, and now may mean anything from a new hat to a cocktail.

Last week I saw an ad for an airline, featuring a large picture of the pilot, with the bold caption: "Jet-Power Missionary." Now a missionary means a person sent to propagate a religious mission, and not an employee who flies a commercial plane around the world.

Another pejorative word is "crucial." A sports story yesterday said: "The Milwaukee Braves' infield faces a crucial test this spring." But "crucial" means "having the form of a cross." It refers to a supreme trial or final choice, such as Jesus' agony upon the cross. It has nothing to do with a baseball team, or any such trivial matters.

I object to this debasement, not because I am a purist about language, but because it robs us of essential words, and deadens their spiritual and emotional significance. If every decision is "crucial," how then can we describe the supreme trial of the cross? If every salesman is a "missionary," what then is a man who carries a religious message afield? If a spring hat is "divine," we shall have to find another phrase for "divine mercy."

In our own time, within the last fifty years, many psychological words have become pejorative — a fact which shocked and disturbed Sigmund Freud, who developed most of them. Today we use "repressed" and "frustrated" as "bad" words, but in the science of psychology they are merely neutral words. Everybody is somewhat repressed and frustrated; what is important is how we *handle* these repressions and frustrations.

Freud never suggested that the goal of psychiatric treatment is to "get rid of our repressions" in the sense that we should behave promiscuously or instinctively; as a highly moral man, he knew this would wreck the social order.

What he meant was *becoming conscious* of our buried

feelings, bringing them to light, and dealing with them realistically, rather than allowing them to control us by unconscious direction. The misinterpretations of Freud in the modern mind are a direct result of our loose, innaccurate, and vulgar handling of the tools of language.

How Time Makes Good Words Bad

I MENTIONED a few weeks ago that our language has more words for bad things than for good things, and therefore it is easier for us to be critical than to be complimentary. Since then I have been doing a little browsing in an old book, Trench's *Dictionary of Obsolete English*, and have made some surprising discoveries.

It turns out that hundreds of words we now use in a bad sense were originally used in a good sense, or at least neutrally. Over the centuries many of these words have drastically changed their meaning for the worse.

"Resent" and "retaliate," for instance, are perfect examples of this. As late as the eighteenth century, "resent" meant to have a feeling of what had been done to us — either a feeling of gratitude for the good, or enmity for the evil; now, of course, we only "resent" injuries to us.

Likewise, "retaliate" once meant returning benefits as well as wrongs; now we use the word solely to describe the return of an attack. Dryden wrote of the people "retaliating kindness to the King."

The word "censure" once designated both favorable and unfavorable judgments, but is now restricted to unfavorable ones. "Cunning" meant knowledge or skill, without any sense of deceit or crookedness. "Lust" was merely any desire, and not specifically a sexual passion. The Bible informs the Israelites that "the Lord had lust unto you and chose you."

In the same way, "lewd" just meant "unlearned," and came from the same root as "laity." It was not until much later that it acquired an obnoxious meaning.

"Officious" meant somebody prompt and kind in the duties of his office; today it means meddling in business that does not belong to you. (Incidentally, "meddle" originally meant "mix" or "mingle" and did not carry the implication of nosiness.)

"Indifferent" meant impartial and fair-minded; now it means uncaring. "Pompous" meant truly magnificent; now it means self-important and ostentatious. "Portly" meant dignified, and not "heavy," as it does now; Shakespeare says that Romeo "bears himself like a portly gentleman."

Among the many other words which have degenerated over the years are "aspersion," "smug," "uncouth," "conceited," "counterfeit," "gossip," "insolent," "libertine," "rascal," "plausible," "reduce," "remonstrate" — and hundreds more which once were neither resented nor censured.

A Lesson in English for Thurber

ALTHOUGH I HAVE considerable respect for James Thurber, both as a humorist and as a stylist in the English language, I felt that he was more cranky than correct in a recent *New Yorker* article about words.

Among other things, he objected to the growing habit of turning nouns into verbs (such as the cigarette slogan, "travels the smoke farther"), and made fun of the hostess who remarked, "We can sleep twenty people in this house in a pinch, but we can only eat twelve."

Actually, part of the great strength and suppleness of the English language is its capacity for turning nouns into verbs. Such common verbs as "awe," "cook," "silence," "time," and "worship" were all nouns to begin with — but they filled a real need, and were transformed into verbs.

English is one of the few languages, in fact, in which the same word in the same form may be all the different parts of speech. Take the word "round," which can perform five distinct operations.

It is a noun in "a round of the ladder"; an adjective in "a round table"; a verb in "the boat failed to round the turning point"; an adverb in "come round tomorrow"; and a preposition in "he walked round the house."

What Thurber fails to do is to distinguish between those words which can handily be turned into other parts of speech, and those which cannot. "The house sleeps twenty people," is a fine construction, and similar usage may be found in Shakespeare; while "we can eat only twelve" is just a silly way of replacing the perfectly good verb "feed."

Purists today object to the use of "contact" as a verb, in the phrase, "I'll contact him tomorrow." Admittedly, it grates on the ears of one sensitive to traditional English, but it is here to stay, not because of barbarism but because it is stronger and shorter than "get in touch with."

Language is as much abused by those who want to maintain all the rigid old forms as by those who have an utter disregard for style and sense. As in politics, both the reactionary and the radical are willing to sacrifice a living reality for some ideal in the past or in the future.

When Shakespeare wrote "such stuff as madmen tongue and brain not," he was taking two nouns and using them as verbs in place of "speak" and "understand." These two usages failed to take because they were unnecessary; but hundreds of others have passed into the language — would Thurber object to "elbowing your way through the crowd"? And why?

In Debate, Get Your Causes Straight

THE MAIN REASON that most arguments get nowhere lies in a five-letter word we frequently use and never think about. That word is "cause."

When we take part in a discussion on "Does Smoking Cause Cancer?" or "Do Slums Cause Crime?" we rarely define which kind of "causation" we are talking about.

Indeed, most persons don't even know the difference between *necessary* and *sufficient* cause; or among *predisposing*, *precipitating*, and *perpetuating* causes; of *unique* versus *convergent* causes; or the idea of *correlation*.

Does smoking "cause" lung cancer? The most we can say now is that there is a definite correlation. Excessive cigarette smoking seems to "precipitate" lung cancer, but the "predisposing" cause may very well be a certain kind of physical constitution that is inherited.

Do slums "cause" crime? Only in a limited sense, otherwise most slum dwellers would be criminals. Of two boys growing up in the slums, one may become a clergyman and the other a criminal. But there is no doubt that slums may "precipitate" and "perpetuate" crime if a boy is emotionally disturbed or subjected to intense family stresses.

Some causes are merely *necessary*, while others are *sufficient*. It is necessary to have gas in your car to go eighty miles an hour, but it is not sufficient — the motor has to be able to take it at that speed. It is necessary to drink liquor in order to be a drunk, but it is not a sufficient cause — which is a fallacy made by the prohibitionists.

Most causes are not *unique*, but *convergent*. What we popularly call a "nervous breakdown," for instance, is caused by a multiplicity of factors: perhaps a weak constitution, plus a bad life situation, plus any number of internal and external pressures. To say "this is the cause of that" is almost always a dangerous oversimplification.

The study of causation is woefully neglected in most academic disciplines, and especially in medicine, where each specialist tends to believe that an illness is caused solely by something in his department, and can be cured by his own special brand of therapy.

Political discussions end in futile bickering for the same reason: each contestant thinks that one factor is the cause of our trouble — inflation, high profits, wage increases, foreign spending — because it is easier to find a devil to blame than to analyze a situation that is compounded of a dozen complex and conflicting causes that defy any simple and swift solution.

You Need an Ear for Words to Write

WHILE READING the entries, as one of the judges in a collegiate writing contest, I was reminded of Mark Twain's annoyed remark that "the difference between the right word and the *almost* right word is the difference between lightning and the lightning bug."

Most persons — and this includes aspiring writers — simply fail to recognize that there are very few true synonyms in the language, no matter what the dictionary may insist .

The dictionary, for instance, gives "devour" as a synonym for "eat." But no woman would care to have it said of her that she "devoured her dinner," which sounds more like an animal than a human. (Indeed, German has "essen" for human eating, and "fressen" for animal eating.)

Again, a woman's eyes may "glow" with affection, but they do not "glitter," although the two words are roughly synonymous. Eyes "glitter" with greed or contempt, but they "glow" with love or compassion.

Distinguishing between two words that seem to mean the same, but have different colors and shapes and suggestions — that is essential to the art of writing, and also of speaking. The dictionary can tell you only what a word points to; it cannot tell you what it feels like.

An interesting example is the word "fat." The unabridged dictionary gives as synonyms: fleshy, plump, corpulent, obese, stocky, portly, tubby, and thick, among others.

Obviously, different people are fat in different ways — a woman may be "fleshy," but a man is "portly." "Obese" carries the connotation of a glandular sickness. "Stocky" involves size as well as shape. We speak of a "plump" or "tubby" baby, but nobody would call him "corpulent."

The same is true of hundreds of words which only superficially resemble one another. "Unspeakable" in the dictionary means the same as "unutterable" — but the former is always used to mean something base or vile, while the latter usually means some rapturous or divine thought or emotion.

The right word is as important to the writer as the right note to the composer or the right line to the painter. Hemingway's prose is so compelling (despite his defects of mind) precisely because he always knows the right word to capture the essence of a situation or the feel of a person. A writer needs an "ear" as much as a musician does.

And without this ear, he is lost and groping in a forest of words, where all the trees look much alike.

"Know"—A Word with a Defect

ALTHOUGH ENGLISH is an admirable language, rich and flexible, it has its own defects. Among the most serious is the double use of the word "know." There are two separate ways of "knowing" something, and our language does not ordinarily distinguish between them. The first way is to know a thing objectively, from the outside; the second way is to know it intimately, from the inside.

As the sociologist Dr. Robert Angell points out in his recent book, *Free Society and Moral Crisis*, different people know a cat in different ways:

"A physicist knows a cat from one viewpoint, a psychologist from another, a physiologist from a third, but the fond child who plays with the cat daily is really acquainted with it."

Both French and German have two words to describe these different ways of knowing: the Germans make a distinction between *wissen* and *kennen*; the French between *savoir* and *connaître*.

The first expression in each pair stands for objective knowledge; the second expression stands for intimate knowledge that includes a shared feeling.

And until we can go from the first kind of knowledge to the second, we really cannot cope effectively with any of the frictions that continually rise in society. As Dr. Angell suggests: "Thus it is that the other man's moral position has little appeal to us unless we see it from all sides as he does, unless we feel a little of the pull it has for him. We are not likely to appreciate his view in this way unless we have come to know him intimately."

As a prominent modern example, many businessmen who have entered government administration quickly find that their viewpoint about "waste" and "extravagance" and "interference" has changed under the impact of daily personal acquaintance with government problems. As participants, they "know" government quite differently from the "knowledge" as outsiders.

This is not to justify government waste, but merely to illuminate the reason men seem to change when they get *inside* a situation. Real knowledge, full knowledge, includes a sharing of feelings — which also explains why a neurotic person may "know" what is wrong with himself, but cannot help himself until he moves from *wissen* to *kennen*, from *savoir* to *connaître*, from the cat as a bundle of reflexes to the cat as a living organism and an object of love.

In Russia It's "It's Chinese to Me"

IN A CHARMING book on language, *Naming-Day in Eden*, the author amplifies a subject that has frequently fascinated me — how each nation attributes distasteful habits and acts to foreigners.

I have commented in the past on the fact that what is called "the French disease" in England is called "the English disease" in France. Likewise, to "take French leave," meaning to duck out without saying farewell, is known as "taking English leave" in France.

The French also used to call a creditor an Englishman (*un Anglais*). When he excused himself from entering a theater or café because he was in debt, a Parisian would say, "*Non, non! Je suis Angle.*" ("I'm broke, I'm in debt.")

When we "gyp" somebody, we are referring to gypsies,

who originally were thought to come from Egypt. And when someone speaks unintelligibly, we say, "It's Greek to me."

The Russians say "It's Chinese to me," the French say "That's Hebrew to me," the Germans say "That's Spanish to me," and the Poles say "I'm listening to a Turkish sermon."

"Each nation," remarks Noah Jacobs, "associates a host of miscellaneous vulgarities, vices, diseases and disagreeable traits with foreign countries."

The Japanese phrase for foreigners means "stinking of foreign hair." The Czechs call a Hungarian a "pimple." In Hungary and Austria, the cockroach is known as a "Swabian," in Poland as a "Prussian," and in Germany as a "Frenchman."

The French refer to a louse as a "Spaniard," and the Italians have at times denoted a privy as an "Englishman." (Does anyone know, by the way, how it came to be called a "john" in American colloquial speech?)

A sharper at cards is a "Greek" to the English and French. The Germans say "proud as a Spaniard," the Rumanians say "stubborn as a Bulgarian," and the Dutch say "boastful as a Frenchman."

In Czech, excessive drinking is "to drink like a Dutchman," but in Holland it is "to drink like a Pole." In Spain, "to work for the English" is to work for practically nothing, and in Yiddish "to repay in Turkish" is to do a dirty trick.

We have come a long way from naming-day in Eden to name-calling day in the capitals of the world.

Strength Can Betray Weakness

IN WRITING, as in life, when we try to add strength, we often betray weakness. The man who asks you to feel his muscles makes you suspect that he really doesn't believe in his virility.

Likewise, the writer who must emphasize every noun with an adjective makes us suspect that his nouns don't carry enough weight. An excessive display of adjectives, like an excessive flexing of muscles, usually indicates some inner doubt of strength.

What called this observation to mind was reading a newspaper bulletin about the "acute crisis" in the Middle East. In his charmingly instructive book, *Plain Words*, Sir Ernest Gowers deals skillfully with this phrase and others like it. He remarks:

> It has been wisely said that the adjective is the enemy of the noun. If we make a habit of saying "The true facts are these," we shall come under suspicion when we profess to tell merely "the facts." If a *crisis* is always *acute* and an *emergency* always *grave*, what is left for those words to do by themselves? If *active* constantly accompanies *consideration*, we shall think we are being fobbed off when we are promised bare consideration. If a *decision* is always qualified by *definite*, a decision by itself becomes a poor filleted thing. If *conditions* are customarily described as *prerequisite* or *essential*, we shall doubt whether a *condition* without an adjective is really a condition at all. If a part is always an *integral part*, there is nothing left for a mere part except to be a spare part.

Adjectives are useful in making meanings more precise; but they tend to weaken the whole effect when used to make meanings more emphatic. The same may be said of adverbs: "I love you" can be a profound and simple statement of fact; "I really love you" introduces an element of doubt. Instead of fortifying "love," it calls it into question.

It is invariably the mark of the poor or inexperienced writer that he seeks to bolster his nouns and verbs, which are the working words of the language. He needs to be reminded that the most powerful and moving verse in the New Testament consists of only two unadorned words: "Jesus wept."

Getting a Look at Two-Faced Words

MICHAEL WAS ANNOYING his young sister, and when I spoke harshly to him, he began bending down and peering under the chairs and tables. "What are you doing?" I asked him.

He looked up at me and grinned. "I'm looking for your temper," he said, "you've lost it."

In such ways do the clear minds of children reveal to us the inconsistencies of speech. Michael didn't know it, but he was analyzing what philologists call "Janus words" — words that face two different ways at once.

Obviously, when we "lose" our temper, we are really gaining it. Children have logical minds, and grammar is illogical — which is why children so often think that adults say silly and contradictory things.

In a book I recommended recently, *Naming-Day in Eden* (which is a both scholarly and charming study of language), Noah Jacobs points out that every language is filled with these Janus words: "One can run fast or stand fast; a fast color does not run at all; fast women are loose; loose is equivalent to unloose, bend to unbend, ravel to unravel and shameful to shameless; to weather is to suffer wear or to resist wear; to be mistaken is to make a mistake or be the victim of one . . ."

In French, he continues, *se marrer* is both to be bored and enjoy oneself; the German *sperren* is both to open and to close; the Greek *skhole* is both leisure and the work which is the result of leisure; the Hebrew *bara* means both to create and to destroy; the Chinese *louan* is both to govern well and to make a disturbance.

As a boy, I wondered about trucks that said "flammable" and couldn't understand how this meant the same as "inflammable." Likewise, "invaluable" means worth nothing and beyond all worth.

Psychologists suggest that all languages contain opposites in the same word (*personne* in French means "nobody" and "a person") because of the element of paradox in the human mind. Such contradictory feelings as love and hate coexist in our unconscious, and our speech tends to reveal these deep clashes of feeling.

Actually, I *found* my temper when I rebuked Michael, and he shrewdly knew it. Janus words can fool grownups into believing the opposite, but the child's grasp of reality goes far beyond language.

"To and Fro" from "Hem and Haw"

A FEW WEEKS AGO I mentioned the phrase "hem and haw" as a marvelously concise description of a certain type of speaking. Afterwards, it occurred to me that neither of these fine little words is used anywhere in the language except as part of that phrase.

Then I began thinking about the Lost Little Words in the English language — words that have been retained in some phrase or proverb or idiom, but which otherwise are not put to use.

For instance, in "hue and cry," the "hue" has disappeared from ordinary speech. It has become what philologists call a "fossil" word.

Likewise, the "file" in "rank and file"; the "whit" in "not a whit"; the "poke" in "a pig in a poke"; the "bay" in "at bay"; and the "loggerheads" in "at loggerheads."

No one knows why these short and useful words have dropped out of everyday speech, except for one special phrase. Then there are also "spick and span" and "tit for tat," containing words that have become meaningless by themselves, even though the phrases themselves are in daily use.

Then, too, there are many archaic and poetic words that no longer cross our lips, except in special idioms that have somehow retained their vitality — such as "*hither* and *thither*," "to and *fro*," "might and *main*," "*rack* and ruin," "*kith* and *kin*," "one *fell* swoop," "on one's *mettle*."

Who can say why "fell," which is a fine adjective, has fallen out of favor? Or why the word "mettle" is no longer a part of our verbal currency? Or who voted "rack" out of linguistic office?

The rich pudding of Shakespeare's plays is filled with thousands of such raisins; and one reason his poetry seems so "difficult" to the modern eye and ear is that he was the master of idiom, utilizing every scrap of phrase he had heard or picked up through his voluminous reading in medieval literature.

He also, of course, coined many phrases of his own, which have passed into the language so completely that we no longer recognize them as "quotations." But the real tragedy of Shakespeare's plays is that in another century they may be unreadable without a "translation" into modern English — so swiftly does our language change its forms and fashions.

There is no logic in language, which only proves that language came before logic — and indicates, perhaps, why words so often confuse a situation instead of clarifying it.

Syd Adores These Divine Words

A SHORT DICTIONARY OF WORD CHANGES:

"Divine" — once meant pertaining to God; religious; holy; proceeding from a deity; now means lovely, cute, charming, attractive, such as "What a divine hat!" and "A perfectly divine luncheon!"

"Fabulous" — once meant fictitious, as in a fable; exaggerated and untrue; not real; now means extraordinary, better than the best, and buy it, such as "Fabulous low price!" and "Fabulous home for sale."

"Adore" — once meant to worship or honor a supernatural being; to regard with reverent admiration; now means like, enjoy, am pleased with, such as "I adore going to the circus" and "An adorable petticoat."

"Passion" — once meant an enduring pain or the suffering of a martyr, from the Latin *passus*, to suffer; now it means what a high school girl feels for a high school boy after their first date; after the second date, it becomes a "grand passion."

"Creative" — once meant producing a work of thought or imagination, especially a work of art; now it often means trivial rearranging or elaborating, such as "creative interior decorating" and "a new hair creation."

"Personality" — once meant the distinctive inner characteristics of a person; the quality of being individual; now it means the obvious social flair, such as "a smile with a lot of personality," and "a fine outgoing personality."

"Enterprise" — once meant an undertaking which involves courage, energy and daring to try the difficult or untried; now it means any business which attempts to make the most profit for the smallest risk.

"Democracy" — once meant (to Jefferson and his colleagues) a system of government in which all the people would be encouraged to rise to the highest level of taste and judgment; now it means a system in which all are expected to sink to the lowest level of taste and judgment; and those who refuse to sink are labeled "undemocratic."

"Enthusiasm" — once meant to be divinely inspired or possessed; to have a zeal for goodness; now it means a "passion" for football or coin collecting or breeding Pomeranians.

"Profession" — once meant a calling of high seriousness, in which the practitioner took a solemn vow to maintain standards of truth and fairness above self-interest; now it means any occupation that is guided by self-interest rather than duty, such as "a professional hockey player" or a "professional bartender."

8

PURELY PERSONAL
PREJUDICES

ONE OF THE rarely considered advantages of growing old is the freedom to tell the absolute truth about anything to anybody; and it is distressing that so few old persons take advantage of this liberty.

*

Next to being insincere, the most exhausting thing in life is being suspicious; the pinched look of the suspicious person comes from emotional fatigue.

*

The best one-word critique of a new book I have heard was expressed by a friend of mine some time ago: "Underwhelming."

*

All incomplete information is, in a sense, false information —for unless we know how it fits into a total pattern, the isolated fact permits us to manipulate it dishonestly for our own partial purposes.

*

A great artist who breaks the rules of his craft has the same privilege as a general who returns a salute sloppily or negligently; it is only the second lieutenants, in any field, who must smartly observe the forms. What I resent in the arts, however, is so many second lieutenants behaving like generals.

*

One way of discovering a man's virtues is by observing his faults: they conform to the same structure of personality, as concavity and convexity belong together.

*

The only truly honest answer most of us should make when asked the common question: "How are you doing?" is "Better than I deserve." (For most of us, this is the only truly religious answer as well.)

*

Being in debt is the worst form of slavery; the ancient slave at least was assured of a place to sleep and enough to eat, but indebtedness beyond normal capacity removes even this security.

*

It may be true that "he travels the fastest who travels alone" — but that kind of trip leaves the traveler right back where he started from, for all achievement without love is circular and self-consuming.

Most revolutions quickly become corrupt and repressive because the very qualities that make men successful revolutionaries are the ones that make them poor executives — the man who can overthrow is not customarily the man who can stabilize.

*

The love of life is not something rational, or even justifiable; it is some spontaneous sense deep in the core of being, and when this sense is lacking or stunted (as in suicidally inclined persons), no logic or argument can awaken it.

*

The same man who discusses his simple tasks as if they were profound also discusses profound matters as if they were simple; he will take an hour to tell you how involved his work is, and then dismiss the knottiest problem in moral philosophy with a bromidic phrase.

*

A personal gift is a sign of warm concern, but a "personalized" gift is just a vulgar piece of showmanship.

*

It is easier for us to confess our sins than our faults; we can be slyly proud of the former, but are only ashamed of the latter — as, for instance, a man may admit he got offensively drunk last night, but will not add that he did so because he felt insecure and inferior.

*

Righteousness is the strongest shield against temptation, but most people settle for cowardice; they are good out of weakness, not out of strength.

Although it has long been a favorite phrase of fiction writers, I have yet to see a person in real life "gnash" his teeth.

*

An ordinary person who boasts of his illustrious ancestors fails to see that he is merely emphasizing the vast difference between them and him. Why call attention to the decadence of a family tree?

*

"Survival of the fittest" does not mean, nor did Darwin mean it to mean, survival of the strongest; often it means survival of the wisest or most tender — for how could human beings have survived and developed unless wisdom and love were passed down from generation to generation?

*

Audiences at an erudite talk are usually divided into those who think the speech is profound because they don't understand it, and those who think the speech is nonsense because they don't understand it; both attitudes, of course, being equally ridiculous.

*

There is nothing to be proud of in speaking the truth; even the Devil speaks the truth, when it serves his purpose to do so; the only truth-telling we have a right to be proud of is the painful kind.

*

When we are younger, we think marriages are divided into two kinds — bad and good; as we grow older, we learn that marriages are indeed divided into two kinds — bad and difficult; for even the "good" marriages are difficult, as young people are never told until too late.

*

I can understand a happy father who wants his son to grow up like himself, in the same sort of setting and vocation; but I fail to understand the countless fathers who want their sons to follow in their footsteps when their footsteps have brought the fathers themselves no real gratification in their personal lives.

*

Women who refer to themselves jocularly as "gals" are simply stressing the obvious fact that they are no longer girls.

*

Most of us are afflicted with what the medical textbooks call "logolalia" — the involuntary repetition of phrases ("you know what I mean") which blemish our conversation as much as if we stuttered.

*

The most dangerous thing about a beautiful woman is that it takes a long time for a man to discover she may have no sense of humor — which is the only characteristic that redeems beauty from dullness.

*

If you are going to take an injury, swallow it whole, like a bitter pill, and don't chew on it — for then you are twice injured: by the injury and by yourself.

There is no greater contradiction of terms in the whole language than a "friendly divorce," which is almost as monstrously ironic as "civilized warfare."

*

It is wrong to do only the things we do well, for this makes us insufferably smug; a man who excels at something should also do something else at which he is a duffer — as a way of curbing his pride and bringing himself down to earth again as a member of common humanity.

*

When a man says, "Let me double-check that for you," he usually means that he hasn't even single-checked it yet.

*

Nothing is easier than to be kind to strangers; this is the least taxing and least expensive of benevolences; but to be kind to those who rub up against us every day — this is the real difficulty.

*

For every one person who is bored with his surroundings, there are a thousand who are bored with themselves, because they have not planted enough foliage in the landscape of their personality.

*

Most people prefer being told what to do, because the compulsion to behave in a certain manner frees them from the painful embarrassment of choice.

There is only one mentally sick patient who cannot be cured: the one who believes himself to be in complete health.

*

We can all see how easily a child of three or four picks up a foreign language without ever being formally taught; yet we persist in being amazed that a child of the same age picks up our attitudes and expressions without being taught — and retains these longer than any of his formal education.

*

Only the thinnest line divides the righteous from the self-righteous; the pure from the priggish; the holy from the holier-than-thou; the virtuous from the repressed — and only God knows where the line is drawn.

*

Excessive grief is a kind of cowardice: the moral unwilling-ness to face the fact that nothing ultimately belongs to us, that we will leave the world as naked as we entered it.

*

More men remain little boys than women remain little girls, for mothers tend to cripple their sons by coddling them, but are more objective about their daughters.

*

To have entertained a great number of differing opinions in the past is usually the sign of a strong and flexible mind; while the person whose opinions have not altered since ado-lescence is often a victim of weakness rather than resoluteness. Final opinions should be *arrived at* rather than *inherited*.

The capitalist who insists that economic factors are the principal and determining motives in human history is a captive of Marxist philosophy, however much he may consider himself an anti-Marxist.

*

What most people ask of religion is that it permit them to live comfortably with their follies; for this they are willing to pay the price of an occasional scolding in a sermon and the pleasant penance of a collection plate.

*

The truest generosity is to give recognition to those who have not yet attained popularity, which is rarely done; for instance, the Nobel Prizes were originally designed to encourage gifted young men, but they have largely degenerated into rewards for older men who have already demonstrated their talents.

*

Goethe was right in asserting that "you can't get rid of what is part of you, even if you throw it away," but he was remiss in failing to add that you can *subdue* it to a better part of you. Psychotherapy does not mean "changing" as much as it means "controlling."

*

There is no delusion more fatal, no folly more profound, than a man's belief that he can kick and gouge and scheme his way to the top — and then afford the luxury of being a good person; for no consequence is more certain than that we *become* what we *do*.

A friend is someone who persists in liking us despite our irritating virtues.

*

One of the most effective ways of absorbing knowledge is to remain steadfastly ignorant of things that are not worth knowing; the mind has only so much room and the more bric-à-brac it takes in, the less space remains for the basic furniture of wisdom. (This is why persons with a great deal of information so often have a minimum of sense.)

*

It takes a sort of bittersweet maturity to accept the fact that we are not nearly as important to anybody as we think we are: I have seen widows desolated by the death of a good husband, and remarried a year later, with all appearance of happiness; when we die, the waters of existence close over our heads with scarcely a ripple.

*

The easiest marriages are those between two persons who are selfish in the same way, and form a common front against the world. What we think of as a "successful" marriage is often just an interlocking of similar egotisms.

*

Literature is not, and can never be, "realistic"; in life, a bore is a person we want to run away from; but in literature, some of the most delightful characters ever drawn have been monumental bores. If an author "realistically" portrayed a bore, we would throw the book down after a few pages.

Ten descriptive words about persons that no good professional writer would ever use, because they are invariably the mark of the amateur, are: *breadwinner, socialite, tycoon, scion, tyke, highbrow, homemaker, sleuth, sawbones,* and *thespian.*

*

Most people secretly believe that poverty is a disease, like some physical ailment; and they try to stay away from the unfortunate, as if failure were "catching."

*

"Semi-classical" music is for people who are ashamed to enjoy popular music, and too shallow to take an interest in serious music. And, like most hybrids, "semi-classical" combines the worst elements of both: the cheapness of popular music, without its vitality, and the pretentiousness of serious music, without its profundity.

*

In the history of ideas, the three most influential and widely known names of the last hundred years are Marx, Einstein and Freud; yet not one person in a thousand can accurately describe what any of them said.

*

Those obsessed with health are not healthy: the first requisite of good health is a certain calculated carelessness about oneself.

*

In language clarity is everything — but it must be the clarity that separates ideas from the passions surrounding them, not the false clarity that offers simple passions as a *substitute* for complex ideas.

*

The disguises some men adopt tell us more about them than the simple candor of others.

*

The most powerful combination of emotions in the world is not called out by any grand cosmic events that are found in novels or in history books — but merely by a parent gazing down upon a sleeping child.

*

The layman today is overexposed to medical knowledge, which only makes him jittery; for even a medical student feels he is coming down with every new disease he learns about in the textbooks.

*

It is a recurrent paradox in history that the weak eventually always overcome the strong; for the basic weakness in strength is that it pushes itself too far and collapses from overambition.

*

If we do not provide the young with good models they can believe in, it must be expected that they will seek bad models; for the most pressing need of an unformed personality is to find some model.

*

Why is it that persons who sleep badly always seem to be so perversely proud of the fact?

Nothing is commonly more dismal than the meeting of two witty minds in company; the result is more likely to be a clash of insults than a crackle of wits, for the one person a wise-cracker cannot stand is someone like himself.

*

Aren't there any tests except that "acid" one?

*

Persons who are addicted to using the phrase "a fun time" aren't generally having as much fun as they think they are. Joy is always diminished by consciousness of it.

*

Humility, as St. Thomas once observed, is a virtue that disappears the moment it confronts itself: when a man says, "I feel humility in this . . ." he is no longer feeling humility, but pride in his humbleness.

*

We dont't mind being wrong so much as we mind being *thought* wrong; it is not fear of error but fear of disapproval that makes for so much uncertainty and timidity in business.

*

No time is riper for the appearance of an original thinker than when all the experts agree on something; this is a sure sign that a revolution in thought is imminent.

*

It's curious that nobody can be quite as self-assertively dogmatic as the man who proclaims his unyielding opposition to all dogma.

The bad qualities we most hate in others are those we secretly suspect we share; practically nobody could get along with an identical twin, accidentally met.

*

Three adjoining ads in a magazine inform us about "Gravy Magic," "Color Magic," and "Motor Magic" — indicating that what we really want from our products is irrational, infantile and impossible.

*

From careful observation of other people, we can learn to avoid their mistakes; but no observation can prevent us from making our own mistakes — and the wise marriage counselor may be heading for divorce in his own way.

*

A truth that has to be proved can never sway men's emotions; we act by slogans, not by syllogisms.

*

Nobody knows himself until he has come face to face with calamity; it is only in crises that we learn our true identity; and many a man has gone through life thinking he was strong, when he was only safe.

*

The drunkard is the object of the world's scorn, but no one is contemptuous toward the glutton; yet the drunkard is commonly a nicer person than the glutton, merely weak where the other is greedy.

Love is a form of intelligence, its highest form; and the evidence is that stupid love usually crushes or deforms whatever it embraces, like an unintelligent parent who cripples a child with a burden of misdirected love.

*

A small town that has only "one good hotel" has no good hotels.

*

When we are young, we find no value in the views we disagree with; as we get older, if we grow in wisdom as well as years, we discover that even an opinion contrary to ours contains a vein of truth which we can usefully assimilate to our own views.

*

Wit and judgment are rarely allied in the same temperament — this is why witty persons so rarely know when to refrain from exercising their tongues.

*

Just as no person can smell his own breath, no person can detect his own bad taste; it is only years later that we can look back and realize how deficient it really was. This inherent blindness is what compels people to defend their taste more passionately than their principles.

*

We are more willing to forgive a man who does us a wrong than one who shows contempt for us; which is why the world has always been more tolerant toward the bully than toward the snob.

When something perplexes us, it arouses a kind of fear: and this fear, in turn, makes us angry; this is why people so often display an irrational anger toward whatever they call "obscure," and prefer a simplicity that really explains nothing.

*

Each class has its own peculiar follies that cannot be understood by an outsider; as William Feather observed: "The petty economies of the rich are just as amazing as the silly extravagances of the poor."

*

It is not true that necessity is the mother of invention; more important discoveries have been made by societies with leisure than by those which were necessitous.

*

Only shallow people think they really know themselves — and perhaps they do, if there is little to know.

*

When action becomes an end in itself, it is as pointless as words that are ends in themselves.

*

People who protect themselves from all hurts also insulate themselves from life; if we are not willing to run the risk of an emotional injury in our relations with others, we have relinquished any real possibility of joy in contact with others.

*

It is easy to be adult, but hard to be mature: to be adult is to know when to seize an opportunity; to be mature means to know when to give up an advantage, which requires a much different and deeper kind of wisdom.

*

Names have a way of coming to mean something much more crude and restricted than their originators meant them to be — the Stoics were not as stoical, the Epicureans as epicurean, or Machiavelli as Machiavellian, as we think they were today. In each case, we have taken one element in their philosophies and distorted it to represent the whole philosophy.

*

No acts are so mischievous in their social consequences as those performed by persons who want to *do* good without first *being* good; too often, a good act is a *substitute for*, not a *symptom of*, good will.

*

The woman who has contempt for the men who admire her is really expressing self-contempt, for she feels unworthy of admiration, and is scornful of those who are duped by her exterior. (This is why such women often end up by marrying brutal men.)

*

Every society has its own approved form of insanity; ours is called Adjustment, which is a circular social movement in which each one is adjusting to another one, and no one knows whom the first is adjusting to.

*

Genuine peace of mind comes only from the conviction that you can rely upon yourself to do the correct and courageous thing at the critical moment; and this is achieved only through habit, not by "faith" or by "fatalism."

*

The most fatiguing activity in the world is the drive to *seem* other than what you are; it is, finally, less exhausting to become what you want to be than to maintain this pretense.

*

It is true that the European has a keener sense of privacy than the American — but much of that is largely *suspicion*, which Americans have not as a whole inherited. What is regarded in Europe as our "excessive and vulgar familiarity" is usually just our wholesome childlike generosity of judgment toward strangers.

*

I can never wholly believe in the honesty of persons who keep diaries, for surely a part of their minds write with the knowledge that this intimate journal may some day become public.

*

It is true, as cynics shallowly suggest, that everybody is "selfish" at one level or another, for only saints can escape the self; but they neglect to point out that there is nothing wrong with being selfish, so long as we recognize (as we rarely do) that the highest interests of the self are most served by forgetting the self.

*

Most readers don't go through books; they let the books go through them; a valuable book has not really been read if its pages are not marked, its paragraphs underlined, its end papers written on, and its margins annotated. Keats's copy of Shakespeare is the prize example of a thoroughly read book.

*

The speaker calling for a "race of supermen" is usually narrow-shouldered, weak-chinned, bandy-legged and pock-marked; would Hitler have been so vehement if he had looked like Eric the Red?

*

Why is it that the people with "photographic" memories usually bring up such dull photographs for our conversational inspection?

*

When a man insists that the majority of people are fools, you may be sure he considers himself a member of the minority group.

*

Confession as such is not necessarily good for the soul unless it is followed by repentance; most people's confessions are like a dump truck getting rid of one load only to make room for the next.

*

Husbands who shoot their wives' lovers are acting on the fallacy that a grown woman can be "led astray" by another man; whereas, in almost all cases, the wayward wife was just waiting for anyone to come along. The individual objects of our passions are less important than we like to believe.

For every one person who gets ahead in the world by his own industry, there are a dozen who get ahead simply by the negligence of others.

*

I tend to be wary of a person who is quick to admit his little faults — the implication being that he is therefore free of large faults. Such candor is a subtle form of deception.

*

The past always looks better than it was, because the mind has a natural tendency to repress memories of pain and only retain memories of pleasure; this is why humanity keeps repeating the same painful mistakes.

*

A "prophet" is just an ancient crackpot who turned out to be less cracked than his smug contemporaries. Society, therefore, should learn to be kinder to its current crop of crackpots.

*

When a weak mind is shaken free from an old dogma, it soon adopts an opposite position that is equally rigid and dogmatic; it is more a psychological fact than a political fact that so many German Nazis became Communists — for the extremist mind cannot rest until it finds an iron cage for itself.

*

Much that passes for "modesty" comes from a supersensitive self that is unwilling to submit its inner features to the scrutiny of the world.

The art of living successfully consists of being able to hold two opposite ideas in tension at the same time: first, to make long-term plans as if we were going to live forever; and, second, to conduct ourselves daily as if we were going to die tomorrow.

*

Couples who quarrel quietly, with deadly politeness, never resolve their basic differences; for as long as they remain "reasonable," the deeply irrational nature of their conflict cannot come to light.

*

You can tell more about a person by what he laughs at than by what he cries at — our tears reveal what we would like to be, but our laughter reveals what we are.

*

It's an ironic result that the man who says "Nothing in the world is one hundred per cent black or white" only succeeds in making the world one hundred per cent gray — and what advantage is that in making value judgments?

*

People who don't understand why true tragedy requires a great and heroic figure should consider their reactions toward a man walking a tightrope stretched four inches above the ground, and one walking a tightrope stretched forty feet above the ground; it is the same rope, and the same skill required to walk it — but the drop from a height is what constitutes tragedy.

*

When a man takes revenge on an enemy, he "becomes even" with him; but when he refuses to take revenge, he becomes superior to him.

If you hear someone boast of having been "cured" by psychoanalysis, it's well to keep in mind that it isn't a cure unless the need to boast has been removed.

*

A truly successful personality knows how to overcome the past, use the present, and prepare for the future — but unless we can first surmount the past, we cannot effectively cope with either the present or the future.

*

As we grow older, we begin to see dimly that the events of our lives seem to arrange themselves in the image of our character; so that, in a sense, everyone receives the events he deserves.

*

Instinct is often wiser than reason: the woman who refuses a man and then accepts his proposal because of his persistence usually regrets it; her mind has given assent, but not her spirit.

*

The fundamental problem in life — as in business, in art, in politics, in most human activities — is how to be stable without becoming stagnant.

*

No other word in the entertainment world has been so abused lately as "festival," which is often just an excuse for three consecutive days of bad music at exorbitant prices.

*

It seems to be a psychological fact that the persons with the most exciting and vital personalities, who always generate activity around them, are at bottom the most lonesome of individuals, and the most inclined to depression and suicide when by themselves.

*

It's hard to know which is worse — to be snubbed by influential people when you are a nonentity, or to be bored by the same people when you are a celebrity.

*

To protect a child from the result of his folly (except in the case of clear and present danger) is to create an adult who will persist in committing follies with no thought of their consequences. Emotionally speaking, there is no salvation without suffering.

*

When a man makes a promise against his nature, I will bet on the nature against the promise.

*

Advising a troubled person to "see your minister or doctor" is ludicrous or futile in most cases — for neither pastors nor physicians are specially trained and equipped to handle basic emotional disturbances, nor do they have the time for intensive personal counseling.

*

A fisherman somehow always manages to make a nonfisherman feel unmanly.

*

Parents should live *for* their children, but not *through* them; the parents whose satisfactions are wholly reflections of their children's achievements are as much monsters as the parents who neglect their offspring. Nothing can deform a personality so much as the burden of a love that is utterly self-sacrificing.

*

We may look for a suitable mate but we will not find one until we first learn what to overlook.

*

The next time some poor devil of a defendant is being badgered on a witness stand, charitably keep in mind that no life could withstand the sharp scrutiny of two hours' cross-examination by a shrewd and well-paid lawyer.

*

In order to justify his behavior to himself, a thief has to believe that everybody steals, in one way or another; thus, we reshape the world to conform to the image we have of ourselves. (Even in the arts, for instance, many persons who cannot appreciate serious music believe that most music-lovers are cultural frauds.)

*

Events follow feelings more than we realize: to brood excessively about a possible failure is one of the surest ways of making it come true.

*

A teacher who tries to be "democratic" is as absurd as a ship's captain who lets his crew cast votes on the course and the destination.

Every unlikable person is, at bottom, disliked by himself; if you want to be liked, the solution is not to be sought in making yourself more attractive to others, but in learning to like and respect yourself in the proper way.

*

The man who is proud of knowing his own mind often doesn't know his own heart; and this is why his mind usually betrays him into dangerous absurdities.

*

When someone else is involved in an accident, we always suspect at least a bit of contributory negligence on his part; when we are involved, we call it a "bolt from the blue."

*

The woman who insists that she never flirts is employing her demureness as a subtle form of flirtation.

*

A nation that knows how to laugh at itself is stronger and has greater survival value than one that takes itself with ponderous solemnity; the weakness of Germany, since Bismarck's day, lay not in its arms but in its incapacity to make fun of its own institutions.

*

I know a convinced liberal, exuding love for humanity from every pore, who is also a misogynist — a man willing to give affection to Hottentots, Eskimos, and Kaffirs, yet withholding it from the 50 per cent of the human race who are women. (Naturally enough, he cannot see the contradiction in his position.)

Some persons seem to do good publicly so that they can build up a supply of "reputation credit" in order to do evil privately.

*

One of the paradoxes of economics is that it is often easier to live within a smaller income than within a larger one; once developed, a taste for luxuries tends to overwhelm the need for necessities.

*

Any man, given enough time and experience, can write sense; but only a genius can write nonsense that will live.

*

An executive who cannot tolerate small mistakes in his subordinates can never inspire them to great achievements; employees who are afraid of little lapses become paralyzed in the imagination.

*

The most important lesson of all is the one it is impossible to get across to young people — that the way into trouble is ridiculously easy, and the way out is inconceivably hard.

*

If we wait until all the facts are in, we shall never make an effective decision; like that brilliant historian, Lord Acton, who spent an entire lifetime collecting material for his "History of Human Liberty," and died without writing it.

*

When an idea cannot be expressed in a simple statement, it is usually a bad idea, or not an idea at all — merely a feeling.

The only way to attain one's ideals is to abandon one's illusions; but this is impossible unless we learn to separate the two.

*

There are moral imbeciles just as there are mental imbeciles; but while the latter are recognized as having an inborn defect and are put where they can do no harm, the former often acquire great power in the world — yet the man born with a deficient moral sense is a thousand times more dangerous than the mental defective.

*

Ancient faith in religion was never so fanatical as modern faith in science: most people today believe that science will eventually solve the basic problems of human existence, which is a wildly superstitious view of life.

*

When a man is out of power in an organization, he calls for "critical overhauling"; as soon as he takes leadership, he calls for "team play."

*

When we try to be better than we can, we often end up acting worse than we should; it is part of maturity to know the maximum emotional load we can bear, for the ligaments of the mind strain as easily as the ligaments of the back.

*

Skeptics like to jibe at religion by saying that if the frogs (for instance) could conceive of a God, they would make Him in the image of a frog — and certainly they would, for if the frogs were endowed with enough reason to be able to think of a God, they would rightly resemble Him.

*

Among the greatest of academic frauds are courses in "Creative Writing"; one can no more be taught how to write "creatively" than to love creatively; one can be taught only to write carefully, gracefully and economically — which has nothing to do with creative power.

*

Why does everyone, including the rich, pay a large sum by check much more lightheartedly than a smaller sum by cash?

*

Why do people who call a certain scene or experience "indescribable" then go on to describe it at length?

*

Why don't we realize that the defects we possess never make us look as ridiculous as the virtues we pretend to have?

*

Why do we call it "healthy rivalry" when we are besting our competitors, but "unfair competition" when they are besting us?

*

Why do we keep searching for more facts, when we generally don't know what to do with the information we already have?

Why are so many of us immoderately proud of the fact that we are poor in arithmetic?

*

Why do we dislike people most for the qualities they cannot help?

*

Why do most men buy hats that don't fit them, when they would never think of buying shoes that don't fit them?

*

Why do we assume that all people should get married when it's perfectly evident that a lot of married couples would be happier living alone?

*

Why is it that the people who say "Charity begins at home" so rarely take it beyond their front door?

*

Why do we complain when adults behave like children, and yet expect children to behave like adults?

*

Why do we generally tell a secret to the kind of person who is least likely to keep it?

*

Why don't reformers learn that glumness is not a necessary prerequisite of goodness?

Why do we sympathize with the person whose social insecurity makes him painfully shy in company, but despise the person whose social insecurity makes him brash in company?

*

Why is it that no one ever includes himself when he speaks of the "mass"?

*

Why are so few women capable of accepting a compliment gracefully?

*

Why is there something that looks so boyishly vulnerable about every man who has just had a new haircut?

*

When will we stop restricting the word "morality" to the matter of sex, and begin using it in its basic sense, as a right relation between human beings in all their interpersonal activities?

*

Our modern emphasis on personal hygiene makes it too easy for a man to confuse a clean shirt with a pure heart.

*

A person who complains that he has been "abandoned" in misfortune by his friends never had any friends; he is a victim of his own delusions, not of their duplicity.

*

Democracy does not mean the silly belief that the majority of the people are right in any given decision; but it does mean the passionate belief that the people have a right to be wrong, and that they have the capacity to correct their mistakes and amend their excesses, in a free and generous spirit which no other form of government can afford.

*

A society has already grown rotten when a person who simply speaks the truth is charged with "committing an indiscretion."

*

I don't know the best time for a honeymoon, but surely the worst time is just after a large, expensive and exhausting wedding; the gay and carefree honeymoon is largely a figment of the women's magazines fiction writers.

*

It is the paradox of civilization that nothing else is as faulty, as cumbersome, as rigid, as inconsistent, as unfair as the law; yet nothing else safeguards us from barbarism and tyranny.

*

The surest way to remain uneducated is to fear exposing one's ignorance; false pride is the greatest enemy of knowledge.

*

The true test of independent judgment is being able to dislike someone who admires us.

*

Women generally get their deepest conversational enjoyment by talking to one other woman at a time, while men much prefer talking with a group of men; this is why grown men rarely have a single "best friend" as most grown women do.

*

It is hard to tell which horrifies the average person most — to hear religion bitterly maligned, or to see it seriously practiced.

*

The guests who stay to the very end of a party are commonly not those who are enjoying themselves most, but those enjoying themselves least; they keep hoping that something exciting and romantic will turn up, and refuse to go lest this happen immediately after they have departed. The final guest at a party is usually the most neurotic.

*

The pathos in life is not that people have to suffer in order to grow, but that so many persist in suffering without growing.

*

When one partner in a dissolving marriage says to friends, "You have to choose which one of us you're going to see; you can't be friends of both," that just makes it easier to choose the other. A person who demands exclusive friendships isn't fit for society.

*

The greatest gift we can give a child is a sense of delight in being allowed to participate in the wonder of the universe, and a sense of proportion which acknowledges that the universe does not revolve around him. Without these balancing rods, children turn into prosy and petulant adults.

*

Positions of great responsibility and authority don't change men, as is commonly thought; they just make big men bigger and small men smaller. The history of the American Presidency is a superb running example.

*

A "clever person" is one who commits none of the minor blunders that are made by fools, but then goes on to perpetrate some crashing error that any fool could easily avoid.

*

I have never understood the smug retort, "I'm not in business for my health," since health — both physical and mental — should be the ultimate goal of all work.

*

In our youth, we are impressed with our singularity, with our striking (and often disturbing) differences from other people; as we get older the inescapable truth is borne upon us that we are dreadfully like everybody else, and what we mistook for individuality was mere egocentricity.

*

It is difficult to get a man to see both sides of a question when his income depends upon his seeing only one side of it.

*

Those who consciously search for "adventures" in life are defeating their own purpose; for, as Martin Buber astutely remarked: "He who aims at the experiencing of experience will necessarily miss the meaning, for he destroys the spontaneity of the engagement."

*

The infallible mark of a false patriot is that, though he professes to love his country, he does not seem to love many of his countrymen very much.

*

So long as "religion" remains a separate area of life, along with "business" and "politics" and other areas, it is largely meaningless; it is only when religion is not concerned with specifically religious acts, but penetrates into every area of activity that it deserves the high honor we pay it.

*

People who are fanatical about "saving for a rainy day" usually get so fixed in the habit, as an end in itself, that they are reluctant to use their savings even in the worst downpour.

*

Nobody thinks himself ill-bred; the ill-bred man calls himself "down-to-earth."

*

The atheist who seriously studies religion in order to attack it is closer to the spirit of God than the bovine believer who supports religion because it is comfortable, respectable, and offers consolation without thought. If God's greatest gift to man is reason, then refusing to exercise reason is the greatest impiety.

An employer who grants a raise slowly and grudgingly is stupid on two counts: first, if it isn't deserved, he shouldn't give it at all; and, second, if it is deserved, he should give it swiftly and cheerfully, or else he forfeits the gratitude and loyalty of the recipient, and the raise is psychologically wasted.

*

Any man who thinks he has lived up to his own ideal of himself had a very low ideal to begin with.

*

When most people blame "science" for something, they really mean "technology" — which is as silly as blaming the multiplication table because our arithmetic has turned out wrong.

*

The trouble with many profound books is that the reader has to have more learning than the author in order to know if the book is right or wrong; and if you have more learning, why bother to read the book?

*

An honest man never complains about the dishonesty of the world; he simply refuses to become a party to it; it is always the unsuccessful crook who rails against the successful ones.

*

If there were no suffering in the world, the arrogance of the human race would become intolerable; even as things stand, the people who haven't suffered much personally tend to be irritatingly smug about their good fortune.

*

When a man lies, it is to seize an advantage; when a woman lies, it is to avoid a difficulty — which I find a much more praiseworthy motive for telling an untruth.

*

All genuine thought is a dialogue between two voices within one's head; when it becomes a monologue, and only one voice is heard, then we have begun to approach a kind of insanity.

*

When the public enters one of its periodic fits of morality, it cannot be satisfied until it punishes a minority for doing openly what the majority does privately. (And this hypocrisy, by the way, explains why so many youngsters believe it is not a shame to do bad, but only to be discovered at it.)

*

In my experience, the men who are most bitter about "women" are really generalizing about one particular woman with whom they had the poor judgment to become involved.

*

Ninety per cent of our personal anxieties come from over-concern with what others will think of us — and we utterly fail to realize that others, like us, are too busy thinking of themselves to bother making much of an estimate of us.

*

It is far easier to learn something when you are ignorant than when you are wrong; just as the hardest crossword puzzle to solve is the one in which we have put a few wrong words, and will not erase them. Most adult education should consist of taking people from error back to ignorance, rather than trying to stuff them with knowledge at first.

*

There is nothing like getting a rare disease for finding out how prevalent it is.

*

No matter what the trouble may be, most bystanders advising a motorist how to get out of a muddy rut will shout: "Straighten your wheels!"

*

What many persons want is not to be happy but to be envied — and they will endure the most private misery so long as they feel that they are publicly enviable.

*

The chief tragedy of the human race is that the war approaching always seems necessary and "inevitable"; it is only twenty years later that it is seen as avoidable and futile. Is the mind perpetually condemned to live two steps behind the passions?

*

The real enemy of the arts is not the lowbrow — who cares nothing about them and is content to leave them alone — but the middlebrow, who is forever trying to debase them, to prettify them, to simplify them; in short, to bring them down to his level of comprehension, rather than making the effort to rise to theirs.

Perfectionists fail to understand that a man's capacities may make us respect him, but it is his foibles that make him loveable; and the person who rigidly represses all his foibles is always puzzled by the world's lack of cordiality.

*

There seems to be so much more evil than good in the world because evil is a short-term infection, while goodness is a long-term influence; thus, it is always easier to see the dramatic effects of evil than the lengthening consequences of goodness.

*

It is a sin to complain when nothing can be done; it is a sin not to complain when something can be done; therefore, all progress depends upon distinguishing between what can be done and what cannot be done. And this is the hardest task in life.

*

Consciousness of our charms makes us less charming: the child is endearing only so long as he is not aware that he is an endearing child.

*

It is one of the paradoxes of the sexes that the strongest man in the world may easily fall apart when his wife gets sick; while the weakest woman in the world often becomes strong when her husband gets sick. Illness tends to bring out the hidden fears in men, and the secret sources of strength in women.

Some people think that because they are clever they cannot be boring; but there is nobody quite so exhausting to listen to as a clever bore.

*

A person without honor thinks that all pride is false pride; this is how he justifies himself.

*

The chief difference between real love and its counterfeit is that in the former each party *wants* to give more than he gets, while in the latter each is *afraid* to give more than he gets. This is why genuine love is the rarest of all relationships.

*

Children never pick up the good habits from their play-mates, but only the bad ones; for the same reason that health is not catching, but disease is.

*

When a person prefaces a statement by saying humbly, "I may not know much about the subject, but . . ." you may be sure he is going to tell you a great deal more than he knows.

*

Many a young matron thinks that all she has to do is wear a sweater, a set of pearls, and speak as though she had marbles in her mouth in order to be considered superior and well-bred.

*

Excessive and compulsive traveling is the alcoholism of the rich, who seek to escape themselves by distance, just as the poor seek to escape themselves by drink.

Those who fear suffering suffer more through their fear than they would through suffering.

*

The only use some women have for their husbands is to flaunt them before unmarried women, as a trophy of no intrinsic value but merely as evidence that they have run the race and won.

*

When we are young we think we could solve the riddle of life if only we could learn the laws of cause and effect; as we grow older, however, we become increasingly uncertain as to what is cause and what is effect. This uncertainty is the beginning of wisdom.

*

What most people ask of religion is that it make them feel comfortable when they embrace its tenets, but that it refrain from making them feel uncomfortable when they violate its tenets.

*

Most history is just gossip that has grown old gracefully.

*

It's odd how the people who insist that you can't have absolute certainty make that statement with absolute certainty.

*

It is easier for most men to submit to a great evil than to suffer a slight vexation; and tyrants flourish by providing the masses with minor pleasures while destroying their major freedoms.

*

Some folks would rather profane their mothers' graves than admit they didn't have a "glorious" time on a vacation; as if having a bad time somehow reflects discredit on their capacity for enjoyment.

*

A woman isn't financially mature until she can refrain from buying an item she doesn't want simply because it has been reduced.

*

What the average business organization seems to be looking for today is a young man of thirty with twenty years of sound business experience.

*

It is the better part of wisdom to accept the inevitable; but it is the best part of wisdom to question what most people call the inevitable.

*

Some people can wipe out an error only by making another one; like a clumsy government that obliterates one bad law by enacting a second equally bad.

*

The most prevalent form of lunacy is given the name of "sanity" in a society; what most of us call "reasonable conduct" is a matter of statistics, not of sense.

A fact does not become a truth until people are willing to act upon it; the fact that war is now a losing proposition for everybody will not flower into an effective truth until we are prepared to make as many sacrifices for our children's future peace as for their present comforts.

*

A woman who tries desperately to keep her looks is sure to lose them more swiftly than a woman who is a little careless about them; grim intensity defeats its own purpose, in looks, in love, and in life generally.

*

There are three delusions that invariably mark the new or inexperienced husband — (a) he thinks he can win an argument by logic, (b) he thinks he can successfully keep a secret from his wife, and (c) he thinks that buying a present makes a woman forget a grievance.

*

The more self-consciously a prayer is said, the less meaningful it becomes; as St. Anthony observed, the perfect prayer is made unconsciously.

*

A "humanitarian" is too often a person who is willing to sacrifice the persons around him in the present for the sake of an abstraction called "mankind" in the future.

*

Since a man of sixty has spent about twenty years in bed, why doesn't he look more rested?

There is a law of diminishing returns in leisure as well as in productivity: the less one has to do, the less time one finds to do it in; which is why the most aimless dowagers are usually the most pressed for time.

*

No argument is harder to refute than a silent look of reproach.

*

We have conquered most of the contagious diseases of the body, but we have scarcely begun to combat the contagious diseases of the mind — bigotry, hate and panic — which have shattered more societies than all the viruses ever known to civilization.

*

The profound difference between the *moralist* and the *moralizer* is that the moralist wants himself to become more like the image of God, while the moralizer wants other people to become more like him.

*

Young women who are enticed into marriage by expensive gifts might do well to remember that the difference between a necklace and a noose is just a couple of inches.

*

A woman is able, eventually, to forgive a man for preferring another woman to her; what she is unable to forgive is a man who leaves her without this excuse; the most resentful ex-wives are those whose husbands fled to singleness, not to the "other woman."

Most opera singers are not musicians; their aim is to conquer the music rather than to interpret it; to amplify the notes they have been given to sing, rather than to subordinate their part to the composer's full intentions.

*

When a writer takes a deep breath and resumes with "in other words," I wish he had written the other words in the first place; why explain something if you must then explain the explanation?

*

The most explosive combination in the world consists of sincerity added to ignorance.

*

It's extraordinary how the same people who are so sensitive toward slights from others are so insensitive about the way others react to them; thus, those who most resent being rubbed are usually rubbing others the wrong way.

*

There is no merit in admitting one was wrong, unless one can admit it without wanting to take credit for being open-minded enough to change one's opinion.

*

Hearing a lie told about ourself is never so painful as hearing the truth; a lie merely fills us with healthy indignation; the truth can paralyze us with dismay.

*

Many friends have found they are not such good friends when they engage in a convivial test of skill — which begins amiably, but soon develops a sharp edge of antagonism beneath the bantering surface. Games tend to bring out both the best and the worst in human relationships.

*

It only seems that the world is getting worse because the facilities for making it worse are more available to more people.

*

The talent for recognizing and appreciating talent that is ahead of its own time is a rare and necessary thing; we have as great need of appreciators as we have of creators.

*

Self-possession is the most precious of all possessions: with it, we need little; without it, we can easily lose all.

*

I heard an ironic commentary on today's culinary skill, by a young married man who had just finished dinner at an older woman's home: "Madam, you cook better than my wife thaws."

*

Nobody is as dull as a man who reads a lot and remembers all of it.

*

It is a curious paradox of femininity that when a woman feels her worst she often looks her best; and, contrariwise, when she takes the greatest pains to look her best, she often turns out looking her worst.

When you desire the good opinion of people whose opinion you do not respect, it's a pretty sure indication that you don't have a good opinion of yourself.

*

The chief difference between dashing fiction about spies and real stories about spies is that in the latter the spies are usually misfits who couldn't make a living doing anything else; they are pathetic and disgruntled, rather than heroic.

*

After an actor has been performing in a successful play long enough, he begins to believe he wrote the lines.

*

A certain amount of monotony is essential to life, and those who always try to flee monotony cut themselves off from a life-giving force; it is the monotony of the sun rising every morning that makes variety possible.

*

There is a great difference between a man being *righteous* and a man being *right*; the truth of an idea has little to do with the character of the person who espouses it.

*

Most prayers are precisely the wrong kind — they invoke God to change His mind about our aims, whereas they should ask the strength to make us change our aims to conform to His will.

*

The parent who always prevents a child from acting up in public is more concerned with public opinion than with the needs of the child; and the price for this rigidity in public is the child's private resolution to even matters up when old enough to do so.

*

I could find it easier to believe in spiritualism and emanations from the afterworld if the shades of departed souls who are materialized at séances didn't seem such dull people and didn't say such silly things, such as "This is your Uncle Harry, and I feel fine." The flaw in "messages" from the beyond is not that they are supernatural, but that they are too prosaically natural. Heaven, after all, is not a resort hotel with rockers on the front porch for the old folks; if it is, it would be insufferably boring for an eternity.

*

Most of us take it as a compliment when an old friend tells us that we haven't changed a bit in twenty years; I would construe it as an insult, for I want my face and bearing to show some signs of the struggle for self-mastery over the years. A smooth porcelain face is a delight at twenty, but a rebuke at forty.

*

Why does modern man so often exhaust himself in pursuit of relaxation, while modern woman so often ages herself prematurely in pursuit of youth?

*

It is easier for most of us to follow a diet, or some other regimen, than to refrain from trying to impose it upon others.

Delinquency is not merely an act, but an attitude; for every one delinquent who actually steals a car, there are a hundred who are convinced that the family car is theirs by right — and this attitude contains the seed of the act.

*

The worst mistakes of judgment are made by people who believe that reason and the passions are opposites; reason does not exist to oppose the passions, but to mediate among them. The man who uses reason to repress his emotions will soon be as mad as the man who permits his emotions to override his reason.

*

Those booties dangling inside the windshields of automobiles must signify the mental age of the motorists who hung them there; I can't imagine what else they stand for.

*

Whenever an advertiser can't think of what else to say about a plain and cheap commodity, he describes it as "sturdy."

*

There must be something perversely pleasant about pain — else why do we persist in aggravating a sore tooth by continually exploring it with our tongue?

*

We would find it easier to respond to the call to make a sacrifice for the country if we didn't suspect that the ones who are making the call aren't making the sacrifice.

Men try to reduce largely for reasons of health; women largely for reasons of appearance; and this is why women are more successful in the effort — because the drive for admiration is stronger than the desire for physical well-being.

*

The most obnoxious affectation is the affectation of blunt candor when it is only malice masquerading as honesty.

*

Most writers are personally timid men; their literary boldness is a compensation for the fears they feel in their face-to-face contact with others.

*

People who are affected are not vain, but suffer from a haunting sense of inferiority; an affectation is a confession that you do not think your natural self is good enough to be displayed in public.

*

All genuine love comes from strength, and is a kind of surplus energy in living; false love comes from weakness, and tries to suck vitality out of its object. Most popular "romantic" songs, with their whining lyrics of self-pity, are embarrassing exhibitions of false love.

*

The rarest creature on earth is a fanatic with a sense of humor; fanatics repel us not by their passionate devotion to a cause but by their incapacity ever to laugh at themselves, which is a deadly flaw in the human animal.

I am convinced that the real reason women live longer than men is that they know how to accept illness with equanimity, whereas a man fights illness and makes himself worse by refusing to come to terms with his health. To women, illness is a fact; to men, a threat.

*

It seems to me short sighted to deplore those persons who marry "beneath them," for some persons can only feel comfortable in a permanent relationship with someone inferior to themselves; an equal or a superior would be too threatening.

*

It is useless to advise people not to worry, unless at the same time you can teach them how to think; worrying is often the only activity that saves them from blank despair.

*

An office manager who can be efficient without being obnoxious is worth his weight in vice-presidents.

*

The private religion of most persons — no matter what they may profess publicly — is that they will promise God not to be too bad if He will promise not to press them to be too good; they want to strike a bargain, not make a commitment.

*

Very attractive women, on the whole, seem to be more humorless than their plainer sisters; perhaps because a plainer woman has to develop a sense of humor as a compensatory device for dealing with men.

Many men attend classes in public speaking to become more eloquent; but it is a perpetual irony that more harm has been done to society by men who were eloquent than by men who were not.

*

People who try to avoid, evade, or push away their problems should recall the fine brief statement made by Robert Frost many years ago: "The best way out is always through."

*

It's a curious social order we live in where a family isn't considered a good credit risk unless it's got a heavy mortgage on the house, is paying monthly installments on an expensive car, and owes money to every department store in town. People who pay cash for everything and buy no more than they can pay for at the time can't borrow a nickel from anybody.

*

More girls get into trouble by wanting to be popular than by wanting to be promiscuous; much of what we call "sin" is simply the fear of lonesomeness.

*

It must be a self-evident truth that life is worth living; it cannot be proved; and therefore a person to whom it does not seem evident cannot be restrained from suicide by arguments, pleas or persuasion.

*

Everybody is "poor" compared with somebody else — and everybody makes the comparison: I have heard one of the ten

richest men in the country complain that he couldn't "afford"
to live as his late father did.

*

We warn an adventurous young man that "a rolling stone
gathers no moss," and then when he forsakes adventure and
grows successful and conservative, and is sitting in his club
chair, we call him an "old mossback."

*

A person who is "hard to know" is generally one who
doesn't know himself very well, and seems an enigma to others
simply because he has refused to confront his own real nature.

*

More lies are told because of laziness than because of ambition; inertia, not greed, is the greatest foe of truth.

*

Geniuses so often seem melancholy because they have come
to an early realization of how well busy fools do in the world.

*

A woman may, after the proper period of penitence has
been made, be content to forget and forgive a man for some
dereliction — but she will never forget that she has forgiven
him.

*

Middle age is so perplexing a time for most people because
it is the only time of life when we hear two voices calling us
distinctly: one voice says: "Why not?" and the other says,
"Why bother?"

The Trojan War was fought over shipping routes, and Helen only provided an excuse; every war has its Helen, although sometimes she is called "Independence," or "Glory," or "Honor," or "Self-Defense."

*

One of the most discouraging aspects of the human condition is that a stranger can know more about our deepest drives in a half hour of casual conversation than we know about ourselves in a lifetime.

*

Mothers tend to worry about their thin children, but it is the fat children who usually have most emotional problems.

*

A hero is often a man who is driven by the terrible fear that he may be thought a coward.

*

All that our present system of punishment does it to make the criminal promise himself to be more careful the next time, not more honest.

*

It's amazing and distressing how a wife who can't remember where she put her car keys a half hour ago can remember exactly the date and the condition her husband came home in late two years ago. A woman's memory may be less extensive than a man's, but it is a lot more intensive.

*

Newspapermen themselves make the worst and most reluctant people to interview: for they know a careless, or unconsciously malicious, interviewer can distort a personality in print; and the art of skillful interviewing is one of the highest (and rarest) of journalistic talents.

*

Those who do things for the sake of gratitude will always find the world ungrateful; it is only when we do not expect thanks that we can be pleased with the modicum we get.

*

No person can help you or understand you who has not suffered something of what you have suffered, who has not felt something of what you have felt; and therefore the thoughtless remark that "all psychiatrists are neurotic" is really an appreciation, although it is meant as a rebuke.

*

An astonishing number of brides devote greater thought to whether the wedding will go well than to whether the marriage will go well.

*

It is part of the perverseness of people to resent a substitute speaker, even when he is better than the one originally scheduled.

*

Historical novels bore me; biographical novels offend me; history and character are cheapened and flattened by being fictionalized, for nothing is more exciting — if well handled — than a real person and a real event.

No greater mistake is made by the average man than believing that peace is the absence of war: peace, like love, is a positive thing, and its chief enemy is indifference.

*

With some men, work is a vice and not a virtue — they drug themselves with work to avoid confronting themselves in the nakedness of their souls.

*

Whenever I begin to think there is some hope for the human race, I run across a man who puts catsup on eggs, and all seems lost again.

*

If we could keep in mind that all young children are in a foreign land, we might then be able to treat them with the forbearance we show émigrées who have not yet mastered our language, our customs and our prevailing hypocrisies.

*

I find the people who take too good care of their bodies as unappealing as those who take too good care of their purses; a touch of carelessness, both physically and financially, gives flair and flavor to a personality which otherwise might become sterile and self-absorbed.

*

One of the great differences between the amateur and the professional is that the former wants to *please* himself while the latter wants to *satisfy* himself.

The most superstitious men in the world are those who have turned materialism into a creed and think that everything can be explained by physical causes; they are simply the reverse of the fanatics who think that everything is explainable in spiritual terms.

*

The paradox of a democracy is that it is willing to risk its life for liberty — but doesn't know what to do with its liberty when it has been attained, except eat too much, work too hard, and play too fiercely.

*

Some people are so proud of their faults that they think a tender heel makes them an Achilles.

*

I prefer a woman who gracefully lies about her age than one who pertly tells you the truth and fully expects you to exclaim, "Why, I never would have thought it!"

*

Many a person who thinks he is "adjusted" is simply resigned.

*

It is a false analogy to believe that a person who writes "beautiful letters" therefore has the makings of a good writer; most professional writers, in point of fact, are wretched letter writers, and there is no necessary relationship between these two talents.

Most parents who can afford it want the "best school" for their children — never stopping to consider what will happen to the school if it doesn't insist on taking the best children. Placing a mediocre child in an excellent school does a disservice to both.

*

Juvenile delinquency will continue to increase so long as youngsters grow up in the cynical belief (too often justified) that the law has two measures — one for persons with influence, and one for persons without. This widespread discrepancy is democracy's greatest failure.

*

Morale is low in some companies because the top officials expect their junior executives to be on their toes and on their knees at the same time.

*

Everybody is a snob about something, whether he knows it or not; and perhaps the only unpardonable snobbery belongs to the person who thinks he is devoid of it, and looks down on all other snobs.

*

We often forget that hatred ties people together as well as love; how many rivals do we see who are locked together in a dance of hatred, each feeling a passion to equal or excel the other in hatred — and each becoming more like his enemy through this reciprocated passion?

A lot of pity is unnecessarily wasted on spinsters: many a woman who can't get a husband is much better off than the women who got the wrong ones.

*

A city slum, whatever its drawbacks, at least has a vitality of its own; it is the suburban slum which looks not only physically bleak but also spiritually deadening.

*

A man's intelligence may be measured almost exactly in inverse ratio to the length of time he is capable of holding a grudge.

*

Perhaps the basic flaw in the human condition can be grasped by the trivial but significant fact that it's always the other person's cigarette smoke at lunch that gets into our eyes — not our own.

*

Women who buy objects for the home as "conversation pieces" must be in pretty sad shape for interesting conversation.

*

When she tells you that she doesn't kiss "on the first date," you know that it isn't because she's moral but because she has a private timetable of liberties to be permitted — which is a kind of prudent immorality of its own.

*

Nothing makes me feel so ashamed of my good fortune as walking through an office building late at night and observing the old women on their hands and knees scrubbing the floors. (Granted, somebody has to do it, but in a sane society it would be the young, just starting out, and not the old, who have earned a little dignity.)

*

There are no *true* synonyms in any language; even "fall" and "autumn" have different auras to them — it is proper to speak of the "fall football schedule," but that nostalgic phrase, "autumn leaves," and that evocative song, "Autumn in New York," would lose their flavor if "fall" were used.

*

The man who is afraid of making a big mistake will never make a big success; more opportunities are lost by overpreciseness than through carelessness.

*

Real communication between friends consists not in saying a lot, but in being able to leave a lot unsaid, although mutually understood.

*

It's sad but true that while alcoholics are the best argument for abstinence, so many abstainers are equally effective arguments for a little drink now and then.

*

Tact, in a man, consists in knowing when to laugh; tact in a woman consists in knowing when not to cry.

*

The reason clever people so often do stupid things is that they are generally so busy talking that they never listen — all they hear is the sound of their own cleverness echoing back at them.

*

The most futile advice is that given by a father to a son: for no son ever really believes that his father felt in the past what the son is now feeling in the present.

*

Brainwashing is as old as creation; it began when the serpent persuaded Eve that she would be "expressing her own personality" by reaching for the forbidden fruit. This is still the main theme of all seductions.

*

The only thing worse than perpetual labor is a perpetual holiday.

*

The better part of valor is knowing how to save it for matters of principle, and not to dissipate it on mere vexations.

*

Life is the art of riding a horse backwards, without reins, and learning to fall off without being trampled. (And there would be fewer personal catastrophes if education placed less emphasis on the skill of riding, and more on the skill of falling.)

*

A lot of congregations need a missionary more than they need a clergyman; the hardest people to convert are those who confuse attendance with attention.

Nothing makes you feel so old as rereading a book you enjoyed twenty years ago and being embarrassed by its naïve exuberance.

*

I can forgive the person who makes snap judgments if he is willing to change them in a snap; but not the person who clings tenaciously to every first impression.

*

There is a tremendous difference between a man talking because he has something to say and a man talking because he has to say something.

*

The hardest art for a man to master — and still feel like a man, not a cad — is learning how to say goodbye gracefully to a woman he no longer cares to see.

*

What a supreme irony that all the nations of the world, on both sides of the curtain, can cooperate for eighteen months on the International Geophysical Year, in a joint effort to examine the universe we live in — while at the same time we cannot cooperate to prevent us from blowing ourselves into the next galaxy.

*

The man who marries "into a family" generally finds that his wife has never married out of it; eventually, he is contending against a clan, and not merely disputing with an individual.

There is no sight more repugnant to the male eye than that of a woman walking down the street, her hair festooned with pin curls that are loosely concealed by a garish babushka.

*

People who habitually preface their statements with "Frankly," "Candidly," or "Honestly," leave me with the uneasy impression that frankness, candor and honesty do not come naturally to them.

*

It's easy to make most motorists understand that they shouldn't drive when they're full of liquor; but it's much harder to make them see that they shouldn't drive when they're full of anger — for I am convinced that more auto accidents are caused by emotional pressure than by alcoholic content.

*

Divorced women who "devote their lives" to their children are too often unconsciously substituting the children for a husband, and thus doing a great disservice to the children, who should not be made to carry so great a burden of devotion.

*

Most "cracker barrel" philosophers ought to get inside the barrel and stay there.

*

One of the best arguments for the abolition of capital punishment is that murder is not a crime of the criminal classes, but in almost all cases is a spontaneous emotional act — and thus is not deterred by any rational thought of punishment.

Real tact does not consist in agreeing with people — this is mere slavishness — but in learning how to disagree without being disagreeable.

*

It's dismaying how many people with high principles have chosen the wrong principles to elevate; I suppose this was the original sin of the Pharisees.

*

A good waitress is not necessarily one who gives fast service — but one who can make slow service seem pleasant by her attitude. After all, the purpose of dining is to get tensions out of us as much as to cram food into us.

*

A dull woman, if she has other virtues, may be tolerable; but the only intolerable female is the one who is so afraid of being dull that she keeps up a continual barrage of bright chatter and exhausts us with her determined gaiety.

*

Most couples who elope do so not for romantic reasons but because they are afraid that if they wait much longer they might return to their senses. The reason such couples generally don't have happy marriages is that an elopement is usually a sign of impatience, and marriage is the supreme test of patience.

*

Nobody can be as self-righteous as a woman who is true to one man simply because she isn't really interested in any men, including him.

Too many people don't punctuate their conversations properly: you think they have come to a full stop, but they have only paused at a semicolon, and as you start to say something they resume talking, which makes for all-round embarrassment.

*

One of the highest paid jobs in America consists of standing in front of a microphone, separating the good records from the bad ones — and playing the bad ones.

*

Some questions in examinations are so vague, general and foolish that only the most stupid pupils can answer them swiftly and with certainty; the intelligent pupil is tempted, quite properly, to hedge his answer with reservations and qualifications — and gets a worse mark because of his more flexible and inquiring mind.

*

Most biographies are inadequate because they show us only one part of the subject; a good biography should show us three things about its subject — the man he was, the man he thought he was, and the man he would like to have been.

*

A wife is a person who is always asking her husband if he likes her hair better this way, and a husband is a person who can't see that it's much different from the way it looked before.

*